One Man, One Woman

Dale O'Leary

One Man, One Woman

A Catholic's Guide to Defending Marriage

SOPHIA INSTITUTE PRESS®
Manchester, New Hampshire

Copyright © 2007 Dale O'Leary

Printed in the United States of America

All rights reserved

Cover design by Theodore Schluenderfritz

No part of this book may be reproduced, stored in a retrieval system, or transmitted in any form, or by any means, electronic, mechanical, photocopying,
or otherwise, without the prior written permission of the publisher, except
by a reviewer, who may quote brief passages in a review.

Sophia Institute Press®
Box 5284, Manchester, NH 03108
1-800-888-9344
www.sophiainstitute.com

Library of Congress Cataloging-in-Publication Data

O'Leary, Dale.
    One man, one woman : a Catholic's guide to defending marriage /
Dale O'Leary.
        p. cm.
    Includes bibliographical references.
    ISBN 978-1-933184-29-6 (pbk. : alk. paper) 1. Same-sex marriage.
2. Marriage — Religious aspects — Catholic Church. 3. Same-sex
marriage — Religious aspects — Catholic Church. 4. Homosexuality —
Religious aspects — Catholic Church. I. Title.

HQ1033.O43 2007
261.8′35848 — dc22

                                                                    2007017447

                    07 08 09 10 9 8 7 6 5 4 3 2 1

*To those who have come out of homosexuality
and to the courageous therapists and counselors
who have dedicated their lives to helping them*

*"Marriage does not exist because of state recognition
or a specific legal system, neither is it created out of whole cloth
by two individuals. Two persons marry when they make mutual
pledges to enter into a life of total sexual community . . .
Two people can only marry if they are capable of
total sexual community . . . marriage is only
possible between a female and a male."*

David Coolidge

Acknowledgments

I would like to thank all those who have tracked the activities of gay activists and posted this information on the worldwide web. In particular, I would like to thank the members of the National Association for Research and Therapy of Homosexuality, Courage, and the Catholic Medical Association for their work in this field.

When I began my inquiries in this area, a friend suggested that I contact Dr. Richard Fitzgibbons. This was great advice. Dr. Fitzgibbons's experience in working with persons with SSA has been invaluable, and he has been a great sounding board for my ideas.

Contents

Introduction

⤚

Clarion Call at Cairo

In September of 1994, the United Nations convened an international conference on Population and Development in Cairo, Egypt. The International Planned Parenthood Federation (IPPF) and its allies had for decades tried to use the UN conference process to declare abortion a universally recognized human right, but they had been frustrated in this effort by pro-life American presidents. Now, with a sympathetic president in the White House, they were confident their time had come. Surely, in Cairo they would achieve their objective.

Pope John Paul II, who saw the dangers and understood the dynamics of the international situation, wrote to the head of every nation, expressing his concern and asking for help. Many pro-life groups took up the call, and one such group, desperate for "bodies on the ground," asked if I would go and help their effort. Journalistic connections helped me quickly secure press credentials and funding, and before I knew it, I was off to Cairo — although not sure exactly what I could do there.

I arrived in Cairo with more than two hundred other representatives from pro-life and pro-family organizations all around the world. Gradually we found each other and began to lobby against the Planned Parenthood agenda — alerting representatives from pro-life countries in the Third World about the First World's plan

to use the conference to push abortion and other anti-family policies on their homelands. And despite being out-funded and out-
organized, in the end, our advocacy succeeded in blocking IPPF
lobbyists from accomplishing their goals.

They and their supporters were shocked, but still determined.
They might have been defeated in Cairo, but another international conference was scheduled for the following year — the UN
Conference on Women in Beijing — and even before Cairo fin-
ished, they were planning and organizing for it.

In Cairo, pro-life activists came to realize that abortion wasn't
the only issue on the table, and that Planned Parenthood wasn't
the only group with which they had to contend. Former U.S. Con-
gresswoman Bella Abzug had gathered around her an influential
delegation of women promoting a radical feminist agenda. They
were organized as the Women's Environmental and Development
Organization (WEDO), but their goals had little to do with either
the environment or development. Their real objective was global
recognition of what they called "sexual and reproductive rights";
their plan was to take the rights articulated in the UN's 1948 Universal Declaration of Human Rights and manipulate their meaning to create an international legal foundation for an unlimited
right to abortion and absolute sexual license. They also sought to
add "sexual orientation" to the categories against which discrimination was prohibited, and to change the globally recognized definition of "family."

The pro-life/pro-family coalition's primary concern at the time
was abortion. We were aware of other threats to the family and parents' rights, but most of us would have preferred to avoid the issue of
homosexuality. Yet it wasn't possible. Whether we were discussing
sex-education materials, or the definition of family, or the prevention of sexually transmitted diseases, homosexuality kept forcing
its way onto the table. This gave us a taste of what was to come.

Beijing Escalates the Conflict

In December of 1994, WEDO held a conference in Glen Cove, New York, presided over by Abzug and attended by UN staff. Documents from the meeting reveal that one of the "bottom-line issues" for which WEDO and its allies would be fighting in Beijing was "recognition of sexual orientation as a fundamental human right within the context of the expanding definition of family."[1]

The following February, the Council of Europe, the cultural arm of the European Union, held a meeting to lay out its agenda for Beijing. The participants at this gathering called for, among other things, recognition of the "right to free choice in matters of reproduction and lifestyle," notably including "sexual preferences" and a specific demand that "the reproductive rights of lesbian women should be recognized."[2]

The Council of Europe delegates also fired a warning shot across the bow of religion:

> The rise of *all* forms of religious fundamentalism was seen as posing a particular threat to the enjoyment by women of their human rights.

It is clear from the context that this statement wasn't meant to refer solely to cultures in which Islam and tribal religions, for example, blatantly subjugated women, but also to the growing political influence of pro-life Catholics and Evangelical Christians in the West.

The preparatory meetings for the Beijing conference took place at the UN building in New York in the Spring of 1995. Pro-family

---

[1] Women's Global Strategies Meeting, December 2, 1994, Working Group 4, Beijing Document, pts. 1, 2.

[2] "Equality and Democracy: Utopia or Challenge?" Council of Europe, Palais de l'Europe, Strasbourg, February 9-11, 1995.

members of Non-Governmental Organizations (NGOs) from South America came with concerns about demands for "sexual rights" that had been made at the regional preparatory conference in Argentina. Its platform had focused on "gender" and "gender perspective" rather than on women, and had nothing positive to say about motherhood or marriage. They were worried that the Western delegates' focus on "gender perspective" and "sexual and reproductive rights" would divert attention from the real needs of women in developing countries, where women needed practical solutions to real problems of oppression, poverty, and disease. Neither promoting abortion and lesbianism, nor redefining the family, was on their agenda.

In Beijing, I heard similar concerns being voiced. One elegant Afghan woman, exiled from her country because of the Taliban, was working to obtain aid for Afghan women who were trapped in refugee camps in Pakistan. She wondered why no one at a conference on women seemed to be interested in the plight of these women. Many pro-life and pro-family delegates, as well as delegates from Muslim countries, soon likewise grew frustrated at having to spend all their time and energy arguing about abortion and sex rather than devising positive ways to help women in need.

That fight came to a head near the end of the conference. Sensing a growing buzz of opposition, UN organizers sympathetic to the sexual-rights agenda scheduled discussion of the most controversial topics, including sexual rights for lesbians, for the final afternoon. The session didn't begin until early evening, and it dragged on into the night. The organizers might have hoped that their opponents would give up and go to bed. They miscalculated. (Muslims, it appears, are accustomed to drinking coffee, smoking cigarettes, and staying up late.)

In the wee hours of the morning, the discussion of lesbian rights finally began. In spite of pressure from the Europeans, the

Muslims refused to budge. Some of the radical feminists were in tears, others enraged, but in the end, there was nothing they could do. The document that emerged from the long night did not explicitly recognize special homosexual rights.

It was those debates at Beijing that provided the initial inspiration for this book. The "sexual rights" proponents were challenging representatives from pro-family NGOs at every turn. The gay-rights supporters, in particular, called us hurtful, cruel, bigoted hypocrites. *And too often, the pro-family speakers did not have an adequate response.*

Most of the world's major religions deem homosexual behavior to be morally wrong. Yet if gays and lesbians had been "born that way," as they claimed, and couldn't change, then how were we to deal with them? Was it enough, as one of the speakers suggested, to tell them to suffer in silence? As I listened to the exchanges, I knew that couldn't be the answer. People of faith had to have a more compassionate response to those with same-sex attractions.

But at the same time, we couldn't sacrifice our belief that homosexual acts are contrary to God's plan. Our very faith lay in the balance: for if we were wrong to hold that homosexual acts were contrary to Nature and the intent of Nature's God, then all religions (including mine) that condemned such behavior would be *ipso facto* guilty of unjust discrimination. And if our revealed texts and teaching authorities were wrong on such an important issue, how could they be an infallible guide in other areas?

This was not a small thing, not an issue from which we could simply walk away because it made us uncomfortable. However much we might wish it were otherwise, our credibility on all other issues hung on our ability to defend this teaching. If this teaching were no longer applicable, why should young people believe that anything we said was morally binding? If God were wrong about this, or if we were wrong about God's teaching, then our credibility would be totally undermined. We would simply be stating our personal opinions — and narrow, mean-spirited opinions at that.

In that moment, I saw clearly that if the pro-family movement was to prevail in the worldwide culture war, we would have to answer the challenge of militant gay activists; and it was equally clear we were ill-prepared to do so. Therefore, in 1996, I began to research the issue of homosexuality, looking for answers to the questions posed by the gay activists. This book is the product of that long search.

I began my search by reading all the literature on the subject I could find — books, journal articles, news accounts. I contacted groups around the country that worked with persons who wanted to come out of homosexuality, as well as other pro-family groups that had come to recognize the rising influence of gay activists. I contacted the National Association for Research and Therapy of Homosexuality (NARTH), and through them a number of mental-health professionals who had been working on the issue for years. I found doctors from the Catholic Medical Association who shared my concerns. I discovered the wonderful work of Courage, a Catholic outreach to persons struggling with same-sex attraction (SSA). And I met many men and women who had found healing from SSA, and peace.

The Goodridge Decision

As years passed and my research continued, I observed a noticeable escalation of gay activism, particularly in the demand for marriage rights. It seemed as if gay activists, confident that their efforts were working, could sense some imminent major victory. Then, in November of 2003, the Massachusetts Supreme Judicial Court ruled in the case of *Hillary Goodridge v. the Department of Public Health* that "barring an individual from the protections, benefits and obligations of civil marriage solely because that person would marry a person of the same sex violates the Massachusetts Constitution."

This was the decision that the defenders of marriage had feared.

The opponents of *Goodridge* began an effort to nullify the decision by amending the state constitution, and were able to gather over 170,000 signatures to that end. But the process revealed deep divisions within communities. Members of pro-family groups, most of them affiliated with churches, were unpleasantly surprised at the number of friends, family members (the younger generation, especially), and fellow congregants who refused to help the effort. Many found it difficult to answer the arguments made by those who would not sign: "Why shouldn't gays and lesbians be allowed to marry?" "They were born that way and can't change." "How does letting them marry hurt other families?"

If this was the reaction to the petition, the organizers wondered, how could the amendment prevail if and when it was finally put before the people? It was then that a group involved in gathering signatures contacted me to ask for help in training people to explain the issue. I developed a seminar and wrote for local Catholic newspapers a series of columns entitled *Truth and Compassion*. In my columns, I tried to answer what I saw as the crucial question: "How can Catholics reconcile their desire to be truly loving, compassionate, and accepting with the unchangeable teaching that homosexual acts are always contrary to God's rules for sexuality?"

Those who refused to sign the petition did so, for the most part, because they saw themselves as compassionate people. They wanted to do the right thing. They didn't like being accused of discrimination or bigotry. They had friends, family members, coworkers, or neighbors with same-sex attractions, and they didn't want them to suffer.

Behind this apparent dilemma, however, there was a false assumption — namely, that persons who experience same-sex attraction were "born that way" and that change was impossible. From my decade of research, I knew that there was no solid scientific evidence to support this claim. There was, on the other hand, substantial evidence that same-sex attraction was a preventable and treatable developmental disorder: an accidental confluence of forces, not a parallel biological destiny.

I realized that before defenders of marriage and people of faith could address the political issues surrounding homosexuality, they had to repent — not for "hate" or unjust discrimination, but for failing to respond to the needs of this population. We hadn't prayed for people with SSA. We hadn't supported ministries that sought to help them. We hadn't educated parents about how to prevent the problem. We had just closed our eyes, and now we were paying a terrible price for our sins of omission.

Persons struggling with SSA have a right to know that they are real men and real women called by God to live their masculinity and femininity to the fullest. They're like someone chained to a tree; cold, hungry, and thirsty. How should we react? Should we bring them a blanket, food, and water? Or should we get a hacksaw? I believe that the hack saw is the correct response. *Freedom* from their condition; not a false compassion that pretends they're not in chains.

⁓

This book is an effort to bring together the best evidence about the nature and origins of SSA, as well as about the agenda and tactics of gay activists — particularly regarding the redefinition of marriage. I hope it can serve as a guide for those who want to be able to respond compassionately, but also intelligently and uncompromisingly, both to the aggressive claims of activists and to the earnest questions of those who remain uncommitted in the battle.

For a battle it is. After a decade of work, I am more convinced than ever that this is the defining issue of our time. Lose here, and we lose the next generation. Prevail, and we lay the foundation for a civilization of love.

One Man, One Woman

Part I

≈

The Politics of Sex and Marriage

"In those situations where homosexual unions have been legally recognized or have been given the legal status and rights belonging to marriage, clear and emphatic opposition is a duty. One must refrain from any kind of formal cooperation in the enactment or application of such gravely unjust laws and, as far as possible, from material cooperation on the level of their application. In this area, everyone can exercise the right of conscientious objection."

Joseph Cardinal Ratzinger
Now Pope Benedict XVI

≈

"There is no going back to the 1950s. Homosexuals are increasingly open and ordinary and will not retreat into the closet."

Jonathan Rauch
*Gay Marriage: Why It's Good for Gays,
Good for Straights, and Good for America*

Chapter 1

⌒

The Political Struggle
Over the Definition of Marriage

How did the movement for same-sex marriage begin?

*What have been the key legal battlefields
in the fight over marriage?*

*Aren't there laws in place that will prevent
same-sex marriage in my state?*

The current battle over the definition of marriage didn't just *happen*. It is the result of decades of efforts by gay activists, who have established clearly delineated objectives, developed comprehensive strategies, and devoted considerable resources toward achieving their aims.

The modern gay-rights movement traces its origin to the Stonewall Riots,[3] which occurred in New York City in June of 1969. The funeral of Judy Garland, an icon for many gay men, had taken place earlier in the day, and emotions were running high.

That evening, a handful of New York City policemen conducted a routine raid on the Stonewall Inn, a "bottle club" that catered to an eclectic crowd of gay men and drag queens. The inn didn't have a liquor license — patrons were supposed to bring their own bottles and sign in at the door as members — but the club illegally served liquor, and police raids weren't uncommon. But that night, the patrons fought back, attacking the police and carrying the disturbance out into the street. The crowd threw bricks and bottles and started fires until the fracas was finally

---

[3] This is true even outside the United States. Iceland, for example, recently chose the anniversary date of the Riots to enact a new civil-unions law.

brought under control at four in the morning, leaving four police-men injured and thirteen demonstrators under arrest.

It was the late Sixties, and revolution was in the air. Tradi-tional morality was under attack. Gay Power fit right in with the spirit of the age, and the Stonewall Riots became a rallying symbol of gay activism. The date is still commemorated every year in Gay Pride activities across the country.

In May of 1970, two Minnesota men became the first same-sex couple to apply for a marriage license in the United States. They were refused.

In 1972, the National Coalition of Gay Organizations held a convention in Chicago and developed the first-ever Gay Rights Platform. Its demands included, among other things:

> • "Federal encouragement and support for sex-education courses, prepared and taught by gay women and men, pre-senting homosexuality as a valid, healthy preference and lifestyle as a viable alternative to heterosexuality."

> • "Repeal [of] all state laws prohibiting solicitation for pri-vate voluntary sexual liaisons; and laws prohibiting prosti-tution, both male and female."

> • "Repeal of all laws governing the age of sexual consent."

> • "Repeal of all legislative provisions that restrict the sex or number of persons entering into a marriage unit; and the extension of legal benefits to all persons who cohabit re-gardless of sex or numbers."[4]

The activists recognized that such sweeping changes couldn't be achieved immediately, but with these ultimate objectives in

---

[4] The entire platform is viewable at numerous websites; for ex-ample, http://www.civilrightsteaching.org.

mind, they set out to pressure sympathetic state legislatures and municipal governments for small changes in law; for example, legal protection against discrimination in public accommodation. Critics of these changes argued that such laws were unnecessary, since homosexuals already frequented the finest restaurants, stayed in the best hotels, and were employed in many glamorous professions. Yet many jurisdictions accepted their demands and added "sexual orientation" to the list of protected classes of citizens.

As soon as the gay activists had won one concession, they demanded another. At each step in this process, they insisted that the changes they were proposing were insignificant — small matters of simple justice whose effects on larger society would be negligible. Their critics warned that the ultimate goal was the redefinition of marriage, but these concerns were dismissed as hysterical bigotry.

But then the activists ran into a problem: as their demands escalated, legislators became less accommodating. The public began to react against the granting of special rights based on sexual orientation.[5] When the issue was placed before voters, the gay agenda usually lost. Gay activists realized that achieving their goals through legislation would require a sea change in public opinion — and the tide was not running their way. So they borrowed the strategy of the abortion-rights movement and turned to the courts.

Counting on activist judges who could be moved by appeals to "privacy" or "choice" to grant what legislatures, public opinion,

---

[5] For example, several municipalities in Colorado had included sexual orientation in laws prohibiting discrimination. In 1993, Colorado voters approved a constitutional amendment that excluded gays and lesbians from all antidiscrimination laws and policies in the state. In 1996, this amendment was later declared unconstitutional (*Romer v. Evans*).

law, precedent, and tradition denied, gay activists presented their demands as a plea for Constitutional rights — and if voters were too bigoted to recognize these "rights," the judges, who knew better, could overrule them. Gay activists succeeded in identifying their struggles with the fight against racial and sexual discrimination, thus entering into a coalition of political allies and winning more public sympathy.

The mainstream media were also largely sympathetic to the gay activists' demands. Picture-perfect, media-savvy same-sex couples applied for marriage licenses in states where they could expect to receive favorable hearings from activist judges. When clerks declined to accept their applications, the couples' legal teams swung into action. Lawsuits and appeals eventually reached state supreme courts.

The first major test of the gay activists' strategy[6] came in the liberal state of Hawaii in 1990, when three same-sex couples applied for marriage licenses and were denied. They sued. In December of 1996, a lower state court ruled in their favor and declared that the statute reserving marriage to opposite-sex couples was unconstitutional. (However, the ruling would never be enforced, because in 1998, voters overwhelmingly passed an amendment to the state constitution reserving marriage to opposite-sex couples.)

---

[6] Of course, pressure to redefine marriage hasn't been confined to the United States. The Netherlands and Belgium have already redefined marriage to include same-sex couples. In 2003, the Ontario Court of Appeal ruled that Canada's marriage laws are unconstitutionally heterosexist and redefined marriage as "the voluntary union for life of two persons to the exclusion of others." In June of 2005, the Canadian Parliament issued a similar redefinition of marriage for the entire country. Spain followed later that summer. We can probably expect more nations in Europe, famously more liberal on sexual matters than the United States, to follow suit in the future.

The Political Struggle Over the Definition of Marriage

In 1996, fearing that Hawaiian courts would grant marriage licenses to same-sex couples, the U.S. Congress passed, by a combined vote of 427 to 81, the Defense of Marriage Act (DOMA), which was signed into law by President Clinton. DOMA provided that no state would be required to recognize a same-sex marriage performed in another state if the law in that state banned same-sex marriage. DOMA also defined the words *marriage* and *spouse* for purposes of federal law to include only male/female couples.

Having failed to achieve their objective in Hawaii, the activists targeted the even more liberal state of Vermont, where the people's ability to amend their state constitution is extremely limited. And on December 20, 1999, the Vermont Supreme Court ruled that the state must institute an equivalent of marriage for same-sex couples: "civil unions" granting all the rights and privileges of marriage without the name. Same-sex couples rushed to Vermont to enter civil unions. Many of their ceremonies included all the trappings of a wedding.

In March of 2000, California voters were presented with a referendum that defined marriage as the union of one man and one woman. Many questioned the wisdom of putting the issue on the ballot in such a politically liberal, socially "tolerant" state. Pre-election polls hadn't been favorable to the amendment, and so it came as a surprise to supporters and critics alike when it won by a two-to-one margin. This referendum victory demonstrated that even in a state that included Hollywood and San Francisco, the people did not want marriage redefined.

Massachusetts' High Court Stirs the Pot

In April of 2001, same-sex couples who had applied for and been denied marriage licenses in the state of Massachusetts took their case to court. In the landmark *Goodridge* ruling of November 18, 2003, the Supreme Judicial Court of Massachusetts issued a 4-3 decision that there was "no rational reason" for restricting marriage to one man and one woman. The court ordered the legislature to change the state law to allow persons of the same sex to marry. In doing so, the court recognized (some might say reveled in) the sweeping effect of this ruling:

> We are mindful that our decision marks a change in the history of our marriage law. Many people hold deep-seated religious, moral, and ethical convictions that marriage should be limited to the union of one man and one woman, and that homosexual conduct is immoral.

The commonwealth had claimed that marriage was instituted to protect children conceived through sexual intercourse, but the court rejected that argument, stating:

> [I]t is the exclusive and permanent commitment of the marriage partners to one another, not the begetting of children, that is the *sine qua non* of marriage.

In the *Goodridge* decision, the Massachusetts justices admitted that they were discarding the "definition of marriage as it has been inherited from common law and understood by many societies for centuries." They felt justified in doing this, they said, because "civil marriage is an evolving paradigm," the current state of which the court claimed for itself the authority to arbitrate.

In his concurring opinion, Justice Greany wrote:

> I am hopeful that our decision will be accepted by those thoughtful citizens who believe that same-sex unions should not be approved by the State. I am not referring here to acceptance in the sense of grudging acknowledgment of the court's authority to adjudicate the matter . . . Simple principles of decency dictate that we extend to the plaintiffs, and

to their new status, full acceptance, tolerance, and respect. We should do so because it is the right thing to do.

"The right thing to do." Defenders of marriage saw these words not as a call for reconciliation, but as a threat. Those who opposed same-sex marriage were not simply on the wrong side of the law; they were wicked, and if they failed to change, they would be guilty of intolerance. Given laws against discrimination and hate crimes, this charge could have legal ramifications.

On May 18 of that year, same-sex couples were officially issued marriage licenses in Massachusetts. Although at least one of each pair was supposed to be a resident of the state, that requirement appears to have been ignored, and a number of out-of-state couples have received licenses, even though their status would not be recognized in their home states.

Today, although Massachusetts has court-imposed same-sex marriage, its opponents continue to work for an amendment to the state constitution defining marriage as between one man and one woman.

A Federal Amendment
and More State Challenges

The federal Defense of Marriage Act and the state DOMAs were designed to prevent what happened in Massachusetts from happening elsewhere, but some felt these wouldn't be enough. They were convinced that without a federal constitutional amendment, activist state or federal courts could force a redefinition of marriage on individual states or on the country as a whole, or insist that other states recognize Massachusetts marriages. After the *Goodridge* decision, President Bush was moved by these concerns, and in February of 2004, he announced his support for the Federal Marriage Amendment (FEMA), which read:

Marriage in the United States shall consist only of the union of a man and a woman. Neither this Constitution nor the constitution of any State, nor state or federal law, shall be construed to require that marital status or the legal incidents thereof be conferred upon unmarried couples or groups.

As politicians and lobbyists debated the FEMA, the issue came before other state courts. In New York, for example, a judge rejected a suit brought by same-sex couples challenging the denial of marriage licenses. The case was appealed to the state supreme court, which, on July 6, 2006, upheld the decision.

Gay activists had argued that there was no rational reason for limiting marriage and its benefits to opposite-sex couples, echoing the argument made in *Goodridge* that the motivation for doing so was ignorance, bigotry, or irrational bias. But in July of 2006, in *Hernandez v. Robles,* New York rejected this argument, stating, "[T]he Legislature could rationally believe that it is better, other things being equal, for children to grow up with both a mother and a father." The court's opinion continued:

The traditional definition of marriage is not merely a by-product of historical injustice . . . The idea that same-sex marriage is even possible is a relatively new one. Until a few decades ago, it was an accepted truth for almost everyone who ever lived, in any society in which marriage existed, that there could be marriages only between participants of different sex. A court should not lightly conclude that everyone who held this belief was irrational, ignorant, or bigoted. We do not so conclude.

The court left the work of defining marriage to the legislature:

The dissenters assert confidently that "future generations" will agree with their view of this case. We do not predict what people will think generations from now, but we believe the present generation should have a chance to decide the issue through its elected representatives.

The Federal Marriage Amendment was brought to a vote in Congress during the summer of 2004, but it did not pass. At the time, its opponents argued that the DOMA was sufficient; that there was no need for something as radical as a constitutional amendment.

Meanwhile, local groups, seeking to prevent their own *Goodridges*, began introducing constitutional amendments in their own states. As of early 2007, eighteen states have passed marriage amendments, including liberal Hawaii and Oregon. Only in Arizona has such an amendment been rejected by voters.[7]

But even state constitutional amendments that passed with overwhelming voter support have faced legal challenges from gay activists. In May of 2005, a federal judge struck down a Nebraska marriage amendment, even though it had passed with seventy percent of the vote. The following May, a country judge in Georgia overturned that state's marriage protection amendment on a technicality, even though it had won seventy-six percent.

These decisions were later overturned, but the battle in the courts continues, as activists continue to try to win from activist judges what they cannot win from voters.[8]

---

[7] Supporters believe it failed because the language on the ballot was confusing, and because Arizona already had a statute banning same-sex marriage.

[8] Interestingly, though, some gay-rights legal activists have become wary of this judicial strategy, warning that if a court were to mandate same-sex marriage in a state with a Defense of Marriage Act or marriage amendment, the other side would cite it as evidence for the necessity of a Federal Marriage Amendment.

One Man, One Woman

⌒

Judging by the results of these referenda, a majority of Americans still oppose the redefinition of marriage. However, most of them have trouble explaining why they hold this belief. They may say, "Well, that is how it has always been," or, "It's natural" or "It's traditional," but they're unable to articulate *why* it has always been that way or *why* it is natural or traditional. Belief in traditional marriage might be widespread, but anecdotal evidence suggests it isn't particularly deep. Without greater understanding of the issues and arguments, people will not be able to hold out forever against the unceasing attacks on marriage. If we are to prevail, we must first arm ourselves with knowledge of the ideology and tactics of the activists who are determined not only to redefine marriage, but to undermine the very foundations of our society.

Chapter 2

The Ideology of the Sexual Left

What motivates proponents of same-sex marriage?

What claims and goals are part of their agenda?

What strategies do they employ to support this agenda?

The battle over the definition of marriage is part of the worldwide Culture War pitting social conservatives against the coalition of radical feminists, sexual liberationists, population-control zealots, abortion advocates, and gay-rights activists that I call the "Sexual Left." Its members envision a society where everyone can engage in the free pursuit of sexual pleasure, without ever having to bear the burden of shame, heartbreak, unwanted children, or sexually transmitted diseases. The Sexual Left believes in an unrestricted right to abortion, virtually absolute sexual freedom, and the abolition of all social distinctions between same-sex and other-sex relationships; indeed, between men and women, period. Since massive public re-education is critical to these goals, they also support early, explicit, and compulsory sex education for children, without parental consent or notification.[9]

Some have traced the rise of the Sexual Left to sexologist Alfred Kinsey and his Institute for Sex Research, founded in 1947. Others point to Margaret Sanger and her founding in 1921 of what would later become Planned Parenthood. Whatever its exact origins, the Sexual Left undoubtedly vaulted into prominence

[9] Those who doubt the Sexual Left's commitment to sex for children should read the popular children's sex manual *It's Perfectly Normal*, by Robie Harris, with its child-friendly drawings of nude adults and children.

in the 1960s, capitalizing on the decade's social upheaval and aligning itself with the political left. It has also found powerful ideological sympathizers in the universities, in the news media, and in the entertainment industry.

The Sexual Left characteristically makes use of deception and euphemism in its propaganda, hiding the more radical elements of its agenda behind carefully crafted public-relations strategies and programs ostensibly designed to foster health, "tolerance," "diversity," or "non-judgmental" attitudes. To promote their explicit sex-education programs, for example, they don't tell parents that they believe children should engage in guilt-free "sex play" in elementary schools. Instead they focus on parents' fears, telling them that without sex-education programs, children will get AIDS.[10]

Parents trust that such programs work, and when they fail — when, for example, sexually transmitted diseases (STDs) spread rather than diminish — it simply allows the Sexual Left to argue for even more explicit sex education, starting at an earlier age; as though more of the disease were the only cure. The relatively few parents who object are told that their "puritanical" attitudes are in fact part of the problem; that children are going to have sex anyway and parents must simply accept it.

The failures of sex education don't bother its promoters, or the philanthropists and politicians who underwrite and empower them. They know that such measures are risk-reduction strategies at best, not prevention programs. What matters to them isn't a short-term reduction in STDs or teen pregnancy, but achieving the Sexual Left's long-term ideological goal: namely, to re-order the younger generation's attitudes toward sex.

[10] Similarly, the Sexual Left has capitalized on the real problem of bullying to push programs that promote the gay agenda under the guise of teaching tolerance and acceptance of diversity.

⤔

A number of years ago, I responded to a column in the *New York Times* that promoted condoms for high-schoolers, arguing instead in favor of abstinence for the same students. The then-head of the Sex Information and Education Council of the U.S. (SIECUS), an advocacy arm of the Sexual Left, responded with disarming frankness that "having sexual relations is normative behavior for teenagers fifteen to nineteen years old."[11]

At the Cairo conference, I attended a SIECUS presentation in which the presenters tried to encourage young Egyptian students to engage in masturbation and other sexual practices. The students were confused, because their limited English vocabulary did not include the explicit terms the SIECUS people were using, and it made for an ugly scene — a corrupted Western sexual ideology being forced on innocents. I objected rather strongly, and the presenters told me to sit down, but I couldn't bear to hear more lies and stormed out, taking half the audience with me. Those Egyptian students were able that day to reject the Sexual Left's seduction, but in the United States, Canada, and Europe, it has infiltrated all too easily — and brought the gay agenda with it.

The Sexual Left and the Gay Agenda

Gay activists are a key constituency in the Sexual Left coalition, and the Sexual Left totally embraces the gay agenda — although, due to public resistance, this support was at first covert. The 1987 book *After the Ball: How America Will Conquer Its Fear and Hatred of Gays in the 90's*, by Marshall Kirk and Hunter Madsen, laid out a strategy for gays to overcome public opposition. They constructed a comprehensive plan for legitimizing homosexuality

[11] Debra Hafner, letter to the editor, *New York Times*, October 30, 1991.

by "overhauling straight America,"[12] the first step of which, Kirk and Madsen warned, was to avoid exposing the movement's Achilles' heel: the sordid and shocking realities of the gay lifestyle:

> [T]he masses should not be shocked and repelled by premature exposure to homosexual behavior itself. Instead, the imagery of sex should be downplayed and gay rights should be reduced to an abstract social question as much as possible. First let the camel get his nose inside the tent — only later his unsightly derriere![13]

Kirk and Madsen encouraged gays and lesbians to portray themselves as "conventional young people, middle-age women, and older folks of all races . . . victims of circumstance and depression." Gay activists were told to portray same-sex attraction as a naturally occurring phenomenon, and gays and lesbians as oppressed victims:

> [T]he mainstream should be told that gays are *victims of fate*, in the sense that most never had a choice to accept or reject their sexual preference. The message must read: "As far as gays can tell, they were born gay."[14]

This simple strategy — create a non-threatening public picture of homosexuality, and then charge anyone who disagrees with intolerance and hate — has been extremely successful. Gay activists craft sound-bite slogans that test well in surveys. They smile and make specious claims. They create myths that serve their

---

[12] Marshall Kirk and Hunter Madsen, *After the Ball: How America Will Conquer Its Fear and Hatred of Gays in the 90's* (New York: Plume, 1989).

[13] Marshall Kirk and Estes Pill (pseudonym for Madsen), "Overhauling Straight America," *Guide Magazine* (November 1987): 8.

[14] Ibid.

public-relations objectives and, with the aid of cooperative media, feed them to the public.

Language, Imagery, and Propaganda

In public-policy debates, language is crucial. This is particularly true in the same-sex marriage debate, and gay activists have been no less crafty in their language than the Sexual Left as a whole. For example, although there is no universal agreement about the definition of *homosexual* (does it refer to certain desires, or behaviors, or convictions, or some combination thereof?), gay activists act as if it were a scientifically designated category of human beings. They have taken further advantage of this ambiguity, always seeking to influence public opinion, by carefully choosing words that frame the issue in their favor. They have eschewed the nineteenth-century term *homosexual*, for instance, and insisted on using *gay* and *lesbian* to refer respectively to men and women who a) identify themselves with their sexual attraction;[15] and b) identify with the gay political agenda.

The language of sexual orientation and "sexual minorities" has also expanded to include bisexuals, transsexuals, transgenders, and transvestites. And thus, the entire constituency is today summed up in the acronym GLBT (Gay, Lesbian, Bisexual, and Transgender) or, alternatively, LGBT. Some also like to refer to themselves as "queer," although others find this term insulting when used by non-members of their community.

However, none of these categories adequately describes all persons with same-sex attraction (SSA): for example, those who have never acted on it. Neither do these categories include those

---

[15] It should be noted that some women identify themselves as lesbian for political reasons, even though they do not engage in sexual intimacy with other women and are sexually attracted to men.

with SSA who don't identify with the gay agenda. For this reason, I find "persons with SSA" to be the broadest and most accurate term, if a somewhat cumbersome one. I try to avoid using the word *homosexual* as a noun, or for that matter *heterosexual*, because these terms create the impression that human beings can be neatly divided into categories based on their patterns of sexual desire. People are either male or female. Patterns of sexual attraction are not their identity and, in fact, can be quite fluid over time. Some gay activists refer to those who are sexually attracted to the other sex as "straight," or derisively as "breeders." I prefer to refer to them simply as men and women.

I do use the word *homosexual* as an adjective, when referring to the various intimate acts that two persons of the same sex can engage in.[16] This allows discussion of the behavior or acts without having to describe them in detail. I choose to avoid such explicit language wherever possible, although occasionally I think it is necessary to name precisely what we are talking about — lest we play right into gay activists' strategy of euphemizing their behaviors.

And we know that there are numerous terms of derision for persons with SSA. All of them reflect badly on those who use them; they demonstrate a lack of charity and should be scrupulously avoided, even if some persons with SSA use such terms in reference to themselves. Persons with SSA are human beings, and they are entitled to all the rights that belong to every human being. This does not include the right to change the definition of marriage.

[16] Technically, of course, the acts that two persons of the same sex engage in are not "sexual acts," because the sexual organs of both persons are not engaged in the same act — that is, sexual intercourse. So, while we may use the term *having sex* to describe homosexual behavior, it isn't really sexual intercourse.

The Strategy of Victimhood

Americans are a compassionate and pragmatic people, who tend to focus on the immediate problem with zeal and sincerity. Unfortunately, this means that they don't always see the long-term consequences of giving in to quick fixes. Members of the Sexual Left, like all proponents of radical social change, have recognized that one way to achieve their objectives is to offer a simple solution based on an appeal to emotion: "Feel sorry for us, we have suffered, give us what we ask for." For their marriage propaganda, they carefully choose sympathetic "victims," loving couples portrayed as struggling heroically against the harm caused by laws, traditions, and institutions that unfairly discriminate against them. The victims — their numbers dramatically exaggerated — must be attractive to look at and listen to, and if possible, surrounded by their sweet, photogenic children. These couples claim to be representative of millions of other victims, and they always position their demands in rights-language; for who can be against "rights"? Why, only mean-spirited, narrow-minded bigots bound to outdated ideas.

Abortion advocates have mastered this strategy. When lobbying for legalized abortion in the 1960s, they claimed that thousands of women were dying every year due to complications from illegal abortions. Women stood before crowds and on TV to tell terrifying tales of "back-alley butchers." Yet the mortality statistics for the period reveal that in the years before abortion was made legal, very few deaths (fewer than fifty a year) could be attributed to illegal abortions. Bernard Nathanson, the era's most famous abortionist (who would later become a pro-life crusader), admitted that they knew their illegal-abortion claims were false, but counted on friendly media not to challenge their appeals to "hard cases."

Today, gay activists have skillfully employed the same strategy to increase public sympathy for their cause while diverting attention from the facts, from the philosophical principles at stake, and from the negative consequences that will follow if their agenda succeeds.

Claims Versus Facts

The gay activists understand how the media works. They know that a false claim can become part of the "accepted wisdom" if repeated often enough — particularly if the claim sounds reasonable or if refuting it takes more than thirty seconds.

Here are some examples of unfounded claims by gay activists that, by sheer repetition, have achieved the status of popular "fact":

CLAIM: *"Ten percent of the population is gay."*

A key initial strategy of gay activists was to inflate public perception of the number of people with SSA. Basing their claim on the results of a 1949 Kinsey study that has long since been discredited, and spreading it with the willing help of the media and schools, they put forward what would become the widely accepted "ten percent" figure.

FACT: No study has ever found that ten percent of the population was actively engaging in same-sex intimacy or self-identifying as "gay." Far from it: several recent population-based studies suggest instead that around two percent of the population falls into this category.[17] The evidence has become so overwhelming that most gay activists have backed away from this myth; unfortunately, it received so much play early on that it still lingers in the popular mind.

---

[17] David Fergusson, John Horwood, and Annette Beautrais, "Is Sexual Orientation Related to Mental Health Problems and Suicidality in Young People?" *Archives of General Psychiatry* 56, no. 10 (1999): 876-888.

CLAIM: *Gay people are "born that way"; there is a "gay gene."*

This is perhaps the most powerful myth, for it appeals to the compassion of all decent people, and it fits their perception that there is something really "different" about persons with SSA and that no one would freely choose it. It also seems reasonable to persons with SSA, most of whom sincerely believe that they were "born that way" because they have always felt "different."

FACT: Feelings are not facts. There is still no replicated scientific evidence for a genetic cause for SSA. The low rate of concordance of SSA in identical-twin pairs makes it virtually impossible for a genetic or pre-natal biological cause of SSA to be discovered in the future.

CLAIM: *People can't change their pattern of sexual attraction.*

Gay activists use the myth of the "gay gene" to support their claim that change of sexual orientation is impossible. Since they're "born that way," they can't change, because deep down they simply *are* gay.

FACT: First, there are many genetic disorders that nonetheless respond to treatment. Even if SSA were genetically predetermined (which it isn't), it doesn't follow that it therefore can't be treated. As for SSA, there are numerous well-documented reports of change of sexual attraction from same-sex to other-sex.[18] Therapists engaged in such work provide real help to people with SSA daily.

CLAIM: *Homosexuals are as psychologically healthy as heterosexuals.*

Gay activists know that it will be much harder to consider SSA a "disorder" if they can foster the perception that persons with SSA are as happy, stable, and healthy as anyone else.

---

[18] Robert Spitzer, "Can Some Gay Men and Lesbians Change Their Sexual Orientation? 200 Participants Reporting a Change from Homosexual to Heterosexual Orientation," *Archives of Sexual Behavior* 32, no. 5 (October 2003): 403-417.

FACT: If same-sex attraction were a neutral condition, we'd expect studies to show no differences in psychological health between persons with SSA and those without. Yet numerous studies show that persons with SSA have significantly higher rates of a number of psychological disorders.[19] Persons with SSA are more likely to suffer from depression, substance-abuse problems, suicidal ideation, sexual addiction, and a number of psychological disorders.

CLAIM: *The problems homosexuals suffer from are caused by the oppression they experience.*

When they fail to convince people of the previous myth (and, in light of their own research, contradict it), activists resort to blaming "homophobic" society for the problems experienced by persons with SSA.

[19] Fergusson et al., "Is Sexual Orientation Related to Mental Health Problems?"; Richard Herrell et al., "Sexual Orientation and Suicidality: A Co-Twin Control Study in Adult Men," *Archives of General Psychiatry* 56, no. 10 (October 1999): 867-874; Theo Sandfort et al., "Same-Sex Sexual Behavior and Psychiatric Disorders: Findings from the Netherlands Mental Health Survey and Incidence Study (NEMESIS)," *Archives of General Psychiatry* 58, no. 1 (January 2001): 85-91; Susan Cochran, J. Greer Sullivan, Vickie Mays, "Prevalence of Mental Health Disorders, Psychological Distress, and Mental Health Services Use Among Lesbian, Gay, and Bisexual Adults in the United States," *Journal of Consulting and Clinical Psychology* 73, no. 1 (2003): 53-61. "These studies [Fergusson and Herrell] contain arguably the best published data on the association between homosexuality and psychopathology; both converge on the same unhappy conclusion: homosexual people are at a substantially higher risk for some forms of emotional problems, including suicidality, major depression, and anxiety disorder. Preliminary results from a large, equally well-conducted Dutch study [Sandfort] generally corroborate these findings" (J. Michael Bailey, "Homosexuality and Mental Illness," *Archives of General Psychiatry* 56, no. 10 [October 1999]: 883).

FACT: If these excess problems were caused entirely by lack of public acceptance of SSA, we would expect to find fewer problems in places where tolerance was high and "homophobia" low. But this isn't the case. Studies done in the Netherlands and New Zealand, for example, where there is generally high tolerance of sexual "diversity," found the same high rates of psychological difficulties as those done elsewhere.[20]

CLAIM: *Homosexuality is as normal as heterosexuality.*

Gay activists not only want to convince the public that SSA is genetically pre-determined and unchangeable, but also that it is a neutral condition, like race, eye color, or handedness. Rather than a disorder, it is just another aspect of human variety.

FACT: SSA does not fit the pattern of genetic mutations that create healthy diversity among the human population. Even if the high rates of psychological disorders found among persons with SSA could be totally attributed to cultural pressures, SSA greatly reduces the possibility of reproduction. A genetic mutation that prevents an individual from reproducing is a defect, not a neutral variance.

CLAIM: *Attempting to change a person's sexual orientation causes emotional harm.*

Gay activists have pressured psychological associations to ban therapy designed to change sexual orientation, claiming it causes psychological distress.

FACT: The very existence of such therapy reveals that many persons with SSA wish to change. Numerous studies have documented change, and treatment for SSA has a similar success/failure rate as that for similar psychological disorders.[21] People who fail to

---

[20] Fergusson 1999, Sandfort 2001, op. cit.

[21] Glenn Wyler, "Anything But Straight: A Book Review," *NARTH Bulletin* (April 2004): 32-45.

achieve their goals through therapy often feel disappointed and might blame the therapy.

CLAIM: *Thousands of gay teens commit suicide every year because of harassment and bullying.*

Gay activists use the tragedy of teen suicide and bullying to push for educational programs that promote gay myths.

FACT: The study on which this claim was based has been totally discredited.[22] Its author invented his results. What responsible researchers have found is that adolescents with SSA who attempt suicide resemble other adolescents with suicidal ideation. They have used drugs, engaged in sex at an early age, and/or come from troubled homes.[23]

CLAIM: *"Coming out" — that is, announcing you're gay — as a teen will help prevent later problems.*

Gay activists claim they aren't recruiting, but merely identifying and helping already "gay" teens to accept their "identities" and to act on them.

FACT: Boys who come out as "gay" during adolescence are at higher risk for a number of negative outcomes, including problems with drugs and infection with STDs.[24]

CLAIM: *Gay teens need condom education to prevent AIDS.*

Gay activists saw the AIDS crisis as another opportunity to push their agenda in the public schools. Only early and explicit sex education, they say, can halt the spread of the epidemic.

---

[22] See Peter LaBarbera, "The Gay Youth Suicide Myth," http://www.leaderu.com/jhs/labarbera.html.

[23] Gary Remafedi, James Farrow, and Robert Deisher, "Risk Factors for Attempted Suicide in Gay and Bisexual Youth, *Pediatrics* 87 (1991): 869-875.

[24] Ibid.

FACT: Decades of intense condom education have not reduced the rate of AIDS infections among men who have sex with men. While condom failure does play a part, the main reason is that men who have sex with men — no matter how much condom education they have received — don't use a condom every time. No amount of education, even very early education, changes this. In fact, young men who begin this behavior before they are twenty-one are at higher risk of becoming infected with HIV.[25]

CLAIM: *Children raised by same-sex couples have no more problems than children raised by their married biological parents.*

Aware that a major impediment to their agenda is public concern about the welfare of children raised by same-sex couples, gay activists have encouraged research to "prove" that there are no differences between children raised by same-sex couples and those raised by their biological married parents. They then offer these to the courts in marriage cases.

FACT: The majority of these studies did not compare children raised by same-sex couples with those raised by their married biological parents, but with children with single mothers or in other problematic situations. Furthermore, a review of these studies shows many of them to be externally or internally invalid. And, in some cases, researchers simply ignored their own findings and skewed their conclusions to fit their agenda.[26]

[25] George Lemp et al., "Seroprevalence of HIV and Risk Behaviors Among Young Homosexual and Bisexual Men," *JAMA* 272, no. 6 (August 10, 1994). Chart on page 451: 15.2 percent of the 79 young men in the study who began anal sex with men were found HIV positive, versus 3.8 percent of the 53 men who began the practice between ages 20 and 22.

[26] Robert Lerner and Althea Nagai, *No Basis: What The Studies Don't Tell Us About Same-Sex Parenting* (Washington: Marriage Law Project, 2001).

CLAIM: *Religious teaching against homosexuality leads to hate crimes.*

Gay activists have conducted a massive campaign to link disapproval of homosexual behavior with violence against persons with SSA, equating it to racism and racial violence. In every interview, press release, and op-ed, they use loaded words such as *discrimination, intolerance, bigotry,* and *hate* when referring to those who, on religious grounds, believe homosexual acts are contrary to God's law, strongly implying that their convictions are fuel for anti-gay violence.

FACT: Hooligans who commit acts of violence against persons with SSA are virtually never regular churchgoers. Most religious groups that oppose the gay agenda strongly condemn — both in word and deed — violence against persons with SSA. In fact, persons who engage in homosexual behavior are more likely to suffer violence from gays and lesbians than from others.[27]

CLAIM: *The Bible doesn't teach that committed homosexual relationships are wrong; its injunctions actually apply only to heterosexuals engaging in homosexual behavior.*

In addition to demonizing religious people who oppose their agenda, gay activists have sought to re-interpret religious texts and traditional moral doctrines that prohibit homosexuality, diminishing (or even reversing) the force of their meaning.

FACT: The biblical prohibition against sexual intimacy between persons of the same sex is clear and unambiguous, and further supported by centuries of Jewish and Christian tradition. It doesn't make provisions for sexual orientation or for "committed relationships."

---

[27] The prevalence of domestic violence among gay and lesbian couples is approximately 25 to 33 percent. Barnes, "It's Just a Quarrel," *American Bar Association Journal* (February 1998); reference found at www.aardvarc.org/dv/gay.shtml.

CLAIM: *At one time, the Catholic Church accepted gay marriage.*

Gay activists, frustrated that the Catholic Church hasn't changed its teachings to keep up with the times, seek to plant in people's minds the idea that, at one time, its teachings were different — even to the point of "blessing" gay unions. A handful of quasi-historical books and articles claiming to prove this have enjoyed ample exposure in the media.

FACT: Gay author John Boswell, who first put forward this claim, purposely mistranslated certain ancient texts to make rituals designed to make men "brothers" or "special comrades" appear to be homoerotic unions or "marriages."[28] It is absolutely clear from the history of the period that no sexual relationship was intended or involved,[29] and certainly not anything approximating a same-sex "marriage."

The Evidence Is One-Sided

When I began my inquiry into the issue of SSA, I sincerely expected to find two equal bodies of evidence, one supporting each side. The claims made by gay activists had received wide coverage in popular articles and books, often accompanied by references to journal articles. I obtained copies of those articles and found that many simply referenced other articles, but eventually I persisted in tracking every claim to its original source. Almost without exception, when I found the origin of the claim, the piece of research

---

[28] Robin Darling Young, "Gay Marriage: Reimagining Church History," *First Things* 47 (November 1994): 43-48: a review of John Boswell, *Same-Sex Unions in Premodern Europe* (New York: Random House, 1994).

[29] The study on which this claim was based (Paul Gibson, "Gay Male and Lesbian Youth Suicide," contained in "Report of the Secretary's Task Force on Youth Suicide," January 1989, but not accepted as peer-reviewed) has been totally discredited. See LaBarbera, "The Gay Youth Suicide Myth."

referenced was a study that didn't prove and, in some cases, didn't even *claim* to prove what it was purported to prove! Many studies contained serious methodological flaws that totally undermined their conclusions.[30] In other cases, the conclusions made by the authors were not supported by their own data. In several cases, statistics were simply created out of whole cloth.

On the other hand, I was able easily to find mountains of information contradicting the gay myths. In-depth studies carefully analyzing each of them have been published by groups such as the National Association for Research and Therapy of Homosexuality (NARTH), the Family Research Council, and Mission America, as well as numerous individual researchers. Yet these seldom receive mainstream media attention, while the least credible claim by the gay activists makes headlines. When the media do report research findings that challenge the gay agenda, the findings are ridiculed or presented in a way that diminishes their credibility. Thus, today there is a growing divide between those who have heard only the gay activists' unsupported claims and a smaller number who have been exposed to evidence that contradicts them.

Gay Activists' Dissenting Voices

Among gay activists, there is also a kind of divide. Although they portray their community as being in complete agreement with the claim that their sexual orientation is something they were born with and can't change, and totally unified in their desire to get married and have children just like other couples, no such unity exists. Some within the gay community know that the

---

[30] For example, the inadequacies in studies of children raised by persons with SSA has been documented in Lerner and Nagai, *No Basis*.

science is inconclusive and believe that resorting to lies and distortions undermines their movement. Others simply *don't* believe they're "just like everyone else," and don't want to pretend they are. For them, gay liberation means *not* having to be like married couples and ordinary families. In a 2003 statement that has been reproduced on numerous websites[31] and forums representing both sides of the debate, gay author John McKellar notes with approval that:

> The modern change in opinion concerning homosexuality, though presented as a scientific advance, is contradicted rather than supported by science. It is a transformation of public morals consistent with widespread abandonment of the Judeo-Christian ethics upon which our civilization is based. Though hailed as "progress," it is really a reversion to ancient pagan practices supported by a counter-culture restatement of gnostic moral relativism.

Others have questioned the reliance of fabricated data. Gareth Kirkby, writing in *Xtra West,* a Canadian publication "committed to the struggle of lesbians and gay men for sexual liberation and human fulfillment," asked why gay activists feel it is necessary to twist the truth:

> Why is it that some of us continue to bend and twist and otherwise play loose with (often outdated) so-called facts? Why for example do we continue to insist that ten percent of the overall population is gay or lesbian? . . . Our personal experience strongly suggests that this figure, despite its omnipresence, just isn't accurate . . . Or how about the argument, admittedly more common in the U.S. than here, that we are all "born this way"? This sounds like a plea that we're

---

[31] For example, http://www.anglican-mainstream.net/?p=1636.

handicapped and deserve pity for our sad misfortune. More to the point, it's painting sexuality with a broad sweep of the brush. Personally, after a number of relationships with women, I chose to be gay.[32]

A Clash of Philosophies

Such frank statements afford us a glimpse at a key truth: the battle over marriage is fundamentally a clash between two incompatible world views. In the end, one must prevail, the other must be discredited. Much more is at stake in this clash than whether a few thousand same-sex couples can call their relationships "marriages." At the core of the Sexual Left and its agenda is an *ideology*. Ultimately what is at stake is whether Western civilization discards or retains one of its foundational principles.

Although most gay activists claim publicly that all they want is merely to extend to persons with SSA the benefits of traditional marriage, there are others who are more forthcoming about their larger aims and the expected effects. Michael Bronski, author of the book *The Pleasure Principle: Culture, Backlash, and the Struggle for Gay Freedom*,[33] has unabashedly advocated sexual pleasure as an end itself. When Pope John Paul II died in the Spring of 2005, Bronski wrote an article in which he attacked John Paul's teachings on sexuality and laid out his alternative view:

Because homosexual sex never has the potential to create children, because it is — in essence — sex for the wonderful sake of sex itself, we have become the standard bearers not just for sexual freedom, but for sexual holiness. If the body and sexuality are holy, then they must be holy in and

---

[32] Gareth Kirkby, "No, No, No to Marriage Rights," *Xtra West* (August 20, 1998).

[33] St. Martin's Press, 1998.

unto themselves. There is no need to justify them with the procreation of children, or to vindicate them with post-coital shame.[34]

I wonder if Bronski knew that the late pope had put his finger precisely on this difference in ideologies over thirty years before. In 1960, as a young Polish bishop named Karol Wojtyla, the future Pope John Paul II wrote a book called *Love and Responsibility*, in which he examined in detail the ideology that makes sexual pleasure the highest good. By reducing other persons to means for one's own enjoyment, this sexual "utilitarianism," he said, contradicts the fundamental law of love: "You shall love your neighbor as yourself," a corollary of which must be, "You shall not use your neighbor as an object." Although Sexual Utilitarianism may sound harmless and even quite appealing — everyone free to enjoy sexual pleasure! — it always ends with one person using another person as an object. This is inconsistent with love and with human dignity.

According to the principles of Sexual Utilitarianism, as long as both (or all) parties are experiencing pleasure and have given consent, any sexual acts are permissible. But what happens when one person ceases to receive pleasure from the relationship? Then, according to the Sexual Utilitarian ethic, he is not bound to consider the feelings of the other, or to honor any promises and commitments he has made. The other has become to him an object he has used and can now cease to use, not a person whom he must continue to love. This is the antithesis of marriage, which is based on a vow to love the other more than self, regardless of whether the other is a provider of pleasure or happiness.

[34] Michael Bronski, "Requiem for the Pope's Penis: How Did the Pope Reconcile His Oppression of Human Sexuality with the Reality of His Own Body?" *Bay Windows* (April 7, 2005).

John Paul II also explains how people rightly feel shame when they view others as sexual objects or allow themselves to be treated as sexual objects — not as a socially conditioned response but as a natural human response. In contrast, Bronski promotes "shamelessness" as the hallmark of the gay lifestyle:

> Homosexuals are often accused of being shameless — and that is precisely the truth. Shame is the antithesis of sacredness[35] and the more shameless homosexuals become — demanding their civil rights, personal integrity, and personal and sexual freedom — the more they exhibit to the world the endless possibilities of sexual pleasure and sexual holiness.[36]

The Sexual Left is offended by religious mores, abstinence education, even warnings about the danger of STDs, because these engender negative feelings of guilt and shame and thereby interfere with the pursuit of pleasure. Somehow they blame the pandemic of STDs sweeping the world on the promoters of chastity, and particularly the Catholic Church. According to them, not promiscuity, but religious rules restricting sexuality are to blame: these make people feel guilty, and so they don't properly prepare themselves for sex (by carrying condoms in their pockets).

Sexual Utilitarianism and Marriage

This isn't a debate about means, but about ends. Should sexual pleasure be the servant of marriage, binding the couple together in love for the sake of each other, their children, and the stability of

---

[35] You might have noticed how Bronski turns words such as *sacredness* and *holiness* upside down, hijacking these ancient ideas and putting them at the service of a philosophy that is actually the antithesis of the moral and spiritual traditions of most major religions.

[36] Bronski, "Requiem for the Pope's Penis."

the community? Or should individual sexual pleasure be an end in itself, with other people merely temporary and interchangeable means to that end? How these questions are decided will affect our entire society. Gay activists often ask, "How can my marriage to the person I love possibly affect you?" But many of them do so disingenuously; for they must know that marriage is not a private institution, and changing the definition of marriage is not a personal decision. Change marriage, and everything changes.

There are eloquent defenders of marriage who know what's at stake. Journalist and social scientist Stanley Kurtz chronicled how changes in marriage law across Europe have affected the foundational culture of the family there. According to him, those who claim that marriage won't be undermined by redefining it to include same-sex couples are not only ignoring evidence from the European experiment, but they're also ignoring the explicit statements of those pushing for such changes. For European activists admit that the change will profoundly affect the way everyone views marriage.

For example, Anthony Giddens, a leading British sociologist, sees a near future in which marriage will no longer be oriented toward monogamy, fidelity, and family; instead all that will matter is the emotional connection between the adults involved: "the pure relationship."

Kurtz explains:

In the *Transformation of Intimacy*, Giddens argues that "episodic gay sexuality of the bathhouse culture type" contains critical positive lessons for heterosexual relationships . . . For Giddens, in an age when the increasingly empty institution of traditional marriage is destined to fall away, gay relationships and gay sexuality serve as the new positive models for heterosexuals. As Giddens notes, while "marriage in the traditional sense" disappears, "it is the gays who are the pioneers." As for children, Giddens advocates laws that oblige parents to provide financially for their offspring, no matter what sort of living arrangements those parents enter into over time. Here, then, we have the cultural meaning of European gay unions, from the man who is arguably Europe's most influential interpreter of the family.[37]

⁓

There is every reason to believe that triumph of the Sexual Utilitarian ethic promoted by the Sexual Left would affect all intimate relationships, not just those between persons of the same sex. If Bronski's "sacred shamelessness" were admitted to the culture's shared marital ethic, then chastity before marriage and fidelity in marriage would become idiosyncratic private choices, no longer shared community values. We've already witnessed the negative impact brought on by other aspects of Sexual Utilitarianism: contraception, abortion, promiscuity, easy divorce — all these have, over time, skewed the shared cultural standards of marriage and sexual behavior and in so doing have helped pave the way to a redefinition of marriage.

In the Culture War, there are many battlefields. It isn't enough to prevent the legal redefinition of marriage; we must defend the ethical basis of marriage. We must remind people that "forsaking all others . . . till death do us part" aren't just nice words; they are solemn vows that people have a duty to honor, even when they don't feel like it. Marriage — faithful, exclusive, permanent marriage between one man and one woman — is the foundation of the family. Strong families make a strong society. This is a battle in which everyone has a stake.

[37] Stanley Kurtz, "Zombie Killers: A.K.A., 'Queering the Social,' " *National Review Online*, May 25, 2006.

Chapter 3

The Debate Over Same-Sex Attraction

What are the combating philosophies in this debate?

How has the clinical view of SSA changed in recent times?

What are the cases for the different theories of SSA's origin?

Homosexual behavior is not a novelty of modern times. It has been reported in many cultures throughout recorded history. However, in almost every past society and era, it has been regarded as unacceptable, immoral, a sign of weakness, unnatural. There have been exceptions, but these appear to have been anomalies produced by extraordinary cultural conditions.

For example, those who promote the gay agenda today often point to classical Greece as a culture in which homosexual behavior was glorified. But would they really want a return to classical Greek values? The sexes were strictly separated. Women were restricted to the home, not educated, and generally regarded as inferior. Adult male citizens were allowed to pursue sexual relationships with the adolescent boys whom they were supposed to educate. Once the boys reached maturity, though, they were expected to marry a woman. What we had then was not an enlightened approach to sexuality, but an organized form of abuse — of both women and boys.

Some writers have noted that there are reports of the emperors Caligula and Nero engaging in homosexuality and even in same-sex "marriage." Yet these reports come to us from the *enemies* of these emperors, eager to demonstrate how depraved and insane they were. Indeed, even in decadent Rome we do not find a cultural normalization of homosexual behavior.

The Religious Debate

Pagan societies might have tolerated most sexual aberrations, but monotheistic religions have from their inception unequivocally condemned all homosexual acts. The Law of Moses condemned in strongest terms a man lying with a man as with a woman, and all religions that honor Moses as a prophet — Judaism, Christianity, Islam, and Mormonism — held homosexual acts as sinful. Traditional Christian religious groups up to the present day, notably the Catholic Church and evangelical Protestantism, have retained these ages-old moral beliefs.

In the last half-century, however, a number of liberal Protestant denominations and liberal branches of Judaism have rejected that tradition and come to accept homosexual behavior and relationships — some even to the point of blessing same-sex couples and ordaining gay and lesbian clergy. Theologians in league with the Sexual Left have produced clever arguments claiming that the key scriptural verses condemning homosexual acts[38] refer only to *heterosexuals* engaging in homosexual acts, not to people who were "born gay" and engaged only in faithful, committed relationships. There's no support for this interpretation either in Scripture or Church tradition, but these theologians begin with the premise that both Scripture and the moral law are made up by men — not revealed by God — and therefore are products of their time and reflect the prejudices of the men who wrote them.

☞

When people in the pews of the so-called "mainline" Protestant churches — Methodists, Lutherans, Episcopalians, and so forth — refuse to accept the "new" theology, dissension results.

---

[38] For example, Lev. 18:22; Rom. 2:26-27; 1 Cor. 6:9-13; 1 Tim. 1:8-11.

For instance, in November of 2003, the American Episcopal Church ordained the openly homosexual (and once-married father of two) Gene Robinson bishop, causing a rupture in the international Anglican Communion. The more conservative churches in Africa were particularly outraged and are on the point of schism. The slow cultural movement toward acceptance of gay marriage has led to the creation of same-sex wedding rites in more and more "gay-friendly" churches. And in many Christian denominations, ongoing moral confusion and institutional scandal have pressed to the fore debates about the ordination of openly gay persons to ministry and church leadership.

The Catholic Church has also been challenged to change or at least soften its teachings on sexual morality, but has consistently refused to do so. In 2006, the Vatican released a document which said that men with deep-seated homosexual tendencies, even if they remain physically chaste, do not possess the emotional maturity to be admitted to seminaries or ordained as priests. But even the Catholic Church is not without dissension, with some priests, lay ministers, and even bishops in some dioceses trying to "moderate" the official Church line in their pastoral writings and practices.

The Evolution of Psychological Opinion

For most of history, homosexual behavior was seen as a moral problem — tolerated in periods where sexual immorality in general was tolerated and condemned harshly where sexual immorality was condemned. In many times and places, it was technically illegal, but the laws were often not consistently enforced.

Then, at the end of the nineteenth century, there was a significant change in attitude toward homosexual behavior, brought about by the invention of psychiatric treatment. What had been previously viewed as a moral problem came to be seen as a psychological disorder.

Psychiatrists now taught that people did not freely choose to be attracted to persons of the same sex; rather, they were driven toward SSA by psychological traumas. Several theories as to the causes and possible treatment of SSA were offered, but it wasn't until the 1950s that the subject received serious study. At that time, a number of mental-health professionals who had treated clients with SSA began to study it seriously. They developed more sophisticated theories to explain the origins of SSA. They experimented with new treatment protocols and reported on successful therapy outcomes. The most comprehensive study, *Homosexuality: A Psychoanalytic Study of Male Homosexuals*, was published by Irving Bieber and associates in 1963. This book compared the treatment of 106 homosexual men with 100 non-homosexual men. According to the study, *"29 patients had become exclusively heterosexual during the course of psychoanalytic treatment"* (italics in original).[39] Many other therapists, using a variety of therapy methods, also reported successful outcomes.[40]

However, in the early 1970s, therapists treating homosexuality as a disorder ran afoul of the burgeoning gay-rights movement. According to Ronald Bayer, author of *Homosexuality and American Psychiatry: The Politics of Diagnosis* and a supporter of the gay agenda, the status of homosexuality ceased to be a psychiatric problem and became "a political question" requiring "a political analysis."[41]

Bayer's book reveals how gay activists pressured the American Psychiatric Association (APA) to remove homosexuality as a diagnosis from its *Diagnostic and Statistical Manual* (DSM) — the

[39] Irving Bieber et al., *Homosexuality: A Psychoanalytic Study of Male Homosexuals* (New York: Basic Books, 1962), 276.

[40] Wyler, "Anything But Straight."

[41] Ronald Bayer, *Homosexuality and American Psychiatry: The Politics of Diagnosis* (New York: Basic Books, 1981), 5.

handbook for mental-health professionals. In 1970 and 1971, gay activists staged noisy protests at the APA's annual meetings, shouting down speakers and accusing the therapists of oppressing them. Many psychiatrists were intimidated by the protesters; however, those who had successfully treated men with SSA defended the diagnosis of homosexuality as a mental disorder, pointing out that it was not based on preconceptions — positive or negative — about homosexuality, but rather, on years of experience with clients with SSA.

Bieber, for example, insisted that his work clearly demonstrated how same-sex attraction in men was rooted in childhood trauma and that no matter how skillfully persons with SSA coped with life situations, no matter how much society learned to tolerate them, their sexual attractions were neither natural nor healthy. Some psychiatrists drew a distinction between the legitimate struggle for civil rights for persons with SSA and the scientific issue of diagnosis. Psychiatrist Robert McDevitt argued poignantly that the declassification of homosexuality was not compassionate but would create "more despair than hope."[42]

But such testimonials were brushed aside, and in 1973 the APA surrendered to pressure, removed homosexuality from its *DSM*, and issued the following statement:

> Whereas homosexuality in and of itself implies no impairment in judgment stability, reliability or vocational capabilities, therefore, be it resolved that the American Psychiatric Association deplores all public and private discrimination against homosexuals in such areas as employment, housing, public accommodation, and licensing, and declares that no burden of proof of such judgment, capacity or reliability

[42] Ibid., 136.

shall be placed upon homosexuals greater than that imposed on other persons.

The statement itself was really quite modest. Both sides in controversy had opposed unjust discrimination against persons with SSA. Both sides agreed that many persons with SSA were successful in their professional work. Both sides agreed that the term *homosexuality* was unscientifically vague. Nonetheless, the change marked a landmark victory for gay activists, one that would have far-reaching effects.

In removing homosexuality from the *DSM*, the APA changed the way it defined psychological disorders. Before 1973, a behavior was considered disordered if it arose from an irrational reaction to childhood traumas or deficits, even if the person with the behavior had found ways to function successfully in society. The new criteria discounted the origins and considered only present distress, disability, and disadvantage. If the person claimed to be "comfortable" with his condition, then it was no longer to be considered a psychological disorder. If he wasn't comfortable, then his discomfort was to be attributed "internalized homophobia" caused by societal oppression — for which "gay-affirming therapy" was the prescribed cure.

The Debate Over the Origins of SSA

This statement by the APA and its removal of homosexuality as a diagnosis from the *DSM* did not settle every issue. The question of treatment, for example, remained open. Should persons who wanted to change their sexual orientation be offered treatment or counseled to accept their homosexuality? More important, the APA's statement didn't address the origins of SSA. This is significant because the question of SSA's origins is the key to the entire debate over the gay agenda, including same-sex marriage.

Gay activists argue that they have a right to marry because they were born "gay" or "lesbian" and are unable to change, and therefore *can't* marry a person of the other sex.

Although the logic of this argument is also open to scrutiny (is marriage a "right" in the same way as life and basic freedoms are? Does society have a duty to modify its longstanding institutions every time they're deemed "unfair" to some?), since popular support for the gay agenda is, in the minds of many, tied to the conviction that persons with SSA are born that way and can't change, this issue of origins is crucial to this debate.

Three Schools

As I studied the competing theories and presumptions about the origins of SSA, I discovered that they all boiled down to one of three basic philosophical approaches: Essentialism, Constructionism, and Developmentalism.

• *Essentialism* regards an individual's pattern of sexual attraction ("orientation") and/or his sexual identity as biologically determined — a fixed and stable characteristic that he's born with and discovers over time. It can't be changed, so it must be accepted as part of essence or nature. Thus, a person *is* gay, lesbian, bisexual, transgendered, straight, or of other sexual orientation. For the Essentialists, SSA is a normal variant of the human race, like skin color.

• *Constructionism* (sometimes called Social Constructionism or Post-Modernist Deconstructionism) holds that sexual identities are shaped by social forces — "constructed out of a historical, cultural context."[43] Constructionists believe that the sexual categories

---

[43] Sari Dworkin, "Individual Therapy with LGB Clients," *Handbook of Counseling and Psychotherapy with Lesbian, Gay, and*

into which people are placed — male, female, homosexual, heterosexual, and so forth — are creations of an oppressive culture. None of them is natural or normal or better than any other. People don't discover their essential identity, but rather, create one for themselves.

This can happen only after the "constructions" have been identified and cast off. Indeed, it can be said that the goal of the Constructionist ideology is to "deconstruct" everything that the oppressor-class insists is natural and normal; say, for instance, the idea that men are to be fathers and women mothers, and that children need one of each. This deconstruction is accomplished by showing how the language of sex and gender serves the interests of the oppressor class and harms the oppressed class — in this case, men and women who don't fit into the heterosexual pattern. Deconstruction is a never-ending task, since the moment something becomes accepted as "normal," it is challenged as oppressive of those who aren't within the norm.

• *Developmentalism* asserts that the human person is neither born a blank slate, free to be whatever he wants to be or else chained by oppressive societal constructions, nor that his pattern of sexual attraction is biologically predetermined. For the Developmentalist, sexual attraction to the other sex is the proper outcome of healthy psychosexual development. If the individual moves successfully through each developmental stage, he will become a psychologically and emotionally healthy adult. But if he does not receive the experiences he needs, if there are deficits or traumas during crucial stages of development, he might become stuck in a particular stage. The result might be patterns of sexual attraction other than the capacity for respectful love of the other

Bisexual Clients, Ruperto M. Perez, Kurt A. DeBord, and Kathleen J. Bieschke, eds. (Washington: APA Books, 1999).

sex. In many cases, for example, SSA occurs when an accidental convergence of circumstances leads to a failure to complete the process of sexual identification.

Developmentalists also factor into this calculation biological characteristics that affect the way a child is treated and the way he responds to experiences, as well as the choices he makes with his free will. Those with a theological perspective will also make room for the action of grace. For the Developmentalist, each person is a unique individual with his or her own personal history, living in a particular culture at a particular moment in history with a particular biological make up, but also endowed with free will and able to make choices, even difficult choices.

At one time, it was thought that once brain patterns were set early in life, change was impossible. New research has demonstrated that the brain, even late in life, has a potential to change.[44] Developmentalists hold that same-sex attraction can be prevented and treated.

Let's critique at the first two theories, commonly held by gay activists, before examining the Developmentalist approach in greater detail in the following chapters.

The Essentialist Strategy

Essentialism is the best-known theory for SSA's origins. Gay activists have based their public strategy on the Essentialist approach — not because there is scientific evidence of the existence of a "gay gene," but because the strategy works. They know that those who believe that some people are simply "born gay" and are

---

[44] Jeffrey Schwartz, *The Mind and the Brain: Neuroplasticity and the Power of Mental Force* (New York: Regan Books, 2002).

unable to change are more likely to support the gay political agenda.[45]

A 1989 study, for example, found that those who believed that persons with SSA were "born that way" held significantly more positive attitudes toward homosexuality than those who believed that homosexuals chose or learned their sexual orientation.[46] In 1992, researchers analyzed how people's attitudes toward homosexuality were affected by reading a summary of research about biological bases of homosexual orientation.[47] They found that those who read material claiming a biological cause for SSA were more likely to favor aspects of the gay agenda.

There have been no replicated scientific studies proving that SSA is biologically predetermined and unchangeable; no studies

[45] Of course, just because a condition is genetically determined doesn't mean it's "normal" and can't — or shouldn't — be treated. For example, babies are tested for PKU (phenylketonuria), a genetic defect affecting the ability to process a particular protein. Early diagnosis allows dietary changes that prevent severe brain damage. If an animal were born with an inherited trait that causes it to avoid reproduction, it would be considered a defect, yet because gay activists presume the Sexual Left's ideology, they insist that same-sex attraction is a physically neutral condition, like eye color.

[46] Kurt Ernulf, Sune Innala, and Fredrick Whitam, "Biological Explanation, Psychological Explanation, and Tolerance of Homosexuals: A Cross-National Analysis of Beliefs and Attitudes," Psychological Reports 65 (1989): 1003-1010.

[47] Julie Piskur and Douglas Degelman, "Effect of Reading a Summary of Research About Biological Bases of Homosexual Orientation on Attitudes Toward Homosexuals," Psychological Reports 71 (1992): 1219-1225. Piskur: "The major finding of this study was that exposure to a written summary of research supporting biological determinants of homosexual orientation can affect scores assessing attitudes toward homosexuals when measured immediately after the reading" (p. 1223).

showing that it is unchangeable. Those who nonetheless promote the myth of the "gay gene," or claim that science has shown SSA to be genetically determined, often reference two studies, one done by Simon LeVay and the other by Dean Hamer, both self-identified gay men.

In 1991, LeVay claimed to have discovered small differences between the brains of men with SSA and those without. However, LeVay had studied the brain tissue of men who had died of AIDS, and the HIV virus is known to affect the brain.[48] Indeed, although the popular media hailed it as a breakthrough at the time, LeVay has since quietly given up research in this area and backed away from the claim that his flawed study proves SSA to be genetically determined.

In 1993, Hamer and his associates published an article in which they claimed to have found a "linkage between DNA markers on the X chromosome and male sexual orientation."[49] According to the article, a certain gene, passed down from the mother, was common to several men with SSA in the same family. Activists touted the study, claiming that they had found the elusive "gay gene." If Hamer had been correct in his conclusion that a particular genetic marker is more common in men with SSA, then

[48] Simon LeVay, "A Difference in the Hypothalamic Structure Between Heterosexual and Homosexual Men," *Science* 253 (1991): 1034-1037. For a scientific refutation of LeVay's claims, see William Byne and Bruce Parsons, "Human Sexual Orientation: The Biologic Theories Reappraised," *Archives of General Psychiatry* 50 (March 1993): 228-239. See also John Horgan, "Gay Genes Revisited: Doubts Arise Over Research on the Biology of Homosexuality," *Scientific American* (November 1995): 28.

[49] Dean Hamer et al., "A Linkage Between DNA Markers on the X Chromosome and Male Sexual Orientation," *Science* 261 (1993): 321-327.

anyone who replicated his experiment should come up with similar results. Yet when a research team conducted the same tests several years later using a larger sample, they did not find a common marker. They concluded that the evidence "did not support an X-linked gene underlying male homosexuality."[50]

In spite of their failure to produce scientifically acceptable evidence for the "gay gene" theory, the LeVay and Hamer studies continue to be widely referenced by gay activists. Chandler Burr, in his book *A Separate Creation: The Search for the Biological Origins of Sexual Orientation*, used the work of LeVay and Hamer to promote his idea that science was on the brink of discovering a biological cause for SSA. Although the book contains a great deal of interesting scientific information about how DNA works, the possibility of treatment for genetic defects, and the sex life of hyenas, none of the evidence Burr presents proves the existence of a gay gene.

That book was published in 1996. More than a decade later, we are no closer to discovering the "gay gene."

Do Our Genes Control How We Live?

Apart from the conclusions of any one study, many people are critical of the very idea that genes could determine sexual orientation. One of them is Edward Stein, a gay activist and author of *The Mismeasure of Desire: The Science, Theory and Ethics of Sexual Orientation*, who notes:

> Genes in themselves cannot directly specify any behavior or psychological phenomenon. Instead, genes direct a particular pattern of RNA synthesis, which in turn may influence

[50] George Rice et al., "Male Homosexuality: Absence of Linkage to Microsatellite Markers at Xq28," *Science* 284, (1999): 665-667.

the development of psychological dispositions and expression of behaviors. There are necessarily many intervening pathways between a gene and a disposition or a behavior, and even more intervening variables between a gene and a pattern that involves both thinking and behaving. The terms "gay gene" and "homosexual gene" are therefore without meaning.[51]

In a 1994 article for *Science* magazine, Charles C. Mann questioned the search of a genetic cause for behavior:

> Time and time again, scientists have claimed that particular genes or chromosomal regions are associated with behavioral traits, only to withdraw their findings when they were not replicated . . . All were announced with great fanfare; all were greeted unskeptically in the popular press; all are now in disrepute.[52]

Despite the spin put on them by gay activists and the media, most of the studies they reference do not actually claim that sexual orientation is genetically *determined*; instead they suggest that sexual orientation might be influenced in part by inherited characteristics. Yet this is no earth-shattering claim. *Everything* we are and do is influenced in part by inherited characteristics: they affect both the way we act and the way we are treated (especially, for our purposes, by parents), and they both in turn influence our psychological development.

For example, an inherited characteristic such as lack of hand/eye coordination in a boy with an athletic father could cause the father

---

[51] Edward Stein, *The Mismeasure of Desire: The Science, Theory and Ethics of Sexual Orientation* (New York: Oxford University Press, 1999), 221.

[52] Charles C. Mann, "Genes and Behavior," *Science* 264 (1987).

to have a problem relating to his son and the mother to overprotect him. If this boy had been born with a more sensitive nature, this treatment might wound him deeply — more deeply than it would a less-sensitive boy — and developmental problems could result. Yet even though the treatment the boy receives and his reaction to it were based on genetically determined characteristics, we wouldn't say that resulting developmental problems would be part of his inborn "nature."

That example might actually be a quite common scenario. Richard Fitzgibbons, who has worked with many men with SSA, is convinced that in our culture, where success in athletics is equated with masculine competence, lack of hand/eye coordination and its effect on a boy's relationship with his father and peers plays an important part in the development of SSA in many men. Lack of athletic skill might hinder the father/son relationship, and the failure in that relationship is the proximate developmental cause of SSA.

Physical and developmental factors aside, we cannot discount the part free will plays in the development of SSA. While gay activists insist that no one would "choose" to be attracted to the same sex and, in the majority of cases, they are probably right, people do make other choices, such as the choice to hold on to resentment, to give in to envy, to wallow in self-pity, to choose self-comfort rather than self-discipline. Such choices build habits that might be difficult to overcome. A child who has not yet reached the age of reason cannot foresee how such small choices are steps on a path that could lead to SSA, so it can't be said that he "chose to be gay." Nonetheless he exercised his free will along the way.

Identical Twins Who Aren't

Identical twins studies are the perfect vehicle for testing the genetic theory. If SSA were genetically determined, then identical twins could be expected to have identical patterns of sexual attraction. Yet in the majority of cases, this isn't so. The most comprehensive research on SSA in identical twins was done by John Michael Bailey and associates, using members of the Australian twins' registry. The study found that if one twin was non-heterosexual, in only eleven percent of cases was the other twin also non-heterosexual.[53]

It isn't surprising that in some cases of identical twins, both individuals would have SSA. Identical twins share the same genetic characteristics and the same environment; even identical twins raised apart display remarkable similarities in many areas. We would, therefore, expect that they would usually show similar patterns of sexual attraction too.

What is surprising is not the concordance, but the relative lack of it. This follows when identical twins are treated quite differently by their parents (something to which identical twins are acutely sensitive), as case histories of twins discordant for sexual attractions reveal. In a case reported by author Richard Green, identical twin Frank Jr. was born first and badly mutilated in the process. He was considered by his parents as a "very ugly baby." Co-twin Paul had big eyes and was perceived as good-looking at birth. Strangers seeing them together commented, "Oh how nice! A boy and a girl."

At age three, Paul contracted an infectious disease that required extensive medical attention. This led to markedly different upbringings for the twins: for two and a half years, his mother drove him to a distant hospital — a two-hour round trip — while

---

[53] John Michael Bailey, Michael Dunne, and Nicholas Martin, "Genetic and Environmental Influences on Sexual Orientation and Its Correlates in an Australian Twin Sample: Personality Processes and Individual Differences," *Journal of Personality and Social Psychology* 78, no. 3 (2000): 524-536.

the father stayed home with Frank Jr. The father engaged in rough play with Frank Jr., but the sickly Paul was coddled.

At age eight, Paul was evaluated for feminine behavior, which included cross-dressing, doll play, female role play, and avoidance of rough-and-tumble play. When asked to draw a person, Paul drew a female and Frank drew a male. In an interview, the twins' mother also commented on the impact of Paul's not being named after his father: "I can see, looking through Paul's eyes, that he [Frank, Jr.] got Daddy's name because he's the one Daddy liked." Paul later developed SSA; his identical twin, Frank, didn't.[54]

In another case, identical twins Sam and Howard differed in weight at birth. Sam, the smaller twin, recalls early feelings of insecurity and vulnerability. He always felt closer to his mother than to his father. On the other hand, Howard recalled feeling secure as a young child. He perceived his father as quiet in disposition but loving, gentle, and strong. Howard was the target of continual maternal disfavor because of his sloppiness, rowdiness, and poor performance as a student. Sam developed SSA; Howard is married with no SSA.[55]

Don't Gay Men Talk Differently, Though?

Many people are convinced that they can identify a man with SSA by his speech patterns, and conclude that this common trait points to a biological cause. It's true that some men with SSA do have an identifiable way of speaking, but this is by no means universal; still less is it evidence that SSA is biologically determined, because speech patterns aren't inherited. When children learn to

[54] Richard Green, *Sexual Identity Conflict in Children and Adults* (Baltimore: Penguin, 1974), 206-207.

[55] Richard Friedman, *Male Homosexuality: A Contemporary Psychoanalytic Perspective* (New Haven: Yale University Press, 1988), 28-29.

speak, they pick up the accent of the people around them. A Chinese child adopted at birth by an American couple will speak English without the slightest accent. But a person who spends his early years speaking one language and later learns to speak another will carry a discernable hint of his first language throughout his life.

In the same way, the lisp, high pitch, and effeminate tones evident in the speech of some men with SSA must be *learned*, likely through imitation of the speech of their mothers — in particular, the way their mothers spoke to them as a baby. Indeed there's an artificial quality to this "effeminate" speech pattern; little girls do not speak in this manner, nor do most adult women.

Some men with SSA insist that the high range of their voice is natural. Yet many speech therapists are convinced that effeminate speech patterns and the high vocal range of some males with SSA — men who otherwise have normal hormone levels and fully developed male sex organs — are psychological in origin, not physical. Interestingly, some men with SSA don't want to hear this. One speech specialist recounted how she was able, through various exercises, to show a client with effeminate speech patterns that he was physically capable of speaking in the lower range that is normal for men. Yet rather than being grateful, the man was furious, and he never returned to the therapist.

In another case, she retrained a man with feminine affectations in his speech to speak as a normal male, although, whenever he spoke with his mother, he would revert to the feminine affectation.[56]

A Myth with Many Takers

It's clear enough why gay activists would employ an Essentialist strategy. But why are myths like the gay gene so popular in the general public?

[56] Private interviews.

Myths flourish because people want to believe they're true. One reason some people want to believe that SSA is genetically determined is because linking SSA to childhood experiences instead seems to some like "blaming the parents." Many people know good, loving men and women who have children with SSA, and it's easier to believe that gay people are hard-wired that way than to conclude that their friends were bad parents.

But, in reality, they needn't conclude that. It's certainly true that in some instances, parental mistreatment is one root cause of SSA. However, most parents of persons with SSA are good people who loved their children and tried to be good parents. But there might simply have been a mismatch between the parent and a particular child. A mother might have been overprotective because she feared male aggression, and her fears might have affected the way she treated one of her sons. A father might have been away from the home at crucial times and not fully understood how his absence affected his relationship with a child's development. In other instances, it might have been a caregiver, a sibling, or another family member who discouraged same-sex identification, or encouraged a child to identify with the other sex.

If blame is to be assigned, it belongs first to professionals who are aware of the research on SSA and its roots in childhood experiences but don't inform parents. Many parents of adults with SSA say they noticed something wrong with their child early on and expressed concern to pediatricians or teachers, only to be told there was nothing to worry about. Many were told their children would "grow out of it," despite substantial evidence that the problem, if left untreated, would make the child vulnerable to a host of problems and could lead to the development of SSA in adolescence.[57]

[57] Joseph Nicolosi, *A Parent's Guide to Preventing Homosexuality;* James Dobson, *Bringing Up Boys;* Fr. John Harvey, *Same-Sex*

"Who Would Want to Be Gay, Anyway?"

Another reason that some men, especially, believe the gay-gene myth is that they know they themselves didn't *choose* to be sexually attracted to women. One day puberty hit, and it just happened, unbidden. Because such men can't imagine being any other way, they reason that any man who isn't turned on by a beautiful woman must have something physically different about him. When he hears a man with SSA tell him that he has "always felt different," it confirms his intuition that the problem must be biological.

Not only do people assume SSA must be natural and inborn because their own attraction to the other sex is unchosen, but they further presume that, given all the troubles that come with SSA — societal disapproval, bias, feelings of loneliness and being "different" — it's ludicrous to think that they consciously chose it. Therefore, SSA must be inborn. What man would *want* to be gay?[58]

This is a variation on the Essentialist strategy, one that depends upon a false dichotomy. The origin of SSA is not an either/or proposition: either "I decided to be gay" or "I was born gay."[59] If the origin of SSA can be found in a person's reaction to early experiences, we have a third possibility, a more nuanced understanding that takes into consideration all that a person is: biology, environment, experience, and free will.

Attraction: A Parent's Guide; Don Schmierer, *An Ounce of Prevention: Preventing the Homosexual Condition in Today's Youth.*

[58] Some activists avoid this argument, which can be taken as a tacit admission that SSA is a second-class situation.

[59] Unfortunately, sometimes defenders of marriage and traditional morality make this same mistake and force themselves into the difficult position of defending the idea that SSA is a "chosen" behavior, pure and simple.

It's certainly true that those of us who are attracted to the other sex don't think of ourselves as "choosing" our sexual orientation. Likewise, persons with SSA are probably being honest when they say they did not choose to be attracted to persons of the same sex. Desires for intimacy with a person of the same sex appeared spontaneously, and only later were they interpreted as sexual desires. It's also true that many persons with SSA report fighting their same-sex attractions, being ashamed of their feelings, wanting to be "straight," and going through various stages of denial, deception, and despair. If SSA in an adult is a result of cumulative experiences and reactions, as many therapists believe, then persons with SSA may theoretically have the freedom to make other choices, but will find it difficult to do so without substantial support.

No baby says, "I want parents who aren't able to meet my needs." None of us chooses his vulnerabilities. We *do* choose how we will respond, but our choices are constrained by our experiences. We are therefore both free and unfree.

"God Made Me Gay"

Another variant of their Essentialist strategy has been to claim that God is responsible for making people gay — basically, the "born that way, can't change" myth recast in religious language. If people are genetically predestined to be attracted to the same-sex, then God, who created them, is responsible, right? And if God makes people gay, then it can't be sinful or wrong or "unnatural." Accordingly, the condemnations of homosexuality found in the holy books and teachings of major religions must be thrown aside as inventions of men — the products of human cultural biases — and SSA should be embraced as a gift from God.

Yet even if SSA were biologically determined, which would, to the theologically minded, present the possibility that God "made them gay," it would not follow that God wants them to engage in homosexual behavior, any more than he wants a person born with a biology that makes them susceptible to alcoholism or obesity or uncontrolled anger to engage in those behaviors. Those who suffer from such problems usually work hard and seek outside help to overcome their biological dispositions; they don't embrace them, citing God's will.

Of course, those who claim that God has reached down and solemnly decreed that certain people should be unchangeably "gay" are often also the same people who insist that the entire universe evolved without divine interference of any kind. This typical inconsistency suggests that "God made me gay" is more a political strategy than a theological statement.

And there might be yet another, forward-thinking motive behind the "God made me gay" claim: it puts SSA in a more positive light. In contrast, a biological explanation involving mutation and natural selection could lead to the conclusion that it's a nonadvantageous genetic mutation: a birth defect. If SSA were proven to be caused by a mutated gene, and such a gene could be identified, then parents could demand prenatal testing and abort the "defective" babies, thus severely curtailing the gay population of the next generation.

Gay activist Larry Kramer once said that if a gay gene were discovered, the religious right would become pro-choice.[60] Such comments slander pro-lifers, who would fight as hard for such unborn babies as they do today even for those with serious physical birth defects. But this scenario, although purely hypothetical (the "gay gene" will never be found) does raise the question of what the Sexual Left would do if forced to choose between supporting gay rights or abortion on demand.

---

[60] Chandler Burr, *Separate Creation* (New York: Hyperion Books, 1997), 280.

The Constructionist Ideology

Listening to the debate over marriage as it's presented in the mainstream media, one would come away with the impression that not only is the Essentialist view the established scientific explanation of SSA, but that all persons with SSA accept it.

It's true that for public consumption, gay activists almost always present themselves as Essentialists and speak of gays, lesbians, bisexuals, transgenders, and straights as though these were clearly defined, permanent categories in which human beings are born and must remain. However, although gay activists and academics might espouse Essentialism in public because it's a useful strategy, ideologically many would consider themselves *Constructionists*.

As gay-rights advocate Ellen Broido acknowledges in her article "Constructing Identity: The Nature and Meaning of Lesbian, Gay, and Bisexual Identity Development," even though "the social constructionist perspective seems to be the dominant viewpoint of those working within the humanities and social sciences,"[61] when it comes time for political strategy, Constructionist activists "have found ways to use essentialist perspectives as effective tools in the struggle to acquire equal rights.[62]

Constructionist gay activists probably see nothing wrong with pretending to be Essentialists, because according to the Constructionist ideology, *every* point of view is "constructed" by

[61] Ellen M. Broido, "Constructing Identity: The Nature and Meaning of Lesbian, Gay, and Bisexual Identity Development," *Handbook of Counseling and Psychotherapy with Lesbian, Gay, and Bisexual Clients*, Ruperto M. Perez, Kurt A. DeBord, and Kathleen J. Bieschke, eds. (Washington: APA Books, 1999).

[62] Celia Kitzinger, "Social Constructionism: Implications for Lesbian and Gay Psychology," in *Lesbian, Gay, and Bisexual Identities Over the Lifespan*, A. D'Augelli and C. Patterns, eds. (New York: Oxford University Press, 1995), 136-165.

its adherents in order to give them a political advantage over their opposition. To them, there's no truth, only useful constructions. According to their view, therefore, pretending to believe in Essentialism isn't a lie, but a normal expression of Constructionism — a pragmatic political response to oppression.

Reading through Construction literature, one feels like Alice through the looking-glass: truth and logic are nothing more than tools to be manipulated in the service of political ends; words cease to have clear meanings.

This makes debating Constructionist gay activists extremely difficult. It also affords them a wide range of duplicitous tactics. Since they're not bound by conventional standards of truth or logic, they see nothing wrong, for example, with telling parents that pro-gay school-based programs exist to help teens who are essentially, unchangeably gay, and likewise telling students confused about their sexual feelings that they should embrace their "gay" identity as who they really are, even though they themselves don't believe such an identity really exists. Similarly, gay-affirming therapists routinely tell clients to give up hope for change and accept that they are by nature "gay," even though they themselves profess an ideology that rejects the idea that we have *any* fixed nature — gay, straight, or otherwise.

A Paradigm of Oppression and Hurt Feelings

Constructionists view all history as a struggle between oppressors and the oppressed. This oppression needn't take the form of denial of basic rights; it can be anything that makes a self-designated member of the oppressed classes (in this case, GLBTs) feel bad. If your feelings are hurt, you're oppressed. Only the oppressed have rights; their oppressors have no rights. Everything that hurts the feelings of the oppressed must be punished. If obvious offenses aren't available, they must be invented.

For example, when actress Jada Pinkett-Smith spoke glowingly about her marriage and her children during a speech at Harvard University,[63] the Bisexual, Gay, Lesbian, Transgender, and Supporters Alliance (BGLTSA) fired back an angry protest. She had offended them because, according to BGLTSA co-chairman Jordan Woods, "Some of the content was extremely heteronormative, and made BGLTSA members feel uncomfortable."

This is classic Constructionist-speak. According to the Constructionist ideology, simply using words such as *mother* and *husband* is to oppress gays, because it demonstrates tacit approval for a sexist, homophobic, patriarchal oppressor-culture that makes GLBTs feel excluded. All such offenders, all those who aid the "heteronormative" social construction, must be publicly humiliated for their "insensitivity."

Constructionist and Proud of It

Not all gay activists are public Essentialists and closet Constructionists. Some proudly and openly embrace the Constructionist ideology, and criticize Essentialist strategy as a sell-out for appealing to "constructs" like "normalcy" and human nature. Dennis Altman, author of *The Homosexualization of America*, is among these critics.

He writes:

[E]ven if there turns out to be a genetic basis for homosexuality — about which I remain skeptical — there is an element of choice about how we live this out.

I do believe human sexuality is largely socially constructed, is fluid and malleable, and that all of us have a far

---

[63] In March of 2005, Hollywood actress Jada Pinkett-Smith was honored as Artist of the Year at Harvard University.

greater potential for sexual experiences than we are likely to act out.[64]

Peter Cohen, a member of the radical gay-rights group Queer Nation, also rejects the born-gay argument as a concession to "heteronormative" constructs:

> I'm disturbed by the assumption that if people are programmed to be gay against their will, we should not see it as their fault and not discriminate against them. Underlying this is the assumption that homosexuality is inferior to heterosexuality . . . I don't see why we have to prove something is biologically caused to give people their rights.[65]

Cohen has pointed out one of the logical inconsistencies of the Essentialist argument: while claiming that SSA is a normal and healthy state, it appeals to the hidden premise that SSA is inferior, and therefore, persons with SSA need special accommodations — their own handicapped life space. They can't be expected to follow the rules that apply to everyone else, because they're helpless victims. Indeed, many people are willing to accede to gay activists' demands, not because they believe that SSA is a normal, healthy variant of human sexuality, but because they see persons with SSA as damaged, and pity them. And although some activists are willing to exploit this pity, others — like Cohen — are offended by it.

---

[64] Stephen Brown, "Defying Gravity: An Interview with Dennis Altman on the 30th Anniversary of *Homosexual: Oppression and Liberation*," *Sexualities* 3, no. 1: 97-107.

[65] C. Eugene Emery, "New Study: Homosexuality Genetic," *Providence Journal* (December 30, 1991). Commenting on J. M. Bailey and R. C. Pillard, "A Genetic Study of Male Sexual Orientation," *Archives of General Psychiatry* 48 (1991): 1089-1096.

The questions for society remain: is pity reason enough to accommodate activists' demands? And is accommodating those demands really the best way to show compassion for persons with SSA?

Most people don't want to be fed myths or constructions; they don't want to be lied to or manipulated. They want to know the facts. Can we answer their legitimate question? What causes same-sex attraction?

Part II

⤙

Understanding Same-Sex Attraction

"Sexual sin is contrary to God's intention, but homosexuality, although often an occasion for sexual sin, is essentially a state of incomplete development. It is the incompletion that is contrary to God's intention here."

Elizabeth Moberly

⤙

"I consider 'homosexuality' an abstraction. There is no such thing as 'homosexuality' per se. When we use the term we are speaking about people — people who happen to be more or less erotically oriented to their own sex, people who are more or less comfortable with this orientation; and people who experience more or fewer difficulties, personal and social, because of their orientation. Always we are speaking of concrete persons, in spite of the limitations of language."

James Nelson,
Pro-gay professor and ordained
minister of the United Church of Christ

Chapter 4

How Sexual Attraction Develops

What really causes same-sex attraction?

What are the essential elements of healthy sexual development?

Are the causes of SSA in men and women the same?

In speaking about the "cause" of same-sex attraction, we must always keep in mind that we're talking about unique individual human beings, each with his own history. In different cultures and different eras, furthermore, there are different circumstances that can push a person down the path to same-sex attraction. And although people seldom consciously "choose" to be attracted to the same sex, human beings nonetheless make many choices, some of which might help lead to SSA. No single pattern will ever explain all cases.

Bailey's research with Australian twins precludes a strictly biological or genetic cause for same-sex attraction, and it also precludes a simplistic causal pattern based on family structure — since twins are born into the same family circumstances at the same time, and share the same general experiences. What twins discordant for sexual attraction *don't* share is exactly the same personal experiences, and exactly the same reactions to them. The origin of SSA, therefore, must lie in these non-shared experiences.

We can think of SSA as an accidental convergence of circumstances. With automobile accidents, we can point to the causes after the fact. We can see how all the circumstances came together at a particular moment to create the crash. We identify, for example, excessive speed as one contributing factor. But we also know that people speed every day and don't get into accidents every time. Often the difference between an accident and a near-miss is another, often relatively minor factor, such as a split-second difference in the reaction time of another driver.

The convergence of circumstances that leads to SSA is like a slow-motion accident. No single event dooms someone to develop SSA; rather, cumulative circumstances conspire against an already-vulnerable child. In order to understand this more thoroughly, it's helpful first to consider how natural sexual attraction to the other sex develops.

How a Baby Learns and Grows

Although the study of early psychological and emotional development is still in its early stages, we've already learned a great deal about what is involved in normal development. We have learned that human beings don't come into the world as blank slates onto which anything can be written, and neither are they fully programmed by their genetic heritage to develop according to an inflexible pattern. Rather, all of us must build the neural connections that govern the way we think, and this building process is triggered by experience. Even before birth, the brain is processing experiences and building brain connections, and throughout our life, it continues to build connections, to prune away unused ones, and to reorganize itself.

The process of early childhood development is not entirely random; rather, a baby appears to be designed to seek out specific kinds of experiences at different stages in his development. For example, he has a brain designed to acquire the language he hears in the first year of life — not simply words but also grammar. Early in life, children learn how to make plurals, for example. They then apply the rule to new words, even if the plural is irregular. A child will say "goose, gooses, mouse, mouses," although he never heard an adult say "gooses."

According to extensive[66] research supporting this theory of human development, the first thing a baby looks for is the light in his mother's eyes.[67] Babies are totally dependent and have a need to develop a connection to another human being in order to survive; normally that person is the baby's biological mother. While still in the womb, it was her heart he heard beating, her voice he heard speaking, her emotions he felt. A healthy mother naturally responds to her baby's needs. She leans over the baby and looks into his eyes, smiles, and coos. This happens not just once, but over and over again. As the mother responds, the baby learns, the brain makes connections.

This process of attachment continues for the first eight months or so, during which time his mother's love lays the foundation for the baby's sense of self as lovable. By the eighth month, the baby becomes more independent: he's capable of crawling away from his mother and engaging in independent actions. The baby comes to realize that he's a separate human being who can manipulate his own environment. But when the baby crawls away, he still needs to know that his mother is there, that she accepts his newfound independence, and that she's pleased with his growing abilities. He looks for her smile, but he's also aware of her frown.

This is because part of healthy development is learning how to deal with stress, failure, and discipline. A good mother doesn't always smile. When the baby does something wrong or dangerous, his mother's eyes narrow: there's no smile. The baby recognizes

---

[66] For a more thorough understanding, I recommend Alan Schore's book *Affect Regulations and the Origin of Self: The Neurobiology of Emotional Development* (Hillsdale, New Jersey: Lawrence Erlbaum, 1994).

[67] Research on early development has found that a baby's eyes are designed to focus at exactly the distance between the baby's face and the mother's face during nursing.

that mother isn't pleased. Parents use frowns and other signs of shame, anger, and disgust to communicate their displeasure and train the child. Different cultures might frown at different behaviors, but the meaning of a frown or a smile remains the same. A good mother follows the "shame face" with a smile or signs of comfort — reconciliation. By balancing smiles with negative reactions, the mother teaches her child that there are limits on behavior and negative consequences for disobedience, but there's also reconciliation and comfort.

Awakening to a World of Sexes

As the baby grows, his father becomes more important. The baby perceives him as "different" from the mother, to whom he had been attached. The father's differentness challenges the baby to separate from his mother and explore the world around him. If from our mothers we learn that we're loved no matter what we do, from our fathers we learn we can win approval for what we do. A healthy balance between acceptance and challenge in the first year of life is important to the development of a healthy personality.

As children develop, they also begin to recognize sex difference, to name people — Mommy, Daddy, Grandma, Grandpa — and to recognize to which sex they belong. Throughout our lives, we have an instinctive need to know a person's sex. Children appear to be preprogrammed to recognize sex difference and to divide the world up into two sexes. And it isn't enough merely to learn, "I'm a boy," or "I'm a girl"; the child learns to *identify* with the sex to which he belongs. He thinks to himself, "I'm like other boys, and I'll grow up to be a man like my father," or she to herself, "I'm like other girls, and I'll grow up to be a woman like my mother." Ideally the child learns to feel good about being a boy or a girl — safe, loved, and accepted. During this period, the child continues (literally) to build his brain, from his experiences making connections that will influence the way he thinks about himself and others for the rest of his life.

For most people, this process of sexual identification proceeds without a problem, and by age three, if asked, "Are you a boy or a girl?" the child will look incredulous, as though the questioner must surely be blind, and reply confidently, "I'm a boy!" or "A girl, of course!"

As children grow, they find they have more in common with children of their own sex than with children of the other sex. Same-sex friendships become extremely important as the child consolidates his sense of masculinity or her sense of femininity. At this stage, familiarity leads to friendship, whereas complementarity — feeling essentially different from another person — creates mystery, which some believe is the foundation of romantic attachment.[68] In adolescence, sexual desires appear and become associated with that mystery.

Where Development Goes Wrong

Of course, no child has a perfect upbringing or parents who knew how to fulfill every single developmental need. But for the vast majority of people, there are enough positive experiences to overcome the negative ones. Healthy development is so ordinary that we tend not to notice it while it's happening. Indeed, it's only when things go wrong — when accidents happen — that people look for reasons why. And for people with SSA, we find evidence in case histories, autobiographical material, and studies that something has gone very wrong indeed.

---

[68] Daryl Bem, "Exotic Becomes Erotic: A Developmental Theory of Sexual Orientation," *Psychological Review* 101, no. 2 (1996): 320-355.

Adults with SSA frequently say, "I've always felt different." As adults, they associate this "always feeling different" with their SSA, and in this they might be correct. Feeling different from one's same-sex parent and/or peers in early childhood appears to be a common element in stories of many people with SSA. The problem is that a child's feelings usually do not fully reflect reality. "Feeling different" from one's same-sex parent and peers doesn't mean that a person *isn't* an ordinary boy or girl who could grow up into an ordinary man or woman. "Feeling different," rather, means that somewhere along the track, the healthy psychosexual development stage of identification with the same sex has not been properly negotiated.

Just as certain intersections might be the scene of numerous accidents, certain family factors seem to put a child at risk for feeling different. In 2001, Peter Berman and Hannah Bruchner conducted a study of sexual attraction in adolescent opposite-sex twins in order to test the various theories for the origins of sexual attraction.[69] They used a large sample drawn from the National Longitudinal Study of Adolescent Health. The results provided what they called "substantial support for the role of social influences" and led them to reject the simple genetic theory, hormone-transfer theory, and a speculative evolutionary theory for SSA.

Specifically, they found that in boy/girl pairs of twins, the boy was more likely to experience SSA in adolescence — but only if he had no older brothers. If SSA is related to early feelings of being different from persons of the same sex and/or being like persons of the other sex, then a boy with only a twin sister is at greater risk of feeling more like a girl (even more so than a boy with only a

---

[69] Peter Bearman, and Hannah Bruchner, "Opposite-sex Twins and Adolescent Same-sex Attraction," Institute for Social and Economic Research and Policy, Columbia University Working Paper, October 2001.

non-twin sister, because of the close community between twins). Having an older brother to identify with, however, helps negate this risk. For the researchers, this clearly pointed to socialization as the dominant factor.

Reparative therapists are convinced that the problem isn't initially related to erotic feelings. In the following excerpt from her blog, a woman with SSA named Eve reveals how, for a child on the path to SSA, feelings of being different are not initially sexual:

> Before there was any sense of sexual difference, there was a dug-in abiding sense of exile, aloneness, of having been cut off from some needed love. Rauch, Sullivan, and I later ended up linking this sense of exile to our sexual and romantic attractions. I suspect that there is some reason for that — this was not merely a random coincidence on our parts . . . But the sense of exile comes first. When I was little I had all these little knickknacks, china cats, and clay unicorns and so forth, who lived on the top of my dresser drawer. They had their own village. One of them, a pale yellowish plastic soldier, always stood at the very edge of the dresser, facing away from the village; for something he'd done (I think his crime changed now and then, as I forget what it was supposed to have been), he was never allowed to return to his hometown or even look back at it. He could only come home when a delegation from the village came out to retrieve and redeem him . . . So yes, homosexuality often serves as a code or stand-in for other exiles.[70]

In the histories of men and women with SSA, we find many such accounts of feeling alone, different, alien. Reading this excerpt, we can't help but feel compassion for that lonely child. It's

---

[70] Eve Tushnet's Blog, June 3, 2004.

important when dealing with the issue of SSA to remember the sense of alienation that lies at its root, and to respond to it with love.

⌒

Not only are all cases of persons with SSA unique, but men and women are different, and therefore it isn't surprising that SSA develops and manifests itself differently in men and women. The next two chapters will deal with the differences and similarities.

Chapter 5

Same-Sex Attraction in Men

What are the factors that often lead to SSA in men?

In what distinctive ways does SSA manifest itself in men?

How can male SSA be prevented?

Since it's a woman who gives birth and forms the first attachment with children of both sexes, the process of identification with the same-sex parent is different for boys than for girls. In the period from eight months to eighteen months of age, a boy will naturally separate from his mother and identify with his father[71] — or, in the father's absence, with some father-substitute. In this regard, even a dead father, if his memory is revered and the son constantly reminded of how he is a man like his father, can be a role model.

How does this occur, in concrete terms? Joseph Nicolosi, who has spent years working with men with SSA, is convinced that this healthy development of masculine identification depends on "shared delight" — those moments during which father and son experience mutual enjoyment in the boy's success. In contrast, "Homosexual men rarely, if ever, recall father-son interaction that includes activities they both enjoyed together."[72]

[71] Allan Schore, *Affect Regulation and the Origin of Self*; Kenneth Zucker and Susan Bradley, *Gender Identity and Psychosexual Problems in Children and Adolescents*. Schore's book reviews the research on healthy development, while Zucker and Bradley explain the roots of SSA.

[72] Joseph Nicolosi, "A Shared Delight: What Is It That My Clients Missed in Their Memories of Their Fathers," *NARTH Bulletin* (April 2004): 29.

According to Nicolosi:

We have all observed a young father tossing his infant son
in the air and catching him. Anyone observing this universal ritual will see that the dad is laughing while the son
looks petrified with fear. Soon the boy begins to laugh because Dad is laughing, while Mother is practically having
an anxiety attack, not understanding any of this. The boy
has just learned an important lesson that older males teach
younger males: "Danger can be fun." More importantly, the
boy learns another lesson; he can trust his father: "Dad will
catch me." And from that early relationship, he learns to
trust other men.[73]

The boy enjoys the physical experience and learns to feel comfortable with his body, and in turn he will become comfortable
playing with other boys. More significantly, the boy also learns
that he can ignore his mother's fears — because he belongs to the
world of men. Mother may say, "Stop, you'll hurt him," but the father and son happily ignore her warnings.

If, however, the mother intervenes and prevents the tossing or
rough-and-tumble play or even verbal sparring, she places herself
between the boy and father and risks derailing her son's development as a man.

Nicolosi explains:

Physical interaction between father and son appears essential in making the father feel familiar, non-mysterious,
and approachable in the boy's eyes. So much of what lies
behind adult same-sex attraction is that deep lingering
unsatisfied desire for physical closeness with a man. With

[73] Nicolosi, "A Shared Delight," 30.

internalization of the father's masculinity, there will be no need to sexualize another man."[74]

If the mother prevents separation, or stands in the way of attachment to the father, or if the father is unavailable for identification or is a poor model, the boy might not successfully complete this important stage of development. He will emerge from early childhood still trying to discover his own masculinity. He will feel different from his father and his peers. He will continue to develop physically and intellectually, but his healthy psychosexual development will have been hindered. Case histories reveal a complex interaction of commonly recurring negative experiences, including a father who is unavailable, persistent interference in the father/son relationship by the mother, and problematic relationships between parents.

There are other ways, besides rough-and-tumble play, for boys to find their masculinity. Non-roughhousing fathers may promote the development of a healthy masculine identification through friendly teasing, verbal sparring, and other non-physical challenges and shared activities. In other cultures throughout history, it has been normal to facilitate separation of boys from mothers and identification with fathers in non-physical ways. A woman born in China, for instance, observed that in her culture, the father of a family would be too dignified to wrestle on the floor with his sons. However, when questioned, the woman admitted that the entire family chipped in to reinforce the son's masculine identification in other ways.

For when a boy's path toward the development of a healthy masculine identity is blocked, he's not automatically destined to develop SSA. However, once he's on the path, negative experiences

---

[74] Ibid.

can start to pile up. A boy who doesn't engage in rough-and-tumble play with his dad, and whose mother is hostile toward masculinity, will have fewer male playmates and might find himself the butt of bullies' harassment (or worse, the victim of pedophiles). This will only increase feelings of being "different." His strong desire for male affection and affirmation might convince him that he was "born gay."

Sometimes Mother Stands in the Way

Some ask, why does one boy identify with the father and his brother not? The answer might lie, in some cases, with the relationship of each boy to his mother. A boy who never properly attached to his mother might have a problem separating from her. Attachment can be disrupted in two ways. In some cases, the mother might be emotionally unavailable or even neglectful, which sets the boy up to expect to be rejected. The boy projects this "reject me" attitude, and others pick up on the child's body language and feel negatively toward him. On the other hand, the mother might over-attach to the child, becoming hysterical at any distance put between them. She might not allow the boy to separate, and will frown on his yearning for masculinity. He might come to feel responsible for her problems and afraid to symbolically leave her and enter the world of men.

Indeed, many adults with SSA express keen awareness of a dysfunctional relationship with their father, but they're often unable to recognize or admit the ways in which their mother might have contributed to it.

For example, in one instance, a mother's feelings of hostility toward masculinity led her to single out her youngest and most emotionally malleable son as her favorite, systematically isolating him from his father and older brothers and preventing a healthy masculine identification. The boy grew to fear his father and identify with his mother. Only after she died was he able to recognize the ways in which she had manipulated him.[75]

The Quest for Same-Sex Love

It's important to understand SSA as a positive drive. That is, the boy is trying to complete his development — and this is healthy and necessary. A boy who misses crucial development steps can't simply move on and forget it. *The drive to complete this developmental stage remains.* He's looking for his masculinity, but he's looking in the wrong place. Psychotherapists refer to this need to complete a missed stage in development as a "reparative drive." An adult who didn't successfully complete an important stage in his developmental process will try to create a situation in the present that will make up for what was missing in the past. In most cases, these efforts at repair do not solve the problem, because the adult doesn't know what he really needs. And so he wanders in a maze of (often self-destructive) behaviors, trying to find the way out but only going back over the same path again and again.

Elizabeth Moberly, in her book *Homosexuality: A New Christian Ethic*, offers the clearest and most compelling explanations of how the failure to identify with the same-sex parent causes a child to feel different, and leads to SSA in adults. In her work with persons with SSA, Moberly realized that her clients were trying, through sexual acts, to meet their legitimate need for non-sexual love from persons of their sex:

> From amidst a welter of details, one constant underlying principle suggests itself: that the homosexual — whether man or woman — has suffered from some deficit in the relationship with the parent *of the same sex*; and that there is a

[75] Private interview.

corresponding drive to make good this deficit — through the medium of same-sex, or "homosexual," relationships.[76]

Moberly further posited that certain negative experiences created these deficits, putting a child on the path to SSA:

[I]n every case, it is postulated, something of a traumatic nature, whether ill-treatment, neglect or sheer absence, has in these particular instances led to a disruption in the normal attachment. This in turn implies that psychological needs, which are normally met though the child's attachment to the parent, are left unfulfilled and still require fulfillment.[77]

In most instances, this trauma can be easily identified. Even therapists who deny that SSA is a disorder, and who treat the problems of clients with SSA with "gay-affirming" therapy, report childhood histories virtually identical to those reported by therapists trying to help clients unhappy with their sexual orientation. They reported the same feelings of being different, the same failure to identify with the same-sex parent. Yet if SSA were a genetically determined condition, we would expect to find a significant percentage of persons with SSA who had positive, supportive relationships with both parents.[78]

---

[76] Elizabeth Moberly, *Homosexuality: A New Christian Ethic* (James Clarke: Cambridge, 1983), 2.

[77] Ibid.

[78] Some gay advocates insist that the boys were different — inalterably "gay" — to begin with, and that caused their fathers to reject them. This chicken-and-the-egg debate can, however, be resolved through study of the family dynamic of boys with Gender Identity Disorder. Adults who have developed SSA may remember little of what happened in the first 18 months to three years of their life, but therapists who treat

Indeed, Bieber's study — the most comprehensive to date on the effect of therapy for same-sex attraction — concluded that such relationships would make the development of SSA virtually impossible:

> We have come to the conclusion that a constructive, sup-portive, warmly related father *precludes* [emphasis in original] the possibility of a homosexual son; he acts as a neutralizing protective agent should the mother make seductive or close-binding attempts.
>
> A mother who is pleased by her son's masculinity and is comfortably related to his sexual curiosity and heterosexual responsiveness to her and other females, encourages and re-inforces a masculine identification. A father who is warmly related to his son, who supports assertiveness and effective-ness, and who is not sexually competitive, provides the real-ity testing necessary for the resolution of the son's irrational sexual competitiveness. This type of parental behavior fos-ters heterosexual development.[79]

It's true, of course, that many men have poor relationships with their fathers yet do not develop SSA. Moberly believes that the way the child *reacts* to the perceived or real rejection is crucial (here the child's temperament and other inherited personality traits are an important variable). Children start on the path to SSA by "defensively detaching" from the same-sex parent. They

young children with GID (usually evidenced by cross-dressing and other gender-confused behaviors) are able to observe the relationship between mother and son, between mother and father, and between the boy and other siblings. And thus, they can see how those troubled relationships contribute to the disorder, not the other way around.

[79] Bieber et al., *Homosexuality: A Psychoanalytic Study of Male Homosexuals*, 311, 313.

actively resist the "restoration of attachment," and the effect of the defensive detachment "long outlasts the initial occasion of trauma."

If a boy sees his father as angry or cruel, he might make an inner vow: "I will never be a man like my father," which can be distorted into: "I will never be a man." Thus, he has detached not only from his father, but also from his own masculinity. A mother might unconsciously encourage defensive detachment by telling her son, "I'm glad you're not like your father." This the boy might internalize as, "I *am not* like my father; I'm different from other men; I'm not a real man."

Thus, the boy, in rejecting his father, is left without a model of manhood. He's driven by developmental forces to attach to and identify with a member of his own sex, but has nothing to attach to. He's caught between two opposing forces. He continues to long for the masculine father-love so that he can complete the process of identification, but the process is blocked by his defensive detachment from his father and from masculinity in general. He might eventually identify same-sex sexual relationships as the solution. But these can only mask the deficits, not solve them.

When Boys Seem Effeminate from the Start

Since the identification process takes place at a very young age, a failure to identify is often apparent early in a boy's development. Failure to identify can manifest itself simply in chronic feelings of unmasculinity, without a female identification, or, more noticeably, in Gender Identity Disorder (GID).

According to the *DSM*, GID is "a strong and persistent cross-gender identification," manifested by cross-dressing and preference for cross-sex roles in play or fantasy, and accompanied by a "persistent discomfort with his or her sex or sense of inappropriateness in the gender role of that sex." The disturbance causes significant distress. GID "represents a profound disturbance of the individual's sense of identity with regard to maleness or femaleness."[80]

Boys with GID might be labeled by parents and peers as "girlish," but they differ from girls of the same age in significant ways. For example, these boys fear and avoid rough, physical play, whereas, although girls might not typically have the same desire for it as boys, neither are they terrified of it. Boys with GID often choose girls for playmates even when boys are available, but their interests are narrower than the average girl's, because they lack the freedom of a normal girl or boy to play many roles. Instead, these boys are driven to take the feminine role exclusively.[81] They're often entranced by dolls with the characteristics of mature women, such as Barbies, or with the villainesses of Disney movies. Whereas normal girls enjoy outdoor play as well as indoor, these boys cling to the home. They enjoy dressing up in Mommy's clothes just as girls do, but little girls don't normally comfort themselves by stroking their mother's lingerie or dressing in her nightgown. And whereas normal little girls might show a certain gender neutrality in their speech patterns, mannerisms, and behavior, GID boys exhibit exaggerated mannerisms imitative of adult women, and lisping speech patterns. GID boys are not "happy little girly-boys"; they're often anxious and fearful, tense

---

[80] *Diagnostic and Statistical Manual of Mental Disorders IV* (Washington: American Psychiatric Association, 1994), 533-537.

[81] Some may fear that encouraging strong same-sex identification in early childhood will create a "rigidity" that will limit a child's potential. But this fear is unfounded. When sexual identity is firmly established early, the child is freer later to explore non-conforming talents and interests. On the other hand, children with GID are not free to explore the full range of options: they are comfortable only when imitating the other sex.

and inhibited.[82] And it is estimated that seventy-five to eighty-five percent of boys with GID will develop SSA or become transsexual as adults.[83]

Kenneth Zucker and Susan Bradley, experts in the study of GID who operate a clinic in Canada for the treatment of children with the disorder, have found that, in many cases, the mothers of boys with GID suffer from various forms of psychopathology that profoundly affect their children — or one particular child.[84] For example, a mother who harbors intensely hostile feelings toward men may frown on her son's masculine strivings and smile when he imitates stereotypical female behavior. If the boy is sensitive, he will want to make his mother smile and avoid making her frown.

Another Scenario for SSA Development

Some men with SSA don't fit the model just described. They didn't exhibit symptoms of GID as children. They didn't identify with females. They didn't display effeminate traits. Richard Friedman and L. Stern studied the childhood experiences of men with SSA who were not effeminate as boys, and "hypothesized that at least one-third of a group of masculine, socially well-adjusted homosexual men would describe normal participation in rough-and-tumble activities during these developmental periods."[85]

---

[82] Zucker and Bradley, *Gender Identity Disorder and Psychosexual Problems*.

[83] Edgardo Menvielle, "Gender Identity Disorder," *Journal of the American Academy of Child and Adolescent Psychiatry* 37, no. 3 (1998): 243-244.

[84] Zucker and Bradley, *Gender Identity Disorder*, 233.

[85] Richard Friedman and L. Stern, "Juvenile Aggressivity and Sissiness in Homosexual and Heterosexual Males," *Journal of the American Academy of Psychoanalysis* 8, no. 3 (1980): 427-440.

Their sample consisted of two groups of seventeen men each, one exclusively homosexual, the other exclusively heterosexual. They excluded any subjects with other psychological disorders, substance-abuse problems, depression, STDs, or suicidal ideation. Their study found that thirteen of the seventeen men with SSA reported that, as boys, they had a "chronic, persistent terror of fighting with other boys":

> The intensity of this fear approximated a panic reaction. To the best of their recall, these boys *never* responded to challenge from a male peer with counter-challenge, threat, or attack. The pervasive dread of male-male peer aggression was a powerful organizing force in their minds. Anticipatory anxiety resulted in phobic responses to social activities; the fantasy that fighting *might* occur led to avoidance of a wide variety of social interactions, especially rough-and-tumble activities.[86]

These boys experienced "a painful loss of self-esteem and loneliness." They were "chronically hungry for closeness with other boys." They had the lowest possible peer status during juvenile and early-adolescent years. The boys had also developed negative feelings about their bodies: "In all cases, the body was perceived as being easily damaged. All subjects expressed a strong fear of physical injury were they to engage in contact sports."

These boys hadn't found their place in the world of men, and they didn't belong to the world of females. They were unable to develop the behaviors that would make them acceptable to their male peers, and unwilling to retreat into the female world.

The universality of the result surprised the authors. Their conclusion:

---

[86] Ibid.

Successful attainment of a minimal degree of aggressivity increases the likelihood that a boy will obtain social supports with peers that further his development of masculine autonomy.

We favor the hypothesis that the wish to be sexually close to males arose in a setting where there were intense longings for general closeness with male peers at a critical period of development. The erotic desire appeared to repair in fantasy feelings of deprivation resulting from inadequate positive social input.[87]

Friedman and Stern's findings confirm what those who work with men with SSA have found and helps to explain the development of SSA in men who were not noticeably effeminate as boys.

The Influence of Sexual Abuse

There's another category of men with SSA that doesn't fit the most common pattern: men who were repeatedly sexually abused at an early age and became accustomed to acting out sexually with males. These men might insist that their early sexual experiences were positive; as boys, they saw themselves not as abused but as privileged, because they were allowed to engage in adult activities at an early age. Such men often become extremely promiscuous and rarely seek psychological help. In several studies of men infected with AIDS, a small percentage reported beginning to have sex with men before age six. Some men with SSA describe incestuous relationships with brothers, uncles, or fathers as "positive," although therapists find them seriously damaged by the experiences.[88]

---

[87] Friedman and Stern, "Juvenile Aggressivity," 436.

[88] Mark Williams, "Father-Son Incest: A Review and Analysis of Reported Incidents," *Clinical Social Work Journal* 16, no. 2 (Summer 1988): 165-179.

Many people think that being sexually molested as a child by a person of the same sex can cause SSA. Therapists differ on the issue. Some think it's a possibility, particularly if the abuse extends over a long period or if the child is very young when it begins. In such cases, a boy might come to believe that because the sensations he experiences with another male become pleasurable to him, he must be a homosexual.

Other therapists, however, believe a failure to identify not only precedes sexual abuse in boys who grow up to develop SSA, but can increase its likelihood. Since boys who have defensively detached from their fathers are desperately seeking male attention and love, they become attractive to pedophiles, who know how to identify vulnerable boys. The incidents of molestation might push the boy down the path toward SSA, but it's a path he was already on. In contrast, a boy whose masculine identity is firmly established by age four will be traumatized by molestation; he will feel guilty and ashamed; he might even worry about his sexual orientation. But his masculine identification will not be undermined.

Various studies have found that about forty percent of men with SSA report experiences of childhood sexual abuse by an adult or an older child. Many more report sexual involvement with other children during childhood.[89] It's important to recognize the part childhood sexual abuse plays in the development of SSA and the need to deal with its effects.

Why Does Only One Son Become Gay?

Some people ask, if a cold, absent, or rejecting father and a conflicted mother in a troubled marriage produce a boy with the

---

[89] Lynda Doll et al., "Self-Reported Childhood and Adolescent Sexual Abuse Among Adult Homosexual and Bisexual Men," *Child Abuse & Neglect* 16 (1992): 855-865.

potential for SSA as an adult, why does only one boy from such a family develop SSA? The simple answer is that parents seldom treat their children identically. In some dysfunctional families, parents might emotionally divide the children between them. A mother might, in such a situation, choose one son to be her favorite — her "substitute husband" — often rejecting her other sons. The boy's natural traits — his appearance, athletic ability, intelligence — can influence the mother's or the father's attitude toward a particular child. The mother might unconsciously favor a boy who is more like her and less like her husband: less athletic, more artistic, more sensitive, prettier. The father might relate more positively to a son who is more like him: less sensitive in nature or physically tougher.

Differences in inborn personality traits also affect how different sons react to their parents' treatment. Zucker and Bradley explain the relationship between the child's temperament[90] and the development of GID:

> For boys our clinical model proposes that Gender Identity Disorder develops from a state of inner insecurity that arises out of the interaction between a boy's temperamental vulnerability to high arousal and an insecure mother-child relationship . . . The boy, who is highly sensitive to maternal signals, perceives the mother's feelings of depression and anger . . . His worry about loss of his mother intensifies his conflict over his own anger, resulting in high levels of arousal or anxiety. The father's own difficulty with affect regulation and inner sense of inadequacy usually produces withdrawal rather than approach. The parents have

[90] For the best current treatment of the classical temperaments, see Art and Laraine Bennet, *The Temperament God Gave You* (Manchester, New Hampshire: Sophia Institute Press, 2005).

difficulty resolving the conflicts that they experience in their relationship.[91]

George Rekers, who has written extensively on these issues, notes that while one boy in a particular kind of dysfunctional family will develop SSA, other boys might develop hypermasculinity. These boys, faced with the same situation as their sibling, might choose to reject the mother as a model and imitate the negative characteristics of the father — becoming "belligerent, destructive, interpersonally violent, and uncontrolled."[92]

Drawing on his experience as a counselor, Roy Masters paints a similar picture of how, in some family units, SSA develops in one boy while another exhibits the opposite behavior [emphasis mine]:

In many years of counseling, I have dealt with countless family situations conforming to the following pattern. Two boys are born into a dysfunctional family, composed of a cruel, confusing mother, and a brutal father (perhaps an alcoholic) who is rarely home. Now, the anger and resentment which the (victim) mother feels for the father is unloaded on these boys. She unconsciously hates men, beginning with her own alcoholic father, but extending now to her husband — and becoming a cumulative traumatic experience for her sons. Because of the different dispositions and status of the two boys, *one rebels from her control and one conforms.* One way or the other, the boys have been traumatized away from their natural center, their true personhood.[93]

---

[91] Zucker and Bradley, *Gender Identity Disorder*, 262-263.

[92] George Rekers, "Gender Identity Disorder," http://www.leaderu.com/jhs/rekers.html.

[93] Roy Masters, *Homosexuality: Opposing Viewpoints* (San Diego: Greenhaven Press, 1993), 30.

What matters in these cases might not be the level of mistreatment, neglect, or manipulation that the child endures, but how the child reacts to the mistreatment. A child who is able to reconcile with his parents or to forgive injuries, or who is fortunate to find an adult who unequivocally supports his masculine development, might escape relatively unscathed from an extremely negative environment, whereas a child in what might appear to be more benign circumstances might become alienated from his true identity. This variable of individual reaction patterns, being rooted in inborn personality traits, strikes some as evidence for a genetic cause for SSA. But it's really part of the more nuanced and realistic Developmentalist understanding of SSA, which considers a wide variety of factors: some inborn, some environmental, some chosen, some accidental.

Preventing SSA in Men

There was a time when parents didn't know the importance of vitamin D in the formation of bones, and as a result, some children didn't get enough vitamin D and developed rickets. Once vitamin D's importance was identified and it was added to milk, rickets virtually disappeared. Likewise, in our day, research has shown us the importance of a father's affirming his son's masculinity, of "shared delight" between the two, and now parents can be taught how to promote the healthy development of sexual identity.

The idea that SSA is preventable infuriates gay activists, and the major media pay little attention to it. But several solid books on the subject are available for parents to use. Nicolosi's *A Parent's Guide to Preventing Homosexuality* offers practical advice on how to help a child develop a secure gender identity and how to treat GID. James Dobson's *Bringing Up Boys* has a chapter on the subject of prevention of SSA. Father John Harvey, the founder of Courage, a Catholic group that ministers to persons with SSA, co-edited

Same-Sex Attraction: A Parent's Guide. Don Schmierer offers a Bible-based guide to raising children: *An Ounce of Prevention: Preventing the Homosexual Condition in Today's Youth.* Not surprisingly, all these books stress the importance of a child's identification with the same-sex parent in early childhood.

The symptoms of GID, often a precursor to developing SSA, are obvious not only to parents but to family, friends, teachers, and pediatricians. Chronic feelings of unmasculinity, while less obvious, can also be discerned by an aware observer. Zucker and Bradley are very positive about the prognosis for children whose problems are identified early and whose parents are willing to work with therapists to resolve their own problems. Unfortunately, many parents aren't willing to embark on such a course. Zucker and Bradley note that in almost every case referred to them, parents did not react negatively to the first symptoms of GID, but let the problem continue until it caused undeniable social difficulties for the child. In some cases, mothers or other female family members interfered by actively encouraging cross-gender identification, or even prematurely labeling the child "gay."

Zucker and Bradley stress the importance of treating GID and related problems in children not just to prevent the development of SSA in adolescence, but also because these children suffer from anxiety and are cut off from the normal interaction with same-sex peers. A boy who is effeminate, for example, is at risk for peer rejection and teasing. Although gay activists insist that the problems manifested by children with GID are *caused* by the teasing they receive, and that the only solution is to teach children to accept those who are "different," Zucker and Bradley point out that although teasing certainly exacerbates the problem, the anxiety and distress exists long before the child goes to school and is exposed to it. Besides, although teasing and cruelty among children should, of course, always be discouraged, observation of the play of young children with GID reveals that children are often not being vicious when they tease. It might be that preschool children recognize there is something wrong and try, in an unintentionally hurtful way, to encourage the gender non-conforming child to act normal.

Indeed, the therapists and physicians of the Sexual Left cause much more harm to children than do teasing peers. Children with GID are troubled. Their behavior is a symptom of underlying fears and unmet needs. Treating them as though their non-conforming behavior were normal and healthy will not solve their problems, but only prolong them. Yet gay activists are putting tremendous pressure on the APA to remove GID in Children from the DSM, just as they did with same-sex attraction. They want GID identified as "pre-homosexuality" and regarded as the normal development pattern for future gays and lesbians. They demand that parents be counseled to accept gender non-conformity and the other symptoms.[94] Zucker and Bradley (among others) have fought this change, insisting that the pathology within families that produces children with GID and the suffering of the children requires treatment.[95]

Sadly, some parents refuse help even when the symptoms are obvious and causing suffering. A daycare provider noticed that a

---

[94] Edgardo Menvielle and Catherine Tuerk, "A Support Group for Parents of Gender-Nonconforming Boys," *Journal of the American Academy of Child & Adolescent Psychiatry* 41, no. 8 (2002): 1010. Miriam Rosenberg, "Children with Gender Identity Issues and Their Parents in Individual and Group Treatment," *Journal of the American Academy of Child & Adolescent Psychiatry* 41, no. 5 (2002): 619.

[95] Kenneth Zucker and Susan Bradley, "Psychopathology in the Parents of Boys with Gender Identity Disorder," *Journal of the American Academy of Child & Adolescent Psychiatry* 42, no. 1 (2003): 3-4.

boy placed in her care was extremely effeminate. His mother routinely bought him girls' toys, dressed him in pink, smiled on his feminine behavior, and frowned when he showed any masculine interests. In contrast, she discouraged her daughter's feminine interests and rarely smiled at her. The marriage had apparently been successful until the birth of the children, after which the mother became more and more disdainful of her husband. Her own mother had been divorced and routinely publicly ridiculed her husband, the woman's father. Her sister was also divorced, extremely hostile toward men, and also had an effeminate son. Initially, her husband had accepted their son's effeminacy, but when he was made aware of the relationship between the way the mother treated the boy and the boy's behavior, he actively tried to encourage the boy's masculinity. The mother was outraged at the father's "interference" and divorced him.[96]

The failure of society to recognize children's needs for same-sex identification and to treat the problems associated with GID has already had tragic consequences. In 1963, Daniel Brown presented a paper on homosexuality and family dynamics. He reviewed the evidence available at the time — evidence that has since been confirmed by numerous studies. He called on his profession to educate parents and teachers about "the decisive influence of the family in determining the course and outcome of the child's psychosexual development." Brown warned that, given what was known about child development,

> There would seem to be no justification for waiting another twenty-five or fifty years to bring this information to the

[96] Private interview.

attention of those who deal with children. And there is no excuse for professional workers in the behavioral sciences to continue avoiding their responsibility to disseminate this knowledge and understanding as widely as possible.[97]

This opportunity was missed. We did not spread this understanding widely, but hid it under a bushel. The results? We can do the math. The young boys who didn't receive help when this warning was given came of age in the 1980s and were part of the first wave of men struck down by the AIDS epidemic.

[97] Daniel Brown, "Homosexuality and Family Dynamics," *Bulletin of Menninger Clinic* 27 (1963): 227-232.

Chapter 6

Same-Sex Attraction in Women

In what distinctive ways does SSA develop in women?

*Why are women with SSA more likely than men to say
they chose the gay lifestyle, as well as to leave it?*

How can female SSA be prevented?

A boy separates from his mother in order to identify with the "male world" at around eight months of age, but a girl's identification with the mother begins at birth. During *her* separation period, a girl baby comes to realize that she's separate from her mother as a person, but also *like her mother*.

This allows girls a greater flexibility. For example, there comes a time in the normal development of many boys where they might absolutely refuse to wear clothes that are obviously designed for girls. On the other hand, girls can comfortably wear styles worn by boys, and play with toys designed for boys, without anxiety. For a girl to be considered a "tomboy" isn't nearly as stigmatizing as a boy's being called a "sissy." Accordingly, most "tomboys" grow up with absolutely no evidence of GID or SSA.

The Importance of Attachment

If a boy with GID typically has had a problem with separation from his mother, a girl is more likely to have had a problem with attachment to hers.

The initial period of attachment is crucial to a girl's emotional development; if her mother is emotionally unavailable during the first eight months of her life, attachment might not fully occur. A number of studies have noted that the mothers of women with SSA are more likely to have been depressed during their daughters' first years of life.[98] Clearly, a depressed woman would be less able to provide the foundational love and affirmation that a baby needs. If a baby girl looks into her mother's eyes and sees only sadness, her need for attachment — her need to look into her mother's smiling eyes and feel love — might go unmet.

In her six years of experience treating women with SSA, counselor Janelle Hallman has discovered four basic elements that she identifies as the roots of SSA in women.

• *A strained, detached, or disrupted bond with the mother,* plus the lack of an available mother-substitute, resulting in a need for secure attachment.

• *A lack of respect and/or protection from men,* often in the form of sexual abuse or rigid gender roles, resulting in a fear or hatred of men.

• *Few, if any, close girlhood friendships,* resulting in a need for belonging and fun.

• Rather than a rich sense identity as a feminine being, *a sense of emptiness and feeling lost,* resulting in a need for a self- and gender-identity.[99]

The mothers of Hallman's clients were troubled women. One would hide under the covers when her husband became abusive or rageful. Another's mother was mentally ill and relied on her daughter to talk her out of committing suicide. Still another didn't

[98] Zucker and Bradley, "Psychopathology in the Parents of Boys with Gender Identity Disorder."

[99] Janelle Hallman, "Clinical Issues within the Lesbian Struggle," *NARTH Bulletin* (Winter 2004): 3.

know the basics of housekeeping or child care. It's understandable that a girl would fail to identify with a mother who was abusive, suicidal, an alcoholic, or who hated being a woman. But the girl's need for mother-love remains. When she grows, she might seek to repair those early wounds through an intimate relationship with another woman.

If, in the first months of her daughter's life, the mother is unavailable for attachment because she is depressed, or otherwise psychologically unable to bond with her daughter, the girl might turn to the father and identify with him. Fathers who have disdain for femininity might encourage masculine behaviors in their daughters and discourage feminine ones. The mother might, in turn, fail to discourage masculinity in her daughter, because she views it as a sign of confidence and strength.

If, instead, her father is cruel and abusive, the girl might develop a fear of men. She might see her mother as a victim who needs protection. Since men are viewed as powerful, she might learn to imitate male traits. In such cases, the daughter might indulge in the fantasy that she's her mother's defender, and when she grows to adulthood, she might find herself attracted to women who need protection — women she can protect in the way she wanted to protect her mother.

A girl might see her mother as weak, dependent, or helpless, and vow, "I will never be a woman like my mother" — which becomes, "I will not be a woman." Or she might see her father abuse her mother and vow, "I will never allow a man to hurt me." This becomes, "I will never allow a man to get close to me." Or she might think, "If I were a man, I could protect my mother." Such feelings become burdens the girl will carry into her adult relationships. Because they lack self-identity and are wracked by guilt, shame, and fear, it's no surprise that girls on the path to SSA often display extreme anxiety.

GID in Girls

Just as with men with SSA, a significant percentage of women with SSA also suffered from Gender Identity Disorder as children. According to Zucker and Bradley, who are experts on GID, such girls differ from ordinary "tomboys" — girls who simply enjoy sports or other rough physical activities — in that they exhibit "an intense unhappiness with their status as females," "display an intense aversion to the wearing of culturally defined feminine clothing under any circumstances," and manifest "discomfort with sexual anatomy."[100]

Zucker and Bradley found that in three-quarters of their cases of girls with GID, the mothers had a history of depression. Some of the mothers had a "history of severe and chronic sexual abuse of an incestuous nature." Many also showed clear evidence of psychological disorders:

> It seemed to us that a girl either failed to identify with her mother or disidentified with her mother because she perceived her mother as weak, incompetent, or helpless. In fact, many of the mothers devalued their own efficacy and regarded the female gender role with disdain.[101]

Another factor was the girls' "experience of severe paternal or male sibling aggression," directed at the girls or their mothers, or both.[102] For these girls, the classic mechanism of identifying with an aggressor appeared to drive their cross-gender identification.

Sexual abuse seems to be both more prevalent among girls already at risk for SSA and can be a contributing factor in its development. A significant percentage of women with SSA report a

[100] Zucker and Bradley, *Gender Identity Disorder*, 252-253.
[101] Ibid., 252.
[102] Ibid., 253.

history of childhood sexual abuse and/or rape. A study of 1,925 lesbians found that "thirty-seven percent had been physically abused as a child or adult, thirty-two percent had been raped or sexually attacked, nineteen percent had been involved in incestuous relationships while growing up."[103]

Other studies have also found that women with SSA are far more likely to have been victims of violence than other women. A pattern of case histories points to the mother's failure to protect her daughter from sexual abuse or incest — or to believe her daughter when informed of it — as a crucial factor in the development of SSA.

A significant percentage of women with SSA showed no symptoms of GID as girls. They develop normal feminine interests, wear female clothing without complaint; in their teens they date, and they might marry and have children — yet at some point, they meet a woman who awakens their need for mother-love. Because they associate the kind of violent passion that they feel for this mother-substitute with sexual desire, they fall into a sexual relationship. This is sometimes referred to as "late-onset lesbianism." It occurs when an adult woman's unmet need for mothering is triggered by a relationship with a particular woman.

It should be noted that, because a mother's depression or other failures and problems might resolve themselves as the years pass, the mother of an adult woman with SSA might be a very different woman from the young mother trying to resolve her own childhood conflicts, cope with a new or difficult marital situation, and take care of a new baby. This can make it more difficult for therapists to identify the mother's role in the development of SSA.

[103] Judith Bradford, Caitlin Ryan, and Ester Rothblum, "National Lesbian Health Care Survey: Implications for Mental Health Care," *Journal of Consulting and Clinical Psychology* 62, no. 2 (1994): 228.

Lesbian by Choice?

Interestingly, whereas the vast majority of men with SSA insist that they didn't choose to be attracted to men, a significant percentage of women with SSA insist that they did indeed freely choose to seek out sex with other women.[104] Many of these are radical feminists who have adopted some form of the Constructionist ideology and see their choice of female sexual partners as part of their political stance.

One of these feminists, lesbian activist Laura Brown, explains why:

> A woman who is strongly politically feminist may make a conscious choice, regardless of feeling, to relate sexually and emotionally to other women because of strong belief in the importance of women bonding with one another or in protest against the dominance hierarchies in which most heterosexual relationships are embedded. In this case her socially defined sexual orientation and lesbian identity exist to some degree detached from her actual experience of arousal or affectional attraction.[105]

Brown rejects the gay advocate's standard Essentialist claim that SSA is biologically determined. So does lesbian activist Donna Minkowitz:

> Remember that most of the line about homosex [sic] being one's nature, not a choice, was articulated as a response to brutal repression . . . [I]t's time for us to abandon this defensive

---

[104] Carla Golden, "Do Women Choose Their Sexual Identity?" *Harvard Gay and Lesbian Review* (December 1, 1997).

[105] Laura Brown, "Lesbian Identities: Concepts and Issues," in D'Augelli and C. Patterson, eds., *Lesbian, Gay, and Bisexual Identities Over the Lifespan*, 5.

posture and walk upright on the earth. Maybe you didn't choose to be gay — that's fine. But I did.[106]

Lesbians who claim to have chosen their sexual behavior have often been influenced by Constructionist writers such as Shulamith Firestone or Judith Butler, whose works — popular in women's studies programs — hold that gender itself is an oppressive social construction. (Firestone championed "an unobstructed pansexuality — Freud's 'polymorphous perversity,' " and demanded that women be freed from the "tyranny of their reproductive biology," while Butler attacks "compulsory heterosexuality" as a system of oppression.) It's easy to dismiss these ideologues as representative of "extreme views," but many of them hold enormous sway in universities, and the young women they indoctrinate will carry their ideas out to the worlds of politics, education, law, and entertainment.

It's a pointless exercise to try to refute their ideology, because they reject all conflicting evidence as constructions of the oppressor class. It might be useful, however, to consider why they espouse what they do. Many of these women have been hurt and might now be trying to solve their personal psychological problems by changing society. In many cases, their fathers were neglectful, abusive, or rejecting; their mothers distant, depressed, and unable to protect them. They were often victims of childhood sexual abuse or rape and blamed their parents for not protecting them or believing them.

The radical feminist ideology explained all they had suffered. Their parents were not neglectful; rather, they had been programmed to accept the oppression of women by the "patriarchal

[106] Donna Minkowitz, "Recruit, Recruit, Recruit," *The Advocate* (December 29, 1992): 17, quoted by Bruce Bawer, *A Place at the Table* (New York: Touchstone, 1993), 177.

sexist society" in which they were raised. And if they couldn't change their parents, they could work to change society, so that future women wouldn't suffer as they had. These women might think that their decision to be lesbian — their refusal to sleep with the enemy — was a freely chosen political stance, but it might have been driven by the same combination of early traumas and unmet emotional needs that lead to SSA in other women.

Indeed, those familiar with the radical feminist movement (distinct from ordinary or classical feminism, with its laudable emphasis on the elimination of genuine legal and social injustice) know that a significant percentage of radical feminists, perhaps even a majority, also consider themselves lesbians. To many true believers in the movement, lesbianism has become a badge of honor — or even a litmus test of feminist *bona fides*.

Change More Common with Women

Although gay activists usually claim that persons with SSA are "born that way" and can't change, the lesbian community is very well aware that many women move in and out of lesbianism. Many lesbians have had satisfying sexual relationships with men. Some women experiment with same-sex relationships and then go on to marry men.[107] Other women marry, have children, and then later become involved with a woman. Same-sex activity in women seems to be far more fluid, more circumstantial, than it is in men. Some women don't even view themselves as lesbians, but as women who just happened to "fall in love" with another woman.

SSA in women also appears to be more amenable to treatment than it is in men. The Bieber study of the results of therapy with

---

[107] This phenomenon is observed with enough frequency during college years that it has its own tongue-in-cheek acronym: LUG, or "Lesbian Until Graduation."

men with SSA found that one-quarter became fully heterosexual,[108] whereas a similar but smaller study found "at least a fifty percent probability of significant improvement in women with this syndrome who present themselves for treatment and remain in it."[109]

One reason for this might be that women are less likely than men to experience sexual addiction. Men who have sex with men are at risk for addiction to sexual fantasy, pornography, masturbation, sex with strangers, sex in public places, and other extreme behaviors. This complicates recovery, because therapy for men with SSA must deal with these addictions in addition to childhood traumas and other root causes.

Sometimes therapists successfully treat SSA in women without intending to. Psychoanalyst Elaine Siegel was asked by leaders of a lesbian community (whose members she described as having a "common need to idealize homosexuality as better than heterosexuality") to treat members of their group suffering from various psychological problems. As a committed feminist, Siegel believed that lesbianism was as normal as heterosexuality for women. She didn't set out in any way to dissuade her patients from their lifestyle.

In working with her clients, Siegel discovered that to treat the presenting problems, it was necessary to deal with the underlying causes, and when these were addressed, the SSA diminished or disappeared — even though this was neither her nor her clients' expectation:

> I came to understand their difficulties as developmental arrests that precluded heterosexual object choices . . . As

---

[108] Bieber et al., *Homosexuality: A Psychoanalytic Study of Male Homosexuals*, 236.

[109] Harvey Kaye et al., "Homosexuality in Women," *Archives of General Psychiatry* 17 (November 1967), 626-634.

conflicts were resolved and distanced from, anxiety was reduced and life became more joyful and productive for all these analysands . . . With the attainment of firmer inner structures, interpersonal relationships also solidified and became more permanent . . .

Siegel was surprised by how her own attitudes were changed by the experience:

To be a liberal and liberated woman and yet to view homosexuality as the result of untoward development seemed at times a betrayal of all I then believed. But viewing my patients through the lens of psychoanalytic thinkers and clinicians soon showed me that allowing myself to be seduced into perceiving female homosexuality as a normal lifestyle would have cemented both my patients and myself into a rigid mode that precluded change of whatever nature.[110]

Although Siegel had "never interpreted homosexuality as an illness," over half the women she treated became fully heterosexual.[111] Her efforts were not appreciated by the other members:

This was taken by the referral source as a "betrayal of the sisters." The homosexual community and the networks to which most of patients belonged reacted very much like the families of disturbed children when the child, as a result of treatment, is no longer forced to express conflict for them.[112]

---

[110] Kaye et al., "Homosexuality in Women."

[111] Elaine Siegel, *Female Homosexuality: Choice Without Volition — A Psychoanalytic Study* (Hillsdale, New Jersey: Analytic Press, 1988).

[112] Ibid., p. xii.

Preventing SSA in Women

As with men, SSA in women is preventable. A big first step would be for educators, pediatricians, and parents to recognize the importance of attachment and to develop effective ways of identifying and treating attachment disorders in girls and depression in new mothers. It is also important that society redouble its efforts to prevent childhood sexual abuse (CSA) — particularly the abuse that occurs within families — as well as to identify abused children and to provide care for girls who have been abused. Since failure to attach and CSA can lead to problems other than SSA, initiatives in these two areas can be taken up without specific reference to the prevention of SSA. These are initiatives, then, on which everyone should be able to agree.

Lastly, people need to be educated to recognize the profound difference between radical-feminist ideology and the legitimate movement for protection of the rights, safety, and aspirations of women. Radical feminists are driven by unresolved anger, not only against men whom they view as oppressive and violent, but against mothers who failed their daughters. These are real problems that need to be addressed; but all men are not monsters, and neither are all women helpless victims. Denying the differences between the sexes and encouraging same-sex relationships is not the solution to the difficulties faced by ordinary women. Trying to use the forces of law and education to "normalize" the effects of their developmental traumas won't make them whole and happy. Real problems can be solved when women and men join together in solidarity to respect the full human dignity of both sexes while acknowledging the real differences.

Chapter 7

❧

SSA Treatment and Change

Can a person really change his sexual orientation?

What does SSA therapy involve?

Why do gay activists oppose SSA therapy?

Gay activists' case for the redefinition of marriage rests on their twin claim that SSA is genetically determined and unchangeable. According to their reasoning, if persons with SSA can't "change what they are," then justice demands that they be allowed to marry others of their own sex; else they are unjustly deprived of the benefits of society.

As we've seen, there's no evidence that SSA is genetically or biologically predetermined. But even if it were, there's also substantial evidence that change is possible. And if change of sexual orientation is indeed possible, then persons with SSA would be barred from marriage not by "nature" but by their own decision not to seek healing for a psychological disorder. Understood this way, gay marriage ceases to resemble a civil-rights issue. Their plea for sympathy loses its foundation.

Change Does Happen

Gay activists aggressively peddle the sweeping myth that no one with SSA has ever truly changed, but there are no scientific studies to support it. This is in part because proving a negative is extremely difficult. A researcher would have to investigate each report of change — and there are many — and conclusively discredit them. This is a hard task that gay activists haven't even attempted; rather, they simply attack the numerous reports of change on ideological grounds, asserting as a premise that change is impossible and therefore SSA therapy *can't* work — and worse, that it's homophobic.

Gay-affirming therapists were not satisfied with writing homosexuality out of the *DSM*; they wanted reparative therapy banned, and its practitioners driven out of the profession. In 1997, Douglas Haldeman, president of the American Psychological Associations Society of the Psychological Study of Lesbian, Gay, and Bisexual Issues, was part of a failed move to bar therapists from providing such treatment to clients who desired it. According to Haldeman, "We wish we could outlaw the practice of therapy, but it is probably more important to dry up the market of people looking for such therapy."[113] (Of course, promoting the myth that therapy never works is one obvious way of discouraging people from seeking such therapy and others from recommending it!) Gay activists have even tried to pressure professional groups to declare that providing therapy for SSA constitutes malpractice. So far, they've failed, but the pressure they've exerted has made it difficult in some places to find a therapist willing to accept a client whose goal is change.

This, despite massive evidence documenting change. For although newspaper advice-givers insist that science has proven that change is impossible, that claim rarely appears in peer-reviewed journal articles where documentation is required. (Instead, those authors merely jab at reports of change and highlight cases of backsliders.)

D. J. West, author of *Homosexuality Re-examined*, concurs: "Every study ever performed on conversion from homosexual to heterosexual orientation has produced some successes."[114]

[113] Terry Wilson, " 'Conversion' Is Still an Alternative in Homosexuals' Psychotherapy," *Chicago Tribune*, sec. 1, August 16, 1997.

[114] D. J. West, *Homosexuality Re-examined* (London: Duckworth, 1977), 359.

Ruth Barnhouse, author of *Homosexuality: A Symbolic Confusion*, reviewed the literature and found that "Approximately thirty percent of those [persons with SSA] coming to treatment for any reason can be converted to the heterosexual adaptation."[115] An additional thirty percent experience relief of symptoms, but do not become comfortably heterosexual. Barnhouse notes that, as with any course of therapy, the more strongly motivated the person is and the fewer other psychological problems he has, the more likely he is to have a positive outcome.

Having successfully treated persons with SSA herself, Barnhouse finds it difficult to understand how people can make the claim that the change is impossible:

> The distortion of reality inherent in the denials by homosexual apologists that the condition is curable is so immense that one wonders what motivates it.[116]

How Do You Define Change?

Some critics of treatment act as though nothing less than a hundred-percent success rate would prove the legitimacy of treatment and change, or that only total transformation from SSA to other-sex attraction, without even a momentary temptation, can be counted as a successful outcome. But therapists point out that such total transformations are rarely the outcome of therapy for other disorders. For example, no therapist treating a person for depression would promise that he would never again have a blue day.

The fact is that there are many psychological conditions that are extremely difficult to treat and from which complete recovery

---

[115] Ruth Barnhouse, *Homosexuality: A Symbolic Confusion* (New York: Seabury Press, 1977), 97.

[116] Ibid., 109.

is rare, but this does not preclude attempting treatment. For example, compulsive hoarding is a disorder that causes victims to be unable to dispose of physical objects — in the worst cases, they hoard animals. To those who have not visited their homes, compulsive hoarders may appear completely normal. The hoarders themselves often deny they have a problem, and they offer elaborate rationalizations for their decisions not to dispose. Therapists are working on treatment strategies, but their success so far has been extremely limited. Yet no one would claim that the therapists' failure or the hoarders' assertion that they don't have a problem means that compulsive hoarding isn't a disorder.

Some gay activists argue that if treatment appears to be successful, it's only because the subjects weren't really "gay" in the first place. But even if this were so, it should be reason enough to encourage anyone dissatisfied with his sexual orientation to seek treatment — since how would he know if he were really "gay" if he hadn't at least given treatment a good try? Even an Essentialist, then, ought to be supportive for treatment, if only to help sort out those who are by nature "gay" from those who aren't.

The debate over SSA has revealed a deep division among therapists over what constitutes a psychological disorder. Some argue that a condition is a disorder only if the person feels dissatisfaction. If the person claims to be happy as he is, then it isn't a disorder. Those who hold this opinion believe that "paraphilias" such as sado-masochism, fetishism, cross-dressing, addiction to pornography, and even pedophilia are not psychological problems, but sexual preferences.

Other therapists contest this assertion. They argue that the main criterion for determining whether a particular condition is a psychological disorder isn't whether the person is happy with his behavior, but the origins of his behavior. Is it, for example, a reaction to a trauma or deficits, or a defense mechanism?

Change Unlooked For

In addition to published reports of change of orientation resulting from therapy, there are numerous reports of spontaneous change — people who report at one time having same-sex attraction or being involved in homosexual behavior and then, without any form of treatment, shedding their SSA and becoming attracted to the other sex. In some cases, this was the result of religious conversion; in others, the products of psychological growth. In still others, such change is an unintended, serendipitous result of therapy for another problem.

In a case reported by Daniel Golwyn and Carol Sevlie, a twenty-three-year-old self-identified homosexual man sought treatment for "severe social phobia." He didn't want to change his sexual orientation: he had been homosexual since he was a teenager and had been sexually active exclusively with men. He blamed his homosexuality on childhood teasing by peers, which had contrasted with the acceptance he received from the homosexual men who courted him.

He was treated for extreme shyness with a drug called phenelzine. During this treatment, he began to have heterosexual fantasies and to date women. The therapist concluded that "social phobia may be a hidden contributing factor" in his homosexual behavior.[117] There's no evidence that prescribing phenelzine for all men with SSA will have the same effect. However, the case reveals the possibility that, for a certain percentage of persons with SSA, same-sex attraction is merely a symptom of another — and, in this case, treatable — problem. For another example, persons with schizophrenia might experience SSA or consider themselves

---

[117] Daniel Golwyn and Carol Sevlie, "Adventitious Change in Homosexual Behavior During Treatment of Social Phobia with Phenelzine," *Journal of Clinical Psychiatry* 54, no. 1 (1993): 173-181.

gay; however, when the schizophrenia is treated, these symptoms can disappear.[118]

In another case, a therapist refused his client's request for therapy to change his sexual orientation. Instead, the therapist convinced the client that his religious beliefs were to blame for his anxiety, and used the therapeutic relationship to change the client's religious perspective. The therapist diagnosed the client's problem as a lack of assertiveness, and the client underwent assertiveness training. Some time after leaving therapy, he communicated to the therapist that he was no longer sexually attracted to men. He dated, married, and reported a complete change of orientation.[119]

Fighting the Anti-Change Establishment

Those who have received effective treatment and have come out of homosexuality have been so frustrated by the denial of their very existence (or charges that they were merely faking change), that in 1999, a group of them organized protests outside the APA's annual meeting. The demonstrators attracted the attention of Robert Spitzer, who had been instrumental in the APA decision to remove homosexuality from the *DSM* more than two decades before. Moved by their testimony, Spitzer began to consider the possibility that change of sexual orientation was possible.[120]

Over the next year, he conducted his own research, and in 2001, he presented findings that showed a substantial number of

---

[118] John Gonsiorek, "The Use of Diagnostic Concepts in Working with Gay and Lesbian Populations," in Gonsiorek, *Homosexuality and Psychotherapy* (New York, Haworth Press, 1982), 12.

[119] Joseph Wolpe, *The Practice of Behavior Therapy* (Elmsford, New York: Pergamon, 1969).

[120] Julia Duin, "New Psychiatric Study Says Gays Can Alter Orientation," *Washington Times*, May 9, 2001.

men and women who reported significant change in sexual orientation, mostly through a combination of therapy and prayer. In his report, Spitzer concluded:

> The subjects' self-reports of change appear to be, by and large, valid, rather than glowing exaggerations, brainwashing, or wishful thinking . . . We therefore conclude that some individuals who participate in a sexual reorientation therapy apparently make sustained changes in sexual orientation.[121]

And in an admirable moment of candor and intellectual honesty, Spitzer acknowledged the error of his past assumptions:

> Like most psychiatrists I thought that homosexual behavior could be resisted, but sexual orientation could not be changed. I now believe that's untrue — some people can and do change.[122]

The report of these findings was modest and nuanced in its claims. Nonetheless, it provoked angry responses from gay activists, and Spitzer found himself in the unpleasant position of being embraced by social conservatives — with whom he had nothing in common — and vilified by his former friends.

One Possible Motive for the Anti-Change Camp

Some gay activists deny the effectiveness of therapy because many of those who advocate and seek therapy are motivated by religious beliefs. It's true that some of those with SSA choose therapy because they want to conform their lives to religious norms (or

---

[121] Spitzer, "Can Some Gay Men and Lesbians Change Their Sexual Orientation?"

[122] Dean Byrd, "Spitzer Study Critiqued in the Journal of Gay and Lesbian Psychotherapy," *NARTH Bulletin* (December 2004): 8.

to family expectations, or for other social considerations), but this doesn't mean that their desires are invalid or should be denied, or that their quest will fail.

Of course, if motivation is to be a criterion for evaluating claims, then it's fair to look at the motives of those who would deny therapy. Clearly some are be motivated by politics. Their first priority might not be protecting clients from disappointment, but protecting a key part of their political agenda — namely, the claim that change of sexual orientation is impossible.

There might even be a deeper reason gay activists deny the possibility of change: they might be afraid of reviving their own desire to change. Many persons with SSA initially rejected the idea that they were "gay" and tried to suppress their feelings of attraction. They didn't realize that the answer to SSA was not to deny their need for same-sex love, but to find it in positive, non-sexual same-sex relationships. It might be painful to admit that others have succeeded where they failed — thus the need to maintain that those who have succeeded are lying or have been duped.

It's also true that any promotion of successful therapy, or acknowledgment of the existence of well-adjusted ex-gays, sends a message to those who are experiencing SSA that being "gay" isn't as good as being "straight." After all, people never enter therapy to be "cured" of their heterosexuality.

What Makes Therapy Work — or Fail

When any kind of therapy succeeds, often it's because the therapist and the client mesh — this particular therapist meets this particular client's needs. Conversely, when a particular course of therapy fails, it could often be the result of a poor client/therapist match; when SSA therapy fails, then, it isn't necessarily evidence that change was impossible.

The fact is, psychosexual developmental disorders are never easy to treat, and many persons with SSA also have other serious problems, such as sexual addiction, clinical narcissism, borderline personality disorder, depression, or substance abuse, which complicate or prevent a full recovery. Failure to achieve success in a treatment program can also occur when the therapist centers in on areas where the client has built up extremely strong defenses. When that happens, the client has a choice: to face his fears or quit. "I don't want to" or "I'm not ready to" is different from "I can't."

As we learn more about which therapy protocols are most effective with which classes of clients, treatment methods will improve and the recovery rate will increase significantly.

The Change Is More than Superficial

Some gay activists will insist that therapy might succeed in changing sexual behavior, but it can't change sexual *orientation*. However, therapists who work with clients who desire change see changing sexual behavior as a step in the process of healing, not necessarily the ultimate goal. One member of the Jewish ex-gay ministry JONAH explains the process of reparative therapy:

> What does it mean to heal same-sex attractions? It is not about "change" in the sense of merely "retraining" yourself sexually, because the underlying problem is not sexual, but emotional.
>
> Most of us fell into this problematic sexual attraction when we felt (or were made to feel) insufficiently masculine, separate or foreign to other men. The sexual attraction is a mistaken, broken attempt to get the male love and approval we didn't get, or an attempt to fill the gap we feel in our own masculinity with another man's manliness.

But here, too the healing is not about "change." Because the truth is that we are sufficiently masculine — just as we are. The only thing that needs to "change" or just be discarded — is our mistaken notion of inadequacy.[123]

There are a number of stages in the healing process. The person might first desist from homosexual behavior with others, then from indulging in fantasy with masturbation, and finally, come to a point when he experiences same-sex attraction only when under stress. At this stage, he learns how to recognize a passing attraction to a person of the same sex for what it is — a reaction to stress — and dismiss it. One man in recovery, for instance, learned to recognize situations that triggered feelings of inadequacy, because such situations would be followed by a sexual temptation. Gradually these temptations become less frequent.[124]

Freedom from SSA doesn't necessarily mean that the person will immediately experience an attraction to the other sex. Some do come to experience a true attraction for the other sex; others don't. The two processes — ceasing to experience same-sex attractions and experiencing other-sex attractions — appear to be separate. Those men who had SSA and after a time became sexually attracted to women say that it "just happened." They felt comfortable and competent as men, and all of a sudden they noticed that women were attractive and had an appealing vulnerability. Some associated their first true heterosexual desire with a desire to protect a female friend. For women, overcoming their fear of men clearly plays a part in the emergence of heterosexual desire.

---

[123] "Thoughts on Rediscovering One's True Self," *NARTH Bulletin* (December 2004): 24.

[124] Spitzer, "Can Some Gay Men and Lesbians Change Their Sexual Orientation?" in Dresher, Zucker, eds., *Ex-Gay Research* (Harrington Park Press, New York, 2006), 48.

But many of those who have engaged in homosexual behavior for many years are often content to complete the first stage of freedom from SSA and don't feel they've "failed" because they don't get married or because they're not sexually aroused by persons of the other sex. This is particularly true for those who also experienced addiction to sexual fantasy or masturbation.

The Road to Change Is Harder Than We Think

The search for freedom from SSA is a lifelong process with many pitfalls along the way. Self-comforting behaviors and sexual addictions are extremely difficult to overcome, and relapse is always a potential problem. Also, since persons with SSA suffer disproportionately from a number of other serious psychological problems, they often find themselves in psychological counseling with therapists who treat them for "internalized homophobia" rather than helping them along their path to healing. "Coming out" and embracing the "gay identity" are supposed to cure their problems. Yet even these gay-affirming therapists admit that, in spite of their best efforts, some clients continue to hold negative feelings about SSA.[125]

On the other hand, some defenders of marriage naively talk as though changing one's sexual desires is easy. "Why," such people ask, "can't persons with SSA just repent? Why should we feel sorry for them? After all, they chose their behavior. Can't they just exercise willpower?" Such a simplistic attitude reveals a lack of understanding about how early experiences and behaviors shape the way a person thinks, reacts, and acts. Although it's possible to change such patterns, it's rarely a quick or easy process. Many people

---

[125] Gonsiorek, "The Use of Diagnostic Concepts in Working with Gay and Lesbian Populations," *Homosexuality and Psychotherapy*, 14.

might also fail to understand the damage done by sexual abuse. It's easy to be shocked by the extreme sexual behaviors that are prevalent among persons with SSA, and not realize that these can, in some cases, be the sequelae of childhood sexual abuse.

☞

For many years, gay activists challenged the studies showing a high rate of other psychological problems among persons with SSA, insisting that the studies were poorly designed and used small samples. But four recent large and well-designed studies (Fergusson 1999, Herrell 1999, Cochran 2000, and Sandfort 2002[126]) have provided convincing evidence that persons with SSA are significantly more likely to suffer from depression, anxiety, substance abuse, and suicide attempts. Indeed, gay-affirming therapists are not unaware of these problems, even if they attribute them to the "painful process of coming to terms with one's homosexuality"[127] in a "homophobic" world.

Although it's convenient for such therapists to blame all the excess psychopathology evident in persons with SSA on "oppression" or "internalized homophobia," studies don't confirm this claim. Were it true, we would expect to find less psychopathology in places where there's a more tolerant attitude toward homosexuality. Yet this isn't the case.

A large population-based study done by gay-rights advocate Theo Sandfort and his associates in the Netherlands — a country that's extremely tolerant of sexual "diversity" — found the same high levels of psychological disorders as studies done in the United

---

[126] Fergusson, et al., "Is Sexual Orientation Related to Mental Health Problems?"; Herrell et al., "Sexual Orientation and Suicidality"; Sandfort et al., "Same-Sex Sexual Behavior."

[127] J. W. Shannon and W. J. Woods, "Affirming Psychotherapy of Gay Men," *The Counseling Psychologist* 19 (1991): 212.

States and in New Zealand.[128] None of these studies included sexual addiction or other sexual problems among the disorders reported on; had they been included, the difference between persons with SSA and those without would have been even more striking. But the results are nonetheless compelling enough to conclude that society is not to blame for the psychological problems that frequently accompany SSA.

It's important to remember that persons with SSA have suffered and struggled. Whether they know it or not, they're seeking a resolution to their problems. For many of them, that resolution can be achieved through proper therapy.

But by demanding that the world pretend that SSA is normal and healthy, and that all their problems are caused by lack of acceptance, the gay community is blocking the path to real recovery. The truth about the human person — namely, that we're born either male or female, and that children flourish when their sexual identity is affirmed by their father and a mother — can't be changed by political strategies or media campaigns, and it's the truth that sets us free. Compassion requires speaking the truth with love.

[128] Sandfort, "Same-Sex Sexual Behavior."

Part III

~

Marriage and Intimate Relationships

"The Church's teaching on marriage and on the complementarity of the sexes reiterates a truth that is evident to right reason and recognized as such by all the major cultures of the world. Marriage is not just any relationship between human beings. It was established by the creator with its own nature, essential properties, and purpose. No ideology can erase from the human spirit the certainty that marriage exists solely between a man and a woman."

Joseph Cardinal Ratzinger
Now Pope Benedict XVI

~

"Ambiguity is a good word for the feeling among gays about marriage. I'd be for marriage if I thought gay people would challenge and change the institution and not buy into the traditional meaning of 'till death do us part' and monogamy forever."

Mitchell Raphael
Editor, *Fab* magazine

Chapter 8

⌒

The Definition and Purpose of Marriage

What does our cultural and legal
tradition have to say about marriage?

What are the biological and
anthropological cases for traditional marriage?

How does traditional marriage benefit society?

In grammar school, children are taught the difference between *may* and *can*. *You may* means you have permission. *You can* means you have the ability. The debate over marriage is often cast as a debate over whether same-sex couples *may* marry, but the more salient question is, "*Can* they marry?" Are they able to fulfill the requirements of marriage, requirements rooted in biological realities and affirmed over thousands of years of human history?

The answer must be no. It's not a simple matter of removing arbitrary legal roadblocks so that they *may* marry; they *cannot* marry. To call their relationships marriages is to change the meaning of the word — to create a world where words do not correspond to reality.

The Tradition on Marriage

Before the advent of gay activism, the question of what makes a marriage hadn't been controversial. Yes, there had been a few skirmishes. In the nineteenth century, Mormons had insisted that polygamy was the form of marriage sanctioned by God. In Utah, they even set up a government that allowed it. But the United States made renunciation of polygamy a requirement for Utah's statehood. Marriage would be between one man and one woman.

In the 1967 case *Loving v. Virginia*, the Supreme Court ruled that laws in southern states banning interracial marriage were

unconstitutional. Those anti-miscegenation laws were an anom-
aly in the history of human culture. Moreover, they were a question of *may*, not *can*. There was no dispute over whether a man
and a woman of different races could fulfill the basic requirements
of marriage. Indeed, it was *because* they were capable of marrying
that racist legislators wanted to forbid it. The Supreme Court
would not allow it: marriage would be between one man and one
woman, regardless of race.

Where does our Western culture get its traditional understanding of what marriage is? Not from religion. As Thomas Aquinas
put it, marriage is first a matter of natural law, not religious dogma:
"The conjugal union of marriage is an institution of nature."[129]
Natural law witnesses to us that "Matrimony is a joining. It unites
the spouses in the task of begetting and raising children, and it
dedicates them to one common life."[130]

What about the definition that the court invented in *Goodridge?* Although we like to think of marriage as being about love
and caring, two people can nonetheless legally marry even if they
don't love one another. And if they stop loving each other, they're
still married. And likewise, although marriage is intimately related to the procreation and caring for children, persons who cannot or will not have children can still marry.

Traditionally in most human cultures, marriage has had two
essential elements: consent and consummation.

1. Consent of the parties. The state issues a license for the parties to make a public, witnessed consent to marry — the wedding
vows. The essential elements to which the couple consents are:

---

[129] Msgr. Paul Glenn, *A Tour of the Summa* (Rockford, Illinois:
Tan Books, 1976), 420.
[130] Ibid., 421.

- *Exclusivity.* They promise to have sexual relations with each other and no one else — *forsaking all others.*

- *Permanence.* They vow to be married not for a month or a year, but forever. And although this promise might not be kept, the couple typically has the intention of forming a permanent bond — *until death do us part.*

- *Commingling of assets.* Persons who marry agree to form a legal unit, and the state agrees to treat them as such. They become legally and economically one — *with all my worldly goods I thee endow.*

- *Children.* They vow to jointly accept responsibility for children conceived through their marital union.

All this assumes that both persons are free to marry, haven't made false presentation, are mentally competent, and aren't making these vows with mental reservations.

2. *Consummation.* The public vows by themselves aren't sufficient to make a marriage. The marriage isn't actualized until it's consummated through a conjugal act. That's why, if the marriage hasn't been consummated, either party can obtain an annulment — a legal degree that no marriage took place.

Although there are various acts in which two or more individuals can engage for sexual pleasure, only one very specific act consummates a marriage. The other acts do not involve the sexual organs of both parties coming together as designed to create a union of the two. The other acts can be engaged in by two persons of the same-sex or by a man and a woman. Such acts involve the hands, either end of the digestive system, or physical objects, but not the reproductive organs of both simultaneously in the same act.

Consummation requires physical complementarity: the reproductive/sexual organs of men and women are different and designed to fit together. When electricians refer to male and female plugs, everyone can easily recognize which is which and why they are so named. Some might object that this definition of marriage is too crude; that love and, therefore, marriage, ought to be able to transcend mundane physical details. Yes, love can transcend the physical, but marriage has a physical foundation. The combination of covenant promises and consummation by means of the conjugal act establishes a family relationship between the husband and the wife. This is what marriage is. Any other relationship, no matter how loving or supportive, isn't a marriage.

Same-sex couples might consent to an exclusive and permanent commitment (although many, especially male, same-sex couples would prefer a kind of marriage that eliminates exclusivity and permanence), but no same-sex couple can consummate their marriage, because two persons of the same sex lack the physical complementarity necessary to become one flesh in the conjugal union.

Is this an arbitrary point? Jonathan Rauch, author of *Gay Marriage: Why It Is Good for Gays, Good for Straights, and Good for America*, thinks so. He argues that the definition is tautological:

> By locating the essence of marriage in the one type of sex which homosexuals cannot have, they have finally managed to draw a line which includes all straight unions in the proper domain of matrimony, while excluding all gay ones.[131]

Gay activists complain that we've chosen to define the requirements of marriage in a way that excludes homosexual marriage.

---

[131] Jonathan Rauch, *Gay Marriage: Why It Is Good for Gays, Good for Straights, and Good for America* (New York: Times Books, 2004), 117.

But clearly this definition of consummation (and thus, marriage) is rooted in natural design. The requirements for conjugal union are what they are; human cultures have identified and codified them based on the natural evidence. The institution of marriage *grew out of them*, not the other way around. Therefore, they exclude gay marriages by way of conclusion, not premise.

Of course, activists would ignore the evidence of natural design, or deny its significance. In this way, the debate over marriage often comes back to a debate over sex difference. Those who want marriage redefined insist that sex difference doesn't matter; that biological differences are accidents of evolution. Although it would seem obvious that men and women are different — and nowhere is this difference more apparent than in the sexual act — for many, the argument from design is no longer convincing.

Thirty years of radical-feminist rhetoric have, in many people's minds, blurred the importance of sex differences, and the difference between the natural and unnatural is lost on this generation. Many no longer fathom how one kind of sexual pleasure can be "natural" and according to the design of the body, and another "unnatural."

Nonetheless, physical complementarity affects the sexual act, even at the most elemental levels. When a man and a woman engage in sexual relations, their intimacy — the touching and caressing — sets off chemical reactions in each, facilitating bonding. The male semen contains hormones that affect the woman's body, producing various positive emotions. Semen carries immunosuppressive agents to protect sperm from the woman's immune system. The woman's vagina is designed to contain the semen to the fallopian tubes and prevent mixing with the bloodstream. Such natural reactions are finely tuned — to create emotional bond between the spouses and, at times, to produce a baby.

Physical Acts Express Personal Love

Some people argue that basing marriage on the physical complementarity of men and women reduces the conjugal love to the merely physical, and that such a limitation is a remnant of outdated sexual stereotyping — the active, aggressive man penetrating the passive, receptive woman, and so forth. Isn't love between two persons, they ask, far more than what they do with their genitals?

Pope John Paul II attempted to address such a criticism by speaking at length about the "language of the body." He didn't separate the love between persons from its physical expression, but *connected* them. According to him, complementarity of the sexes bespeaks a natural (and ultimately divine) design, in which the body expresses personal, conjugal love in a singular and powerful way. He explained how in the

> spousal union of the married couple, the body itself "speaks." It speaks by means of its masculinity and femininity.[132]
>
> The spouses' bodies will speak "for" and "on behalf of" each of them. They will speak in the name of and with the authority of the person, of each of the persons, carrying out the conjugal dialogue proper to their vocation and based on the language of the body, reread in due course opportunely and continually — and it is necessary that it be reread in truth! The spouses are called to form their life and living together as a communion of persons on the basis of that language . . . [T]he spouses — by means of their conduct and comportment, by means of their actions and gestures — are called to become the authors of such meanings of the "language of the body."[133]

[132] John Paul II, *Theology of the Body: Human Love in the Divine Plan* (Boston: Pauline Books, 1997), 359.

[133] Ibid., 364.

Tragically, many modern men and women are often deaf to this language. All they've experienced in sexual exchanges is using and being used. They're therefore unable to understand why two bodies of the same sex cannot speak the language of conjugal love to one another.

According to John Paul II, if you're using a person for your own pleasure, when they stop providing pleasure, you have a right to end the relationship — even if it hurts the other person — because your pleasure is primary:

> "Love" in this Utilitarian conception is a union of egoisms, which can hold together only on the condition that they confront each other with nothing unpleasant, with nothing to conflict with their mutual pleasure.[134]

Many would prefer not to think about what actually happens when two men or two women engage in homosexual acts. Such reticence is understandable; it's better to keep some images out of our mind. However, in this debate, it's important to make clear that the acts in which two persons of the same sex can engage *cannot* unite them as one flesh in a mutual gift of self. Only the conjugal union, in which the man speaking the natural language of his body enters the woman, who receives him with the natural language of her body, can do that.

Homosexual acts are things that one person does *to* another person; the conjugal union is an act in which both parties participate as equals according to their personal nature, symbolically expressed by their bodies when they use their reproductive organs as they were designed.

Accordingly, Bishop Fred Henry of Calgary called on fellow citizens to resist the redefinition of marriage, because:

[134] Ibid., 39.

[F]uture spouses are not free to alter marriage's essential purpose or properties. These do not depend on the will or the sexual orientation of the contracting parties. They are rooted in natural law and do not change.

The committed union of two people of the same sex is not the same human reality as the committed union of one man and one woman. A same-sex union is not a physical union that transmits human life, producing children. A same-sex union is not the joining of two complementary natures that complete each other. Simply stated, a same-sex union is not marriage. The idea that homosexuals can create same-sex "marriage" through their individual choice is false. All the packaging in the world doesn't alter substance.[135]

The State Has an Interest in Stable Families

The conjugal act's potential for conceiving a child is another compelling reason human cultures have long defined marriage as a union between one man and one woman. Every society has an interest in protecting the welfare of children (and the women to whom their care tends to fall) and in ensuring stable social structures. Legal marriage is the mechanism by which society assigns the duty of fatherhood. Children born to a married woman are assumed to be the offspring of her legal husband, and he is made legally responsible for their support.

Gay activists frequently argue that the state doesn't prohibit the marriage of infertile couples or couples too old to conceive, so why should laws discriminate against same-sex couples who can't conceive? The reason is that even male/female couples who can't conceive children due to defect or age can still consummate their relationship and thereby fulfill an essential requirement for marriage.

---

[135] Bishop Fred Henry, Pastoral Letter, January 15, 2005.

Same-sex couples cannot consummate a marriage; their inability to conceive a child naturally isn't due to defect or circumstances, but simply follows from this fundamental deficiency.

Marriage links the father, emotionally and financially, to his biological children, creating the biological family unit. The state allows married couples to commingle assets in advantageous ways in order to protect children and women who devote themselves to the care of children. The legal protections of marriage protect these commingled assets and lend further stability — again resulting in both emotional and economic benefits for families and for all society.

Governments have traditionally placed legal restrictions on marriage, each in some way an affirmation of marriage's traditional meaning or purpose. Children are generally considered too young to consent to marriage, and so states set minimum age requirements. Laws prohibit marriages between close blood relatives. You may marry only one person at a time. Other such laws — prohibiting contraception, adultery, and easy divorce — have also been part of the state's traditional purview over marriage, even if in most Western nations today, they've been eliminated or gone unenforced.

⌒

Marriage is such a positive good and offers so many benefits that it isn't surprising that persons with SSA want to marry and feel deprived when they're denied society's approval. That's why we must be able to communicate why calling same-sex relationships "marriages" would be harmful not only to marriage as an institution and to the society that sanctions it, but also to persons who seek to "marry" someone of the same sex.

Chapter 9

≈

Why Redefining Marriage
Will Harm Persons with SSA

*How are intimate same-sex
relationships different from marriages?*

*How do same-sex couples deal
with the lack of complementarity?*

*What observations do we make
about long-term same-sex couples?*

Even though their sexual orientation isn't genetically determined, even though they're capable of change, if persons with SSA could benefit from redefining marriage, their demand would at least merit consideration. But the opposite is the case. Legally validating same-sex relationships — treating them as though they were real marriages — would not serve the best interests of the persons involved. Indeed, it would harm them.

For if SSA is evidence of a deficit, and not a normal variant of humanness, if it's associated with numerous underlying psychological disorders and related to early traumas or developmental failures, then a "marriage" between two persons of the same sex would amount to a covenant between them to remain unhealed.

Society can't force those with such deficits to seek help, of course, but neither should it lock them into their disorder by granting legal status to same-sex relationships. Redefining marriage would only reinforce their illusion that SSA is just like attraction to the other sex, and that same-sex intimacy is just like the conjugal union between husband and wife. It would also allow them to continue under the illusion that society is to blame for their many problems. They would be caught in a never-ending battle against perceived oppression.

We can acknowledge the natural desire for the good that is marriage, but at the same time, we must refuse to call a counterfeit the real thing. Same-sex couples may pretend among themselves, but they have no right to force others to participate in their self-deception. That is precisely what the campaign to redefine marriage amounts to.

The Search for Psychological Completeness

Persons experiencing SSA might be intellectually mature, but this doesn't mean they're psychologically complete members of their own sex. Many persons with SSA emerged from childhood with uncompleted developmental tasks. Some might be looking for the parental love they were deprived of as children, others for peer bonding. Some feel inadequate and are looking for a partner who is an ideal image of what they want to be. Now, of course it's good to love your father and mother and to care deeply for same-sex friends, but these relationships are not meant to be sexual. It's good to have a positive self-image, but being sexually intimate with a person whose qualities you admire is not the way to achieve it.

As Elizabeth Moberly puts it:

> A form of marriage to sanction the homosexual relationship would be inappropriate, because the relationship is inherently self-limiting, and because marriage is not right for a relationship analogous to that between a parent and child. Marriage is a heterosexual "institution. As the homosexual reparative drive is itself a striving for the same-sex psychological completeness that is heterosexuality, homosexuality cannot be considered on a par with heterosexuality.[136]

The attraction between a man and woman is the fruit of a mature sexual identity. Each recognizes the other as different and therefore desirable. On the other hand, when same-sex attraction

---

[136] Moberly, *Homosexuality: A New Christian Ethic*, 37.

springs from a desire to complete the developmental stage of identification with the same sex, it cannot be the foundation of a
healthy relationship. For Moberly, the homosexual condition is "as
a state of psychological incompletion and a corresponding striving
for completion."[137] Same-sex sexual relationships offer the persons
involved a false hope for that completion, but various obstacles
prevent it. First, the partners will tend to have similar psychological needs — meaning that each will be unable to meet the other's.
Also, those "deep dependency needs" are exceedingly difficult to
fulfill in adulthood. This can lead to unhealthy situations in
which one adult must continually play the part of the parent, because the other needs to be a child. Or worse — in which both
want to be the dependent child.[138]

But perhaps the most significant reason same-sex sexual relationships don't resolve the need for same-sex love is that

> the defensive detachment that was originally responsible
> for checking the normal process of growth may re-emerge
> and disrupt the renewed attachment. The instability of
> many homosexual relationships may well stem from this
> fact.[139]

Defensive detachment occurs when a child feeling rejected (in
this case, by the same-sex parent) reacts by rejecting the rejecter.
For example, an angry little boy says in his heart, "I will never be
like my father," and even if, in later years, the father tries to mend
the relationship, the door is closed and locked. If SSA springs from
a defensive detachment from the same-sex parent, as the child
grows into an adult, he will carry anger toward that parent — and

[137] Ibid., 27.
[138] Ibid., 19.
[139] Ibid.

anyone who resembles that parent — into subsequent relation-ships, poisoning them.

Many adults with SSA carry the deep wounds of childhood re-jection. Rejection experienced in childhood and unhealed creates an interior emptiness that even the most attentive partner can't fill. This is true in husband/wife relationships, and even more so in same-sex relationships, where the likelihood of one or both hav-ing experienced severe rejection is greater. No matter how many times the partner says, "I love you," or how much affection is shown, this empty place remains; a sinkhole that swallows up love yet remains unfilled. Eventually, the partner grows tried of trying to fill it, and if, as often happens, both partners come into the rela-tionship wounded, each will further resent that his own needs aren't recognized.

Sometimes a same-sex couple — usually female — will sustain their relationship by focusing on something outside the relation-ship, such as perceived oppression. These couples achieve unity by redirecting their anger onto a society that refuses to "accept" them. This shared sense of oppression does create a bond, but it seldom, if ever, leads to the healing they need. Instead, it leads the couple to see oppression even where there is none, leading to an "us-against-the-world" posture[140] and a phenomenon that thera-pists call *enmeshment* or *fusion*. What follows is an inability to ac-cept *separateness*, making it hard to achieve that mature kind of intimacy characterized by "the dynamic balance between close-ness and separation acceptable to both partners."[141]

---

[140] J. Krestan and C. S. Bepko, "The Problem of Fusion in the Lesbian Relationship," *Family Process* 19, no. 2 (1980): 277-289.

[141] Karen Bridges and James Croteau, "Once-Married Lesbians"; quotation is from B. McCandlish, "Therapeutic Issues with Les-bian Couples," in John Gonsiorek, ed., *A Guide to Psychotherapy*

Persons with SSA can't be faulted for wanting to be part of a family. After all, human beings are meant to live in families, and for persons with SSA, the drive for familial intimacy is likely even magnified by the deficits of their childhood. Moberly views persons with SSA indeed as psychologically "orphaned" by their defensive detachment from the same-sex parent. She advocates helping them to understand their real needs and find appropriate non-sexual same-sex love:

> Homosexuality is not "anti-family," but rather it is a paradoxical confirmation of the need for the family and of the importance of the child being able to receive parental care . . . The homosexual has a greater need for relationships than a single heterosexual, because the former involves a child's need for his parent rather than the need of one adult for another. To be a single adult is one thing; to be a parentless child is quite another.[142]

Same-Sex Relationships Force Persons into Unnatural Roles

As we noted earlier, sex difference creates complementarity: a positive tension that supplies the internal dynamic on which male/female relationships are based. Complementarity allows the man to be all that he is as a man, the woman all that she is as a woman. For the sake of unity, each may sacrifice selfishness and self-centeredness for the other, but they don't need to sacrifice their true selves. Same-sex relationships, in contrast, suffer from a redundancy that creates an unhealthy tension. To compensate for the lack of complementarity, in order to sustain a same-sex relationship, the participants must sacrifice a part of their true selves.

with Gay and Lesbian Clients (New York: Harrington Park Press, 1985), 73.

[142] Moberly, *Homosexuality: A New Christian Ethic*, 34.

One Man, One Woman

If the same-sex relationship mimics a husband/wife relationship, for example, one of the partners must sacrifice his natural vocation (male/husband and father, or female/wife and mother) to adopt the role of the opposite sex. Although this might initially be embraced, the one making the greater sacrifice might later come to resent the role he's forced to play. If the same-sex relationship is an attempt to recreate a parent/child relationship, one partner must sacrifice his natural growth and maturity and remain a perpetual child. If the partners try to merge their personalities into an undifferentiated unity, both must sacrifice their individuality. In same-sex relationships that evolve in friendship, sexual intimacy between the two often diminishes or disappears. When a person settles for someone of the same sex because a member of the opposite sex isn't available, he sacrifices natural heterosexuality. None of the sacrifices are in the best interest of the persons making them, and neither is it fair for the other partner to ask for such sacrifices.

Let's look more closely at each of these scenarios.

• *Pseudo husband/wife relationship.* Many people look at same-sex couples and assume that one plays the part of the husband and one the wife. Slang words identifying these roles are today part of our everyday vocabulary. And yet many gay activists consider this a demeaning stereotype. According to Janice Bohan, author of articles on feminism, lesbianism, and Constructionist theory, the stereotype reflects heterosexist assumptions:

> [T]he notion that in same-sex couples one partner plays the role of "wife" and the other, the role of "husband" clearly reflects our deep-seated incapacity to conceive of a relationship between equals.[143]

---

[143] Janice Bohan, *Psychology and Sexual Orientation: Coming to Terms* (New York: Routledge 1996), 36.

Whether or not this stereotype "reflects heterosexist assumptions," it nonetheless serves gay activists' political ends, making same-sex couples appear conventional, recognizable, even wholesome. However, it has little basis in the reality of the lives of couples with SSA, especially men, as David McWhirter and Andrew Mattison, authors of the book *The Male Couple: How Relationships Develop*, point out:

> Near the top of the list of old beliefs about male couples is that one of the partners is more masculine while the other has more feminine characteristics. Next on this list is the belief that one plays the husband and assumes the manly duties while the other becomes the wife and functions accordingly. This stereotypical notion is held by many in the general public and reinforced by numerous writers in the past. Our couples manifested very little evidence of stereotypical behavior.[144]

Among female couples, the wife/pseudo-husband scenario isn't as uncommon. "Butch/femme" relationships are well known within the lesbian community. In such couples, the pseudo-husband adopts a stereotypical masculine appearance, always wearing pants and often sporting a male haircut. The "wife" maintains a softer appearance, making her often indistinguishable from other women; she's often very pretty. When such a couple decides to conceive children artificially, it is the "wife" who bears them.

For a high-profile example, when media personality Rosie O'Donnell "came out" as a lesbian, for a time she put away feminine clothing and hairstyles, dressed in clearly masculine clothing, and talked about her "wife." Her partner, Kelli, the biological

---

[144] David McWhirter and Andrew Mattison, *The Male Couple* (Englewood Cliffs, New Jersey: Prentice Hall, 1984), 231.

mother of some of their children (some are adopted), is obviously feminine. We can see how the lack of complementary plays out in two-woman families in comments made by O'Donnell on her talk show, *The View*. The panel was discussing breastfeeding, and Rosie announced that Kelli had breastfed their baby conceived through artificial insemination — but for only one month, because Rosie had demanded that Kelli stop. Rosie explained that breastfeeding allowed Kelli to develop an intimacy with the baby that Rosie couldn't be a part of, and the other women on the show were clearly shocked that Rosie saw nothing wrong with allowing her jealousy to deny the baby the positive benefits of breastfeeding.

It isn't surprising that Rosie and other pseudo-husbands would have maternal feelings; although they might want to adopt the male role in the relationship, they're unable wholly to sacrifice their natural desire to mother. Being a mother is simply more natural to a woman than being a father.

Some women with SSA combine mannish dress and behavior with extreme anti-male attitudes. This seeming contradiction might be the result of early traumas: women who saw their mothers abused, or were abused themselves, might view femininity as weakness and associate power and security with maleness. But since men can't be trusted, they must adopt the male role of protector to other women.

• *Pseudo parent/child relationship*. Whereas the general public might view most same-sex relationships as pseudo-marriages, a significant percentage of them actually resemble parent/child relationships. Where SSA is related to a failure to bond with the same-sex parent, the younger, dependent partner in a same-sex relationship might be attempting to repair this failure by seeking union with a replacement parent. The older partner — particularly in pseudo father/son relationships — might be attracted to the youth and beauty of the younger, hoping to recapture his own youth. In female couples, the age difference might not be as significant as the maturity difference: the pseudo-mother exercising her desire for motherhood and at the same time offering the pseudo-daughter the mothering she didn't receive in childhood. In some cases, both partners might be looking for parenting, which further complicates the relationship.

Ideally in marriage, both partners should want what's best for the other. But in a pseudo parent/child relationship, the older partner doesn't want what's best for the younger — namely, that he mature into an independent adult. For the relationship to continue, the younger must remain dependent and immature. Furthermore, in most pseudo father/son relationships, there's a large difference in income and assets between the two. In these couplings, the commingling of assets proper to a true marriage seldom occurs; rather, the older man supports the younger. (Many people, influenced by stereotypes of the male/female relationship, mistake these psychological parent/child relationships for pseudo husband/wife relationships, because they see the provider pseudo-parent as a husband and the dependent pseudo-child as a wife. In so doing, they miss the real dynamic of the relationship.)

In some cases, pseudo-father/son relationships keep the "son" in a dependent position in which he provides sexual services in exchange for a lifestyle that would otherwise be far beyond his means. Researcher Richard Steinman conducted a study on social exchanges in same-sex relationships between older and younger men. He reported, "In an age-stratified relationship, the youthful persona of the younger partner may be offered in exchange for certain benefits from the older partner."[145]

---

[145] R. Steinman, "Social Exchanges Between Older and Younger Gay Male Partners," *Journal of Homosexuality* 20 (1991): 181.

These age-different male couples might stay together for an extended time, but according to Steinman, the older partners often grow dissatisfied with the sexual aspects of the relationship:

> The condition of older partners wanting more sex than their alluring younger partners afforded them, as in the case of Peter and Glen, was quite widespread in the study. This was even evident between some partners as young as thirty-three and twenty-one years old, respectively. Many younger partners were unable to maintain the unwritten and usually unspoken contract. While their older partners were living up to the letter of the contract — providing ample extrinsic resources — these younger men fell short of satisfactorily delivering the sexual component of the intrinsic, thereby rendering the social exchange quite inequitable. In gay male culture, from time to time, one hears older gay men say about a hypothetical younger partner, "If he didn't 'put out,' I'd *throw* him out."[146]

In newspapers, female couples applying for marriage licenses are often pictured looking lovingly into each other's eyes. The assumption is that these women have been able to capture and preserve the romance that characterizes the first stages of a male/female relationship.

Yet there might be another explanation: the women in such a relationship have recreated the mother/child bond. Where SSA in a woman is the result of a failure to attach to her mother in early childhood, a woman who has otherwise considered herself completely heterosexual might quite suddenly look into another woman's eyes and see there a solution to her unrecognized need for the attachment to the mother she missed.

[146] Steinman, "Social Exchanges," 198.

But although she might need the healing that accepting love from a woman can bring, this isn't a sexual need, and a forty-year-old woman isn't a dependent child. A mother/child bond, intrinsically non-sexual, can't be the foundation for an adult sexual relationship. A true mother expects her baby to grow up and become an independent person.

• *Mirror images/merged personalities.* Another form the same-sex relationship can take is that of the mirror-image or merged couple. Like girlfriends in elementary school, this couple may dress identically and share all activities. Any difference, no matter how slight, might be seen as a betrayal. In a normal marriage, sexual complementarity allows the equality of balance, but without natural complementarity, the merged same-sex couple struggles to achieve an equality of *measure.* Yet since two individuals are never identical, this is virtually impossible.

It's well known that in almost all male same-sex relationships, sex precedes friendship; in many cases, it might even precede an exchange of names. Occasionally these encounters result in an immediate bonding — the partner is exactly what each has been looking for. Such couples might move in together shortly after the first encounter.

McWhirter and Mattison found that most of the male/male relationships they studied began with merging — each man seeing the other as an extension of himself:

> The intensity of the merger allows each to take on the new partner's qualities, as if those qualities were his own. Each person sometimes without conscious awareness, now feels able to own qualities of the beloved which he heretofore lacked.[147]

[147] McWhirter and Mattison, *The Male Couple,* 23.

According to one study respondent:

"It was as if we became one person . . . When I walked down the street wearing Patrick's gold chain, I felt like my English improved and I could stay at the Ritz." To which Patrick responded, "And when I wore Joe's work boots, I swear my biceps grew two inches . . . I was him."[148]

In contrast, a man and a woman might fall deeply in love, but they do not merge in this manner. Their complementarity, both sexual and psychological, allows them to become one flesh without becoming one person. It allows them to grow closer without losing their individuality; indeed, the closer they become, the more each is complete as man or as woman.

The respondents found the experience of merging extremely satisfying, probably because it fulfilled the unmet developmental need to identify with same-sex peers. Yet it's clear from McWhirter and Mattison's account that this merging is only temporary, an illusion that vanishes as each partner inevitably begins to exhibit his natural individuality.

Where this arrangement endures for a period of time, the sexual component eventually disappears, and the partners might seek outside sexual gratification while reserving non-sexual affection for each other.

Eric Marcus, author of *The Male Couple's Guide*, recognizes the problem:

There are couples who no longer have sex together. If you're in such a relationship and both you and your partner are satisfied, then there is really no problem.[149]

[148] McWhirter and Mattison, *The Male Couple*, 23.

[149] Eric Marcus, *The Male Couple's Guide* (New York: Harper Perennial, 1999), 165.

Marcus also counsels couples on "making nonmonogamy work."[150]

In female/female merged relationships, the women might struggle with issues of control. In order to create the illusion of merger, each must suppress what is different about herself. One partner might fear separateness, the other fear losing the self. According to Barbara McCandlish, who has treated lesbian couples, this can lead to problems:

> Lesbian couples often discover in the course of therapy that they may have assumed "rules" against being separate. Each partner will tend to treat as rejection any attempts by the other to have separate friends, be emotionally distant, or have a different world view. Sometimes even talking or dressing differently is viewed as a threat. Having secrets, thoughts, and feelings that are not shared is especially threatening. Any attempts at separation are undermined with the communication "You don't love me." Even when one partner attempts to leave the relationship or have additional intimate relationships, she will persist in undermining attempts by the other partner to be separate.[151]

McCandlish's case histories illustrate how female couples bring deep unresolved problems to the relationship: unmet needs, deep anger, and an inability to trust. Women who have been in unsatisfying previous relationships with men are often "surprised and saddened" to find they haven't left strife behind. Whereas even in difficult male-female relationships, sex difference creates a natural "separateness" that can co-exist with intimacy, therapists have

---

[150] Ibid., 43.

[151] Barbara McCandlish, "Against All Odds, Lesbian Mother Family Dynamics," in Frank Bozett, *Gay and Lesbian Parents* (New York: Praeger, 1987), 77.

noted that in female/female couples, "the lack of acceptable ways to separate undermines the existing intimacy and forces the partners to use defensive modes to gain a sense of self."[152]

Reading through the case histories provided by therapists who work with these couples, one can't help but notice how, after outlining the various problems and offering a reasonable analysis of how childhood experiences and the very nature of the same-sex relationships contribute to them, the therapists invariably try to shift the blame to "heterosexism" or "internalized homophobia."[153] Their sympathy with the gay political agenda makes them unable to recognize what is right before their eyes.

• *Non-sexual friendship.* As I studied literature produced by the gay community, I was surprised to find story after story of same-sex couples whose sexual intimacy decreased dramatically over time, or even ceased altogether. An ordinary marriage in which, after just a few years, the partners no longer engaged in sexual activity with each other would be considered seriously deficient, even if the parties claimed to remain "best friends." Yet this appears to be what happens with many same-sex relationships, which often begin with intense sexual activity but quickly become non-sexual.

As friendship between husband and wife grows over time, complementarity and mystery remain, and sexual intimacy can become even more satisfying. But as friendship between two men grows, their awareness of each as another man like himself increases, and sexual excitement tends to fade concurrently. Fr. Jeffrey Keefe, a psychologist who has worked with men with SSA, discovered from his clients that as true friendship develops between the partners, homosexual behavior is inhibited:

[152] McCandlish, "Against All Odds," 76.

[153] Joan Sophie, "Internalized Homophobia and Lesbian Identity," *Journal of Homosexuality* (1987): 53-65.

In my clinical experience, it is not uncommon that a male homosexual cannot continue having sex with a partner as affection deepens.[154]

This decline in sexual desire leads many same-sex couples to engage in ever more extreme sexual practices. Male couples, especially, might engage in intimacy with each other only when a third person is present, or when they are high on drugs. According to McWhirter and Mattison, among the couples they studied who had been together eleven to twenty years:

There is little or no sexual activity together for many couples. Some manage to maintain sex together by introducing other partners and experimenting with new outlets together.[155]

The cessation of sexual intimacy is also common among female couples (common enough that it has a slang name: "lesbian bed death"), but women are less likely than men to tolerate infidelity. If one partner comes to the point where sexual intimacy is no longer important, while the other wants it to continue, the relationship tends to dissolve rather than "branch out."

In an article on psychotherapy with lesbian couples, therapist Sallyann Roth notes:

[S]ome lesbian couples go without genital sex for considerable lengths of time. The greater the duration of these times, the more mutually avoidant of sex the partners become.[156]

---

[154] Jeffrey Keefe, "A Sharper Focus on Homosexuality," in Fr. John Harvey, *The Homosexual Person* (San Francisco: Ignatius Press, 1987), 74.

[155] McWhirter and Mattison, *The Male Couple*, 111.

[156] Sallyann Roth, "Psychotherapy with Lesbian Couples," in Emery Hetrick and Terry Stein, *Innovation in Psychotherapy with Homosexuals* (Washington: APA 1984): 99.

Some gay activists try to put a positive spin on this phenomenon, claiming that it shows same-sex partners can remain devoted to each other even when the sexual dimension dries up and disappears, but most blame it on society's subjugation of women.

This problem is rarely discussed in public, since it would likely harm the campaign to redefine marriage. It might also be that persons with SSA, and their therapists, are truly confused and embarrassed by it. Some couples might hope that if their relationships were legally recognized, sexual desire would return. But this is only once again to locate the problem in societal oppression, rather than its true sources.[157] If indeed it's the case that declining sexual intimacy follows naturally from the growth of same-sex friendship or primal bonding or merging, then calling same-sex relationships "marriages" will not solve their problems, but only increase their shame and disappointment when it fails to.

It should be pointed out, of course, that there's nothing wrong with two persons of the same sex living together without sexual intimacy. I'm aware of several same-sex couples — both male and female — who have had Christian conversions and come out of homosexuality, but continued to live together in chaste friendship. For a man and woman who had been previously intimate with each other, such an arrangement could be very difficult and temptation-filled, but same-sex couples who take this path are able do so precisely because they are *no longer* tempted to sexual intimacy with each other. Their deep friendship, affection, and the habits of common life remain — but these do not amount to a marriage.

[157] It is interesting that one of the first couples to legalize their relationship in Canada separated almost immediately, and the Goodridges, who gave the name to the Massachusetts case that led to the redefinition of marriage in that state, are now separated.

The Subversion of Friendship

The debate over marriage has led, sadly, to popular confusion over the nature of friendship. Many people today can't conceive of deep same-sex friendships without homoerotic overtones. For example, the biblical relationship between David, the shepherd-turned-giant-killer, and Jonathan, the king's son, is certainly one of the most beautiful literary-historical examples of male friendship. But some gay activists insist on reading a sexual element into that relationship, and many others like it. This demonstrates their failure to understand the intensity of true friendship.[158] As C. S. Lewis wrote in his book *The Four Loves*, "Those who cannot conceive Friendship as a substantive love but only as a disguise or elaboration of Eros betray the fact that they have never had a friend."

Paul Guay, in an article in *Crisis* magazine entitled "Setting Freud Straight: Homosexuality as Repressed Friendship," argues that those followers of Freud who see friendship as latent or repressed homosexuality have the whole thing upside down. The reality is "that homosexuality is itself latent or repressed friendship."[159] The male with SSA is looking for the male friendship that he missed in childhood.

The late Christian author Sheldon Vanauken, in an article entitled "Homosexuality's Hidden Cost: The Undermining of Friendship," lamented how the suspicion of latent homosexuality

---

[158] Of course, many persons with SSA develop solid non-sexual friendships with other persons with SSA. Some relationships that begin with a sexual encounter evolve into enduring friendships based on shared interests. Some admit to treasuring their friends more than their lovers. Many men with SSA experienced the self-giving of true (non-sexual) friendships when they cared for friends who were dying of AIDS.

[159] Paul Guay, "Setting Freud Straight: Homosexuality as Repressed Friendship," *Crisis* (May 1990), 30.

has made both men and women fearful of their natural feelings of deep affection and love for persons of the same sex. Such relationships founded on shared interests were once considered an essential part of the human experience. But the modern overemphasis on the sexual has made people afraid to express these feelings, depriving them of an important source of love.[160]

The understanding of how same-sex relationships become nonsexual friendships might also be the key to understanding how same-sex couples — males, especially — are able to tolerate gross and repeated sexual infidelity. Once the relationship has moved into the friendship stage, infidelity doesn't threaten it. Two friends' shared interests aren't undermined by either one's outside sexual activity. For these men, homosexual acts don't constitute a total gift of self, but mutual erotic gratification. This contrasts with male/female marriages, in which sexual intimacy is preserved by complementarity and presumed to be exclusive; thus, even one act of infidelity can be ruinous.

• *Substitutes.* Another category of relationships involves persons who consider themselves heterosexual but wind up in a same-sex relationship. In some cases, this is because they can't find a partner of the other sex and fall into a same-sex relationship out of loneliness or similar reasons. In some cases, each partner comes to the relationship wounded, lonely, or lost; each sees the other as the only person who has ever cared for him. In other cases, a relationship can develop between persons in same-sex environments such as prisons, schools, all-male work environments, women left behind in communities from which the men have migrated, persons living in societies in which men and women are strictly segregated (in the past, harems), men who took up prostitution for

[160] Sheldon Vanauken, "Homosexuality's Hidden Cost: The Undermining of Friendship," *Crisis* (September 1992): 39.

financial reasons and became accustomed to it, women involved in prostitution who seek comfort from other women, persons who couple with transsexuals of the same biological sex, and persons with sexual fetishes and sexual addictions.

Such persons might consider themselves heterosexual, but find a same-sex relationship that meets their needs. For example, men involved in bodybuilding are attractive to some men with SSA because they have "ideal" male bodies. The bodybuilders, although they insist they're totally heterosexual, might become involved in a form of prostitution. Since sexual behavior can be addictive, the men, having been habituated to this behavior, might find it difficult to return to a relationship with a woman.[161]

The common denominator in each of these relationship patterns is that none of them fosters the good of both partners — none of them helps either of the partners to live as a mature and fully complete person according to his or her natural sexual identity. Each involves a sacrifice of something essential. Each involves a tacit mutual promise to remain unhealed — never to be the full man or woman they were created to be. The most positive scenario — two adults living together as chaste friends without outside sexual relationships, loving and caring for each other — might indeed serve real needs, but it's neither identical to nor a substitute for marriage.

Of course, ordinary marriages have troubles too. In some marriages, one or both of the spouses might try to use the other to fulfill childhood needs or to resolve emotional traumas. People with

[161] Alan Klein, "Managing Deviance: Hustling, Homophobia, and the Bodybuilding Subculture," *Deviant Behavior* 10 (1989): 11-27.

SSA aren't the only ones carrying around deep wounds. But the difference is that in a dysfunctional marriage, psychological growth can improve the relationship over time, making it more intimate, more conjugal, more a true marriage. But in a same-sex relationship, real psychological growth and healing tend to resolve the need to act out sexually with a person of the same sex. Friendship might remain — even deepen — but sexual intimacy diminishes or disappears, making the relationship even less like a true marriage.

Chapter 10

Why Redefining Marriage Will Harm Society

*How would same-sex marriage
change society's ideals of marriage?*

*How could this redefinition
of marriage harm society?*

*Do gay activists really want same-sex
marriages to be just like traditional ones?*

In 2006, representatives from a number of pro-family groups meeting together in Princeton, New Jersey, recognized that the battle over the definition of marriage was part of a larger assault on marriage and the family. They prepared, as a battle plan for countering it, a statement called "Marriage and the Public Good," which laid out a clear definition of marriage and highlighted its importance to civil society. The ten principles it enumerates can serve for us as a starting point for understanding the importance of marriage in our culture.

Many of the points (three through seven in particular) are backed up by a growing body of social-science research that demonstrates conclusively that marriage consisting of a husband, a wife, and their children has economic benefits for the participants and for society in general.

1. *Marriage is a personal union, intended for the whole of life, of husband and wife.*

2. *Marriage is a profound human good, elevating and perfecting our social and sexual nature.*

3. *Ordinarily, both men and women who marry are better off as a result.*

4. *Marriage protects and promotes the well-being of children.*

5. *Marriage sustains civil society and promotes
   the common good.*

6. *Marriage is a wealth-creating institution,
   increasing human and social capital.*

7. *When marriage weakens, the equality gap widens,
   as children suffer from the disadvantages of growing
   up in homes without committed mothers and fathers.*

8. *A functioning marriage culture serves to protect
   political liberty and foster limited government.*

9. *The laws that govern marriage matter significantly.*

10. *"Civil marriage" and "religious marriage" cannot
    be rigidly or completely divorced from one another.*[162]

Although some gay activists claim in public that allowing same-sex couples to call their relationships "marriages" will strengthen marriage as an institution, the less-publicized comments of others suggest that these claims are disingenuous and that many gay activists hope that changing the definition of marriage will weaken support for many of its traditional characteristics, particularly fidelity, permanence, and the norm of the father/mother/children family.

Proud of Being "Non-Possessive"

The principles just listed are grounded in a long and deep cultural tradition based on natural law. When the Massachusetts high court ordered the recognition of same-sex marriages, it justified the

[162] "Marriage and the Public Good: Ten Principles" (Princeton, New Jersey: Witherspoon Institute, June 2006); http://www.princetonprinciples.org.

decision by creating out of whole cloth its own novel definition of marriage. The "*sine qua non* of marriage," it said, is not the sexual complementarity of the partners, but the "exclusive and permanent commitment of the marriage partners to one another."[163]

Evidently, the court ignored the universally recognized fact that male/male partnerships are rarely exclusive or permanent. In reviewing six books on same-sex marriage, the authors of an article in the *American Political Science Review* found that not one of them affirmed sexual exclusivity or sexual fidelity as the expected norm in a same-sex marriage.[164] Researchers David McWhirter and Andrew Mattison studied 156 couples for their book *The Male Couple: How Relationships Develop*. They likewise found that:

> Only seven couples have a totally exclusive sexual relationship, and these men all have been together for less than five years. Stated in another way, all couples with a relationship lasting more than five years have incorporated some provision for outside sexual activity in their relationships.[165]

Most married people see sexual exclusivity to be an essential part of marriage — even if, due to human weakness, some fail to uphold it — and they can't comprehend the ability of male couples to tolerate repeated "adultery." However, as was noted in the previous chapter, this fits in with the psychological model of most male same-sex partnerships. Outside sexual excursions simply do not threaten many of the substitute-relationship forms these partnerships take. What *would* threaten them isn't outside sex, but outside sex combined with deep friendship. Thus, so long as the

---

[163] *Goodridge* decision.

[164] David L. Tubbs and Robert P. George, "Redefining Marriage Away," *City Journal* (Summer 2004), quoting "Queer Liberalism?" *American Political Science Review*, June 2000.

[165] McWhirter and Mattison, *The Male Couple*, 252.

unfaithful partner engages in uncommitted sex with multiple partners, the primary relationship isn't threatened.

This helps explain the seemingly counterintuitive evidence
that men in committed relationships are more likely to become
infected with STDs than those who are not.[166] In a bizarre way,
promiscuity — with its increased health risks — is the key to pre-
serving their main partnership.

According to McWhirter and Mattison, male-male relationships pass through stages, and at each progressive stage, there's a
lessening of "possessive" feelings.[167]

> As a result of this study, we believe that the single most im-
> portant factor that keeps couples together past the ten-year
> mark is the lack of possessiveness they feel. Many couples
> learn very early in their relationship that ownership of each
> other sexually can be the greatest internal threat to their
> staying together.[168]

Those who favor total sexual liberation frequently denigrate the
"possessiveness" of marriages. And yet the sense of belonging to
one's spouse is a positive benefit of making a sincere gift of self, one
that (seemingly paradoxically) increases freedom. Those who see
themselves as, in a sense, belonging to one another can trust the
other, and that trust forms the basis for healthy separateness.

---

[166] M. Xiridou et al., "The Contribution of Steady and Casual
Partnerships to the Incidence of HIV Infection Among Homosexual Men in Amsterdam," *AIDS* 17, no. 7 (2003): 1029-
1038. Most new HIV infections among homosexual men in
Amsterdam occur within steady relationships. Prevention measures should address risky behavior, specifically with steady
partners, and the promotion of HIV testing.

[167] McWhirter and Mattison, *The Male Couple*, 103.

[168] Ibid., 256.

Gay activist Dennis Altman confirms McWhirter and Mattison's findings: "Among gay men a long-lasting *monogamous* relationship is almost unknown."[169] But for Altman, this isn't a negative. Like many gay activists who reject "heteronormative" standards, he regards the open infidelity of men with SSA as a virtue, characterizing it positively as:

> a degree of fluidity that allows for considerable variety and autonomy. What often appears to straight critics as an obsession with sex is more accurately a preoccupation with constructing relationships that can meet our needs for security and independence, commitment, and variety.[170]

Variety, in this case, meaning outside sexual partners.

Gay activist Bruce Voeller thinks men with SSA ought to stop apologizing for their behavior:

> We should put an end to our embarrassment about transcending monogamy, for by moving beyond it we have also transcended the possessiveness and jealousy adopted from traditional heterosexual relationships in which males "own" women, who are in turn dependent. By openly and honestly incorporating recreational sex into our relationships we have tapped a rich quarry of "resistance," that essential quality needed for rewarding, ongoing sexuality . . ."[171]

This attitude isn't confined to men. Lesbian activist Donna Minkowitz also defends sexual infidelity as a laudable, desirable, intrinsic aspect of being gay. For her, persons with SSA are:

[169] Dennis Altman, *The Homosexualization of America* (Boston: Beacon Press, 1982), 187.

[170] Ibid.

[171] Bruce Voeller, "Stonewall Anniversary," *The Advocate* (July 12, 1979).

a sexually adventurous, gender-defying bunch. We have also come up with configurations for relationships and families that go a long way toward solving the problem that has kept heterosexuals sad for centuries — how to combine emotional fidelity with sexual freedom. One of the right wing's goals in making these attributes into smears is to force lesbians and gay men to abandon the most defiant, least heterosexual aspects of their lives. If we become the straightest gays in world history, they have already won half the battle.[172]

According to Minkowitz, social conservatives are correct when they say that gay activists pose a danger to traditional cultural institutions. But for him, this simply means that they

threaten the family, male domination, and the Calvinist ethic of work and grimness that has paralyzed most Americans' search for pleasure ... Remember that most of the line about homosex being one's nature, not a choice, was articulated as a response to brutal repression ... [I]t's time for us to abandon this defensive posture and walk upright on the earth.[173]

Even the strongest advocates for the redefinition of marriage don't expect male couples to be faithful.[174] In fact, they view a male couple's ability to tolerate infidelity (which might well destroy a male/female marriage) as a positive quality.

---

[172] Minkowitz, "Recruit, Recruit, Recruit."

[173] Ibid.

[174] Some activists contend that the prohibition of marriage is what feeds the gay culture of infidelity, and they wishfully assert that allowing them to marry will cause it to change. But proponents of this so-called "conservative case" for same-sex marriage are a small minority.

Why Redefining Marriage Will Harm Society

In light of the language of the *Goodridge* decision, we see again how disingenuous the gay activists' strategy is. They paint a picture of same-sex marriage that's indistinguishable from traditional marriage in the "*sine qua non*" areas of love, permanence, and exclusivity. Politicians, the media, and the courts uncritically accept this characterization. Yet to each other, many of the same activists admit with some pride that same-sex relationships needn't be exclusive — in fact, that their special genius is precisely their *non*-exclusivity.

Gay activists like to focus on marriage's failures. They're quick to point out that male/female marriages are often far from loving, or faithful, or exclusive. It's true that throughout human history, men and women have failed to live up to marriage's meaning; the human condition is fallible. And in recent times, the rise of the Sexual Left, of which (we note without irony) the gay activists are a part, has greatly undermined cultural support for fidelity and permanence in marriage. Divorce, infidelity, and even polyamory are increasingly seen as non-scandalous behaviors.

Nonetheless, for husband/wife married couples, exclusivity is still the *desired norm*; infidelity remains the undesired exception. But for a large percentage of same-sex couples (especially male ones), infidelity is accepted and valued — something which, they say, makes them special — even superior. And thus the two relationships remain fundamentally different.

So, while the courts might talk of "an exclusive and permanent commitment to love each other," the effect of the decision to redefine marriage to include same-sex couples would further undermine support for the exclusive and permanent nature of the marriage vows. It will introduce into the cultural consciousness a version of marriage that differs fundamentally from traditional marriage in its most critical facets.

Redefining Fidelity

One way for gay activists to deflect such charges is to redefine *fidelity* so that it no longer strictly prohibits other sexual partners, but simply serves as a point of negotiation about the nature and extent of outside relationships. This passage from *The Male Couple* explains how they justify this redefinition:

> Our culture has defined faithfulness in couples always to include or be synonymous with sexual fidelity, so it is little wonder that [male] relationships begin with that assumption. It is only through time that the symbolic nature of sexual exclusivity translates into the real issues of faithfulness. When that happens, the substantive, emotional dependability of the partner, not sex, becomes the real measure of faithfulness.[175]

Observe how these gay authors have totally redefined the essence of the marriage relationship. The sexual union between man and woman in marriage signifies a complete gift of self, each saying to the other by their actions, "I am giving to you and to no other, my whole self, including my body." A homosexual act, on the other hand, is something that one person does to another. Each is using the other as an object.

Gay activists would respond that there's nothing wrong with a man in a relationship using a third man as a sex object, so long as his partner can count on his "emotional dependability." But a man who uses men other than his partner as objects of pleasure chooses these men based on attractiveness, and rejects those who do not perform. He isn't "there," even as a friend, for the men he is using. These sex objects will not be valued as persons or even treated with respect. There's no offering of "emotional dependability,"

---

[175] McWhirter and Mattison, *The Male Couple*, 252.

unless we count the mutual agreement that they're both in it only for pleasure.

There's an old saying that "bad money drives out good." This altered understanding of "fidelity" will, if allowed to flourish, make true fidelity merely an option rather than the expected norm. It's only a small step to a situation in which the partner who is offended by infidelity will be condemned for having unrealistic expectations.

Liberal clerics champion this redefinition of fidelity. For example, James Nelson, an ordained minister in the United Church of Christ and a supporter of the gay agenda, claims that it's "insensitive and unfair to judge gay men and lesbians by a heterosexual ideal of the monogamous relationship." Nelson suggests a more flexible standard, under which

> infidelity does not have a simply biological meaning (sex with someone other than the permanent partner). Rather, infidelity means the rupture of the bonds of faithfulness, trust, honesty, and commitment between the partners . . . [W]hile the weight of Christian tradition is on the side of sexual exclusivity, there are also risks when a couple's relationship becomes marked by possessiveness.[176]

Rather than coming out and saying that they favor infidelity and adultery, the Sexual Left criticizes "possessiveness." But we can see from Nelson's comments that not only does he think society should tolerate same-sex couples' adultery, but that there's something fundamentally wrong with non-exclusivity, because it could become "possessive." Here Nelson fails to distinguish between

---

[176] James Nelson, "Religious and Moral Issues in Working with Homosexual Clients," in Gonsiorek, *Homosexuality and Psychotherapy*, 123.

pathological possessiveness, which demands total control, and healthy "belonging one to the other," which is essential to true marriage.[177]

Europe's Advocates Are More
Forthcoming About Their True Goals

Advocates for the redefinition of marriage in the United States recognize that they must present themselves in public as supportive of the values of fidelity and permanence. But European gay activists are not so reticent. Stanley Kurtz, closely following the debate over marriage in Europe, notes that, whereas the standard line among American gay activists is that redefining marriage won't change the institution, European activists and academics alike are happy to proclaim that it will be the final nail in the coffin of traditional marriage. For example, in his book *The Transformation of Intimacy*, influential British sociologist Anthony Giddens pushes the idea of "the pure relationship," in which marriage is reduced to a purely emotional bond between two adults. Monogamy would be an option, adopted by negotiation — not an essential part of marriage. He sees same-sex couples as "pioneers" for this new kind of marriage.[178]

To see what lies at the end of the trail being blazed by these pioneers, we need only to look at Scandinavia and the Netherlands. The result of the acceptance of *de facto* gay marriage in those countries can be seen in the state of marriage and family life there. The percentage of people marrying and staying married in those places has dropped precipitously. More children are born out of

---

[177] Ironically, pathological possessiveness is a not-uncommon problem for same-sex couples, particularly female couples.

[178] Stanley Kurtz, "Zombie Killers: A.K.A., 'Queering the Social,' " *National Review Online* (May 25, 2006).

wedlock, without social stigma, giving rise to numerous accepted alternative family forms.[179] In other words, the traditional institution of marriage is dying.

Such examples show us that when almost any relationship can be called a kind of "marriage" and is thought to be a suitable framework in which to raise children, couples will be less likely to marry — even couples with children. And indeed, the trends all across Europe are for lower marriage rates and marrying at an ever-later age.

The Female Couple's Futile Quest for Equality of Kind

While male couples are more likely to idealize "non-possessive" infidelity, female couples lay claim to a different virtue that supposedly sets them above traditional marriages: "equality." For radical feminists, a female couple is more "equal" than a husband and wife because two women are free from the evil of "male dominance." According to this ideology, same-sex relationships eliminate the physical and emotional oppression, and the forced dependency, that make traditional marriages an instrument of "sexist, patriarchal oppression." Since they're the same — right down to their physical equipment — two women can be a model of equality that women in relationships with men can only dream of.

This might sound good in theory, but in practice, absolute equality is virtually impossible. For example, lesbian therapist Sallyann Roth notes how women in same-sex relationships struggle with the fact that one is richer or earns more than the other. This violates their political ideal of complete equality.

Lesbian couples develop extraordinarily creative financial arrangements to avoid power imbalances in financial decision

---

[179] Stanley Kurtz, "The Death of Marriage in Scandinavia," March 9, 2004, http://www.preservemarriage.org.

making and planning and to maintain a sense of interdependence without losing independence. It is common to keep money separate for the early years of the relationship and to keep detailed accounts of exactly who has spent how much for what, with attempts made to keep contributions for living expenses exactly equal. Often large "debts" are built up, debts that may never be paid but that allow the illusion or promise of equal contribution even as the actual practice is clearly quite different.[180]

No matter how carefully the couple monitors their actions, the illusion of equality is all but impossible to maintain. It's inevitable that one will earn more money, work longer hours, do more work around the house, or spend more time caring for the children. Specific roles and patterns of behavior will emerge, the reality will not match the ideal, and shame and resentment will follow.

In clear contrast, the natural sexual complementarity between man and woman affords the opportunity for equality-in-difference. If one person has apples and the other also has apples, in order for there to be equality, there must be constant calculation, apples-to-apples. However, if one has apples, and the other has ingredients for crust, they can contribute equally — although in different ways — to making a pie. In the same way, the complementary differences between men and women allow a husband and wife to divide the work and responsibilities of a family in ways that recognize the individual talents of the partners. A true, satisfying sense of equality is possible.

For same-sex couples, both male and female, the constant need to calculate each one's contribution can lead to difficulties. For example, according to McWhirter and Mattison:

[180] Roth, "Psychotherapy with Lesbian Couples," in Hetrick and Stein, *Innovation in Psychotherapy with Homosexuals*, 104.

Boys learn to be providers. Gay men learn this and bring the yearning to provide to the developing relationship. With each partner bringing this need to provide while believing that he should provide for himself, one might expect trouble on the horizon as the two men each try to take charge of all the providing.[181]

Male couples are able to work this out by meticulous attention to how money and work are divided. But often — especially in the father/son paradigm — such an arrangement can't be achieved or, if it is, can't be maintained for long. One of McWhirter and Mattison's respondents was twenty-two years younger than his partner and soon became embarrassed by and dissatisfied with his dependency:

> It seemed rosy for the first two years. I kept the house gorgeous, got the cars serviced, even made the hors d'oeuvres when we entertained his cronies. Unlike my sister, who did the same for her executive husband, the time came pretty fast when I couldn't stay locked in to the "pretty but dumb" spot forever. More important, I wanted to become his equal and he wanted it too. He didn't want a pretty boy. He could have rented one if he did.[182]

Unsurprisingly, partners in same-sex relationships often avoid commingling assets — in part, because there's a realistic expectation that the relationship might not be permanent, but also because commingling assets isn't appropriate for a parent/child relationship or for a friendship. Even those couples who initially "merge" emotionally don't commingle assets. Similarly, lesbian couples

[181] McWhirter and Mattison, *The Male Couple*, 32.
[182] Ibid., 35.

who seek to live as perfect "equals" do so by carefully metering the assets they contribute to the relationship, not by commingling them.[183]

But when a man and woman marry, it's assumed that they'll immediately commingle their assets. Husband/wife unions have long been granted certain economic benefits precisely because it's assumed that they're a single unit contributing in monetary and non-monetary ways to the welfare of the family. Marital law, likewise, has traditionally recognized the difference in contribution, by protecting the interests of and granting benefits to women who don't work outside the home.

For many same-sex couples, then, another of the essential aspects of marriage — the "with all my worldly goods I thee endow" part — is missing.

Making a Gay Family

Gay activist Jonathan Rauch praises marriage's "near magical ability to create kin out of thin air, to turn passion into commitment, to make people healthier and happier . . ."[184] He insists that "legalizing same-sex marriage would indeed strengthen the meaning and mission and message of marriage."[185]

It's understandable that some people with SSA would view marriage as the solution to their problems, but without the complementarity of sex difference, the "magic" can't happen. A man and a woman become "kin" because they become one flesh in the

---

[183] Although in practice, many women in same-sex relationships exhibit a need to control their partner. Deeply rooted in unresolved childhood trauma, this need to control can drive one partner to make excessive demands on the other, forcing her into a permanent submissive role.

[184] Rauch, Gay Marriage, 32.

[185] Ibid., 86.

conjugal act and one flesh through the conception of children. They commingle their assets; they usually take on a common surname. They make a covenant to be faithful until death, no matter what. It's true that some couples don't keep their vows, or might enter into marriage with mental reservations, but these represent deviations from the norm — the norm of behavior, but more important, the norm of expectation. Redefining marriage to include same-sex couples, on the other hand, would fundamentally alter the norm.

Those who don't understand this simply haven't been listening to what the gay community itself is saying. Their goal is not to conform same-sex relationships to the traditional norms of marriage, but to conform the norms of marriage to the ideology of the Sexual Left. Gay activist Michelangelo Signorile, for example, makes it clear that the redefinition of marriage is only a means to an end, and that end is the total transformation of society:

> A middle ground might be to fight for same-sex marriage and its benefits and then, once granted, redefine the institution of marriage completely, to demand the right to marry not as a way of adhering to society's moral codes, but rather to debunk a myth and radically alter an archaic institution . . . The most subversive action lesbian and gay men can undertake — and one that would perhaps benefit all of society — is to transform the notion of family entirely . . . It's the final tool with which to dismantle all sodomy statutes, get education about homosexuality and AIDS into the public schools, and in short to usher in a sea change in how society views and treats us.[186]

---

[186] Michelangelo Signorile, "Bridal Wave," OUT Magazine (December/January 1994): 161; "I do, I do, I do, I do, I do," OUT Magazine (May 1996): 30.

Likewise, Paula Ettelbrick, executive director of the International Gay and Lesbian Human Rights Commission, says she's willing to work for the legal redefinition of marriage — but only because the change will "radically reorder society's view of reality":

> Being queer is more than setting up house, sleeping with a person of the same gender, and seeking state approval for doing so . . . Being queer means pushing the parameters of sex, sexuality, and family; and in the process, transforming the very fabric of society . . . We must keep our eyes on the goals of providing true alternatives to marriage and of radically reordering society's view of reality.[187]

＠

Those who read the preceding quotations might accuse me of picking out the most radical statements I could find. Surely, they might say, the average person with SSA just wants to marry, like any other man or woman in love.

In response, I can only say that in reviewing hundreds of articles and publications, I couldn't find one instance where a pro-gay writer was willing to settle for a society in which the traditional norms of fidelity, exclusivity, and permanence in marriage would be promoted and taught to children. Although some hoped that their relationships would become more stable if called "marriages," none suggested that this stability would result from adopting marriage's traditional virtues.

Although it's difficult to calculate the number of persons with SSA living as couples, in those countries where they're allowed to establish civil unions or are granted marriage licenses, only a very

---

[187] Paula Ettelbrick, "Since When Is Marriage a Path to Liberation?" in William Rubenstein, ed., *Lesbians, Gay Men and the Law* (New York: The New Press, 1993), 401-405.

small percentage of same-sex couples apply. This further suggests that gay activists do not view legal recognition of their relationships as an end in itself, but rather part of a grander strategy for changing public attitudes toward sex, marriage, and parenting.

Part IV

꒰

The Effects on Children

*"Marriage expresses a public judgment that every child
deserves a mom and a dad. Same-sex marriage,
by contrast, says that sexual and emotional needs of
adults count for more than the needs of children."*

Jeff Jacoby
The Boston Globe

*"My worry is that a purely affectional conception
of marriage will tend to favor a purely affectional
conception of parenthood. And I think that denying
the importance of biological parenthood leads us to
violate the fundamental rights of children."*

J. David Velleman
Professor of Philosophy, New York University

Chapter 11

Same-Sex Parenting
Places Children at Risk

*What inherent dangers does
same-sex parenting create for children?*

*What are the particular risks associated
with different same-sex parenting scenarios?*

*Does the adoption system often
show favoritism to same-sex couples?*

A recent cover story for the *New York Times Magazine*, "Growing Up with Mom and Mom," featured a woman named Ry Russo-Young, who, according to the headline, was "raised from birth by trailblazing lesbians."[188] The predictably sympathetic article sought to showcase Ry, then twenty-two, and her twenty-four-year-old sister, Cade, as glowing poster children for successful same-sex parenting. It ends with the tender scene of Ry's mother wiping her eyes and saying, "It's like our whole lives together have been this one big, messy, incredible experiment and it worked."[189]

And yet, even in this idealized, hand-picked example, it was clear that there were many ways in which the "experiment" had failed.

Both Ry and Cade were conceived with sperm from openly gay men. Ry remembers her father, Thomas Steel, as affectionate — but not like a parent. They had a positive relationship as Ry grew up, until he asked for permission to take Ry to see his parents and grandmother in California. When Russo and Young refused, Steel filed for paternity rights. He made some headway in the case, but then abruptly dropped his suit when he realized that the litigation

---

[188] Susan Dominus, "Growing Up with Mom and Mom," *New York Times Magazine* (October 24, 2004).

[189] Ibid., 144.

had caused him to lose Ry's affection. Years later, "a hint of a wistful tone creeps in" when Ry talks about her biological father (now dead from AIDS) — except when her "mothers" were present. Then she would become "almost uncharacteristically tough."[190]

One gathers from the article that Ry's "mothers" were part of an active radical feminist community that held extremely negative views about marriage, and that these views affected their daughters. At one point, Ry says she was "repulsed" by heterosexual relations and afraid of the "sexist soul-losing domain of oppression." At age sixteen, she had written:

> It took me a lot of struggle to realize that I really was attracted to men, yet now it is really hard for me to deal with men as human beings, let alone sexually . . . I cannot understand or relate to men because I am so immersed in gay culture and unfamiliar with what it is to have a straight relationship.

When she was a teen, Ry had a crush on a boy, and her mother encouraged her to have sex with him. She did, but felt conflicted about it, because it meant "growing up and away from my mothers." Since then, she has become more confident with men, but still feels as though she is "passing" for straight.

Indeed, the girls did not receive from their "mothers" either clear models of femininity or an appreciation of masculinity. They were forced to cast about for guidance to fill in the gaps of their sexual development. Ry remembered her sister "poring over *Seventeen* [magazine] as if it contained a code she needed to crack." (Cade apparently didn't find what she was looking for and, at age eighteen, announced she was a lesbian.) In fact, as the article's author observed, "For most of her life, Ry has been both parent and

---

[190] Dominus, "Growing Up with Mom and Mom," 84.

child to her mothers." If this is supposed to be a success story, what of the failures?

The Problem with Donor Dads

The *New York Times Magazine* followed up the Ry-and-Cade story with a long piece on gay donor dads — men with SSA who agreed to donate sperm (or, in one case, help create a baby the old-fashioned way) to lesbian women who wanted to start a family.[191] One of the men interviewed had agreed to be the donor to a bira-cial couple who wished to have the black partner inseminated by a white man and the white partner inseminated by a black man. "R.," the white donor father, really wanted the experience of fa-thering, but after the insemination, the couple refused to give him regular visitation. The situation improved, however, when the couple broke up, and the white partner married a man and had a child with him.

According to the article:

> The current family tree is a crazy circuit board: The black woman has a new female partner. The white woman is now living with a man, and the two have had their own child. So, as R. said, between the one child that R. has with the black mother, the twins borne by the white mother with a black donor and the newest, fourth, child born to her with her new male partner, all of whom have some sort of sibling relation to one another, things can be a little confusing. "They're quite a little Petri dish of a family, as you can imag-ine," R. told me. The children go from the white mother, who lives in a SoHo loft, to their black mother, who lives in a nice, middle-class row house in Crown Heights.

[191] John Bowe, "Gay Donor or Gay Dad?" *New York Times Maga-zine* (November 2006).

Participants in these bizarre arrangements justify experimenting with children's lives by comparing their children's situation with that of other children from failed marriages. But there's a critical difference: these adults entered into these experiments willfully, without consideration for the predictable catastrophes to follow. It's clear from the article that the feelings of the adult participants, not the needs of the children, were the prime consideration.

⁌

The debate over same-sex marriage necessarily includes the question of same-sex parenting. Judges may claim, as in *Goodridge*, that the begetting and raising of children isn't an essential aspect of marriage, but gay activists' claim of a "right" to marry is nonetheless accompanied by the claim of a "right" to adopt, foster, artificially create, or assume custody of children. Defenders of marriage point to social-science research to argue that a married mother and father form the best foundation for raising happy and healthy children, and that any other arrangement puts children at risk. Opponents contend that their experiments with sperm donation, surrogate motherhood, and multiple parents can do the job as well or better.

This is an important question to resolve. Children don't ask to be born. Adults have a duty to provide the best possible situation for any children they conceive. Society has a duty to encourage optimum parenting, since the society frequently must bear the costs of parental failures.

The Duty to Protect Children

In 2006, a thirty-member, multi-party commission of the French National Assembly submitted a report on the family. Citing the U.N. Convention on the Rights of the Child, the report rejected the call for open marriage for same-sex couples, stating, "The interests of the child must outweigh the exercise of freedom by adults . . . whatever life choices are made by the parents." It further stated, "Marriage is thus not only the contractual recognition of a couple's love. It is a demanding framework with rights and obligations designed to welcome the child and provide for his or her harmonious development." Therefore, the male/female nature of marriage should be preserved because it

> corresponds to a biological reality — the infertility of same-sex couples — and to the vital need to construct an identity for the child necessarily resulting from the union of a man and a woman.[192]

This report underscored a key truth: if we are to put the best interests of children first, we must respect a child's right to be born into a family consisting of his biological father and mother, who are united in a permanent and exclusive marriage.

Separation from Biological Parents

Gay activists argue that all a child needs is two loving adults; but the fact is that *biology matters*. The development of reproductive technologies hasn't reached the point where a same-sex couple can conceive a child who is the biological offspring of both of them. Thus, all the children in the care of same-sex couples have been separated from one or both biological parents. This might have occurred because the children were:

- Born during a previous marriage or relationship;

- Adopted from a local agency or from a foreign country;

[192] Parliamentary Report on the Family and the Rights of Children, French National Assembly, Paris, January 25, 2006, http://www.preservemarriage.ca.

- Placed with them for foster care;

- Conceived by artificial insemination with an unknown donor, a known donor, or a donor who wished to participate in the child's life;

- Born to a surrogate mother, who was paid for her services or who planned to participate in the child's upbringing.

Now, these scenarios can exist for husband/wife couples too, of course. Even then, each one brings challenges and risks. But these risks are greatly exacerbated when such children are raised by a same-sex couple — unjustly and premeditatedly exposing children to unnecessary risks.

- *Children born during previous marriage or relationship.* In the past, most children being raised by same-sex couples had been born when one parent was married or in a relationship with a person of the other sex. These children had to undergo the trauma of divorce or separation and then the trauma of their parents' "coming out." However, many children in this situation had the experience of living with a father and a mother before the divorce, and many continued an ongoing relationship with both biological parents.

Numerous studies have demonstrated the negative effects of divorce on children. Judith Wallerstein, a well-known expert on divorce, documents these effects in her books, *Second Chances: Men, Women, and Children a Decade After Divorce*[193] and *The Unexpected Legacy of Divorce*.[194] Wallerstein wanted to know how

---

[193] Judith Wallerstein and Sandra Blakeslee, *Second Chances: Men, Women, and Children a Decade After Divorce: Who Wins, Who Loses — and Why* (New York: Ticknor and Fields, 1989).

[194] Judith Wallerstein, Julia Lewis, and Sandra Blakeslee, *The Unexpected Legacy of Divorce: A Twenty-Five-Year Landmark Study* (New York: Hyperion, 2000).

long it took children to recover from a relatively uncomplicated no-fault divorce. She was surprised to discover that even twenty-five years after the divorce, many of the 131 children in her study were still dealing with emotional fallout. Not one escaped unscathed. Wallerstein found that no matter how many children suffer the trauma of their parents' divorce, the pain remains very personal:

> People like to think that because there are so many divorced families, adults and children will find divorce easier or even easy . . . [but] although the stigma of divorce has been enormously reduced in recent years, the pain that each child feels is not assuaged. Each and every child cries out, "Why me?"[195]

We shouldn't be surprised when children forced to endure the compound trauma of divorce and parental "coming out" — especially if the parent who comes out insists that he was "born gay" and that sexual attraction is genetically determined — ask not only, "Why me?" but, "Am I gay?"

Although Wallerstein tries to be an objective observer of the effects of divorce, she clearly finds it hard to hide her anger at parents who ignore the real suffering their decisions have caused their children. Comparing Wallerstein's case histories with the first-person accounts of same-sex parenting recorded in the book *Lesbians Raising Sons*, we can see the effects of the double trauma. Sons seem to suffer more greatly than daughters, because many in the lesbian community are openly hostile toward masculinity, toward male society, and even toward small boys.[196] This creates a dilemma

[195] Wallerstein, *Second Chances*, 303.

[196] Jess Wells, *Lesbians Raising Sons* (Los Angeles: Alyson Books, 1997).

for male children. They feel either guilty for their natural male instincts or openly angry in defense of their masculinity. Often the anger will be directed toward the mother's partner. Older boys might choose to live with their father or leave home prematurely.

Ghazala Javaid, author of a small study of the children of women who were married and "came out," suggests that the length of time the children lived in an intact family and the degree of on-going involvement with the father affected the children's development of sexual identity:

> One small group of children were unsure regarding future marriage and having children. Four children in this sub-group indicated an uncertainty regarding a gender-appropriate body image, as reflected by their drawings and accompanying comments. Three of this group also had a negative relationship with their fathers, having felt angry at early abandonment.[197]

According to Javaid, the relationship between the mother and her sons often suffered:

> [T]he homosexual mother intuitively felt that her son would not understand, so mutual discussion and direct dealing with her lifestyle were lacking; the sons could not identify with her homosexual experience; a mutual distancing could evolve. This was reflected in the study by the fact that more boys chose to live with their fathers.[198]

Karen Lewis provided therapy for children whose mothers divorced their fathers to live with a woman. Several of the boys were

---

[197] Ghazala Javaid, "The Children of Homosexual and Heterosexual Single Mothers," *Child Psychiatry and Human Development* 23, no. 4 (Summer 1993): 245.

[198] Ibid., 246.

furious at their mother's lover. Some were embarrassed by the "stereotypical butch/femme relationship" between the two. Several of the children reacted with a "brief experimentation with homosexuality." Many of them, she notes, worried that they might be homosexual:

> Several girls thought they might turn to women if they did not have a satisfying relationship with a man. One added, "That's what my mother did." She said, in regard to her dating, if she complained to her mother about boys, "she would tell me to try girls." This response not only sets up the daughter to fulfill her mother's prophecy; it also denies the girl maternal support in problem solving.[199]

True to form, gay activists insist that the problems faced by children whose parents divorce and then "come out" are caused by the "homophobic" society in which they live. If only society changed, they say, the problems would disappear. Yet society's acceptance of divorce hasn't diminished the pain it causes children; why should we assume that even in a totally accepting society, permanently and purposefully fatherless or motherless children will simply "adjust"? And it's clear from case histories, even those from pro-gay sources, that the pain felt by children was deeply personal and internal — not caused solely by outside influences.[200]

Advocates for the redefinition of marriage frequently hold up a group of studies of children being raised by same-sex couples to support their claim that there are no differences between these children and children raised by heterosexual couples. However,

[199] Karen Lewis, "Children of Lesbians: Their Point of View," *Social Work* (May 1980): 200.

[200] Lisa Saffron, *What About the Children: Sons and Daughters of Lesbian and Gay Parents Talk About Their Lives* (London: Cassell, 1996); Wells, *Lesbians Raising Sons*.

the studies they cite don't compare children raised by same-sex couples with children raised by their married, biological parents, but rather, with children raised by single mothers or in some other suboptimal situation. This is a tacit admission that children raised by same-sex couples can't be compared with children raised by married, biological parents.

Moreover, researchers have also found such studies to be either internally or externally invalid.[201] According to Steven Nock, an expert in research methodology, "[N]ot a single one was conducted according to generally accepted standards of scientific research."[202] Most of them used such small, poorly selected samples that their conclusions were meaningless; or worse, they drew conclusions contrary to their own findings.

• *Children adopted from a local agency.* At one time in the United States, only married couples were accepted as potential adoptive parents, but that has changed. In many jurisdictions, single persons are now allowed to adopt older children; some of these have been persons with SSA. (Florida is the only state that bans such adoptions.) Several states allow same-sex couples to adopt, and a majority allow the partner to adopt as a co-parent. This has all led to a large recent increase in the number of adopted children living with same-sex couples — which is remarkable in itself, given the general shortage of children available for adoption. How are so many same-sex couples able to adopt, in particular to adopt healthy babies, for whom there are usually long waiting lists?

Case in point: in spite of the high demand for adoptable newborns, Dan Savage, a gay activist who authors a sex-advice column, was able to adopt (with his partner) a newborn baby boy in

---

[201] Lerner and Nagai, *No Basis*.

[202] Affidavit of Steven Lowell Nock, in *Halpern v. Attorney General of Canada*, 2002.

Oregon. Savage wrote a book (*The Kid: What Happened After My Boyfriend and I Decided to Go Get Pregnant*[203]) about his experience that reveals a disdain for the birth mother and a frighteningly cavalier attitude toward the process. Savage and his partner were in competition with married husband/wife couples, and Savage believes that the birth mother, a young woman with a troubled past, chose him and his partner over available married couples as a way of rebelling against her family of origin and the baby's father. One has to ask how the relevant authorities could agree to allow a clearly unstable young woman, motivated by spite, to give her baby to a man who, by his own admission, entered into the process because he thought it might make a good subject for a book.

Children's Rights and Needs Should Come First

While the public likes to romanticize adoption, the fact is that being surrendered by one's biological parents is a wounding experience. In spite of many reassurances from the adoptive parents and all their love and care, the adoptive child often asks, "Why? Why did my mother give me up? Where was my father?" These questions often persist well into adulthood and can motivate a search for the biological parents. It takes emotional and psychological stability on the part of the adoptive parents to allow the child to explore these questions. And so adopted children need the best possible placement — a father and a mother who are committed to each other and to the child and who have the internal resources to cope with the many problems that adoption brings (in addition to the ordinary trials of parenting). In such cases, it seems obvious that placement agencies should first consider the best interests of the child, not any social or political agenda.

---

[203] Dan Savage, *The Kid: What Happened After My Boyfriend and I Decide to Go Get Pregnant* (New York: Plume 1999).

Adoption by a happily, faithfully married husband and wife provides a healing environment for the child who has been surrendered by his biological parents. The faithful, committed love of the father for his wife and children teaches the adoptive child that all men do not walk away from their responsibilities to their children. The adoptive mother's strength under pressure teaches the child that even though his biological mother surrendered him, his adoptive mother is strong enough to face any crisis and will never stop loving him. The day-to-day experience of seeing a loving married father and mother sacrifice and persevere gives the adopted child an image of true marital and parental love that can serve as a model for his own life.

This is undoubtedly why, in spite of the initial wound, many adopted children grow into healthy and happy adults who marry wisely and become good parents. But it's never easy, and pretending that adoption is just like having your own biological child — that there are no additional problems to be overcome — does a disservice to the adoptive child's struggle to understand his situation and to the adoptive parents' heroic love.

As the French report on the rights of children put it, "the primary aim of adoption is to provide a child with a family, and not a family with a child . . . [G]iven the original trauma he or she experienced, an adopted child requires the kind of legal and emotional security that only married parents can offer." Because children surrendered for adoption have already suffered one major loss, it's crucial that they be placed in the most stable situation possible. But same-sex couples have built-in problems and deficiencies that make them less stable right from the start.

For example, evidence suggests that women with SSA are far more psychologically fragile than other women. Numerous studies have found that women with SSA are more likely to experience depression or other mental health problems. One study found that sixty-six percent of self-identified lesbian-bisexual women had availed themselves of some form of mental health care in the previous twelve months; one-third of the group had experienced major depression in that same period. A study by gay activist Theo Sandfort and associates in the Netherlands found that among women who had sex with women, the lifetime prevalence of major depression was over forty percent.[204]

A mother's psychological state has a direct impact on her children. Married women who adopt sometimes report that even though they didn't go through the physical process of birth, they experienced a kind of post-adoption depression. They had anxiously anticipated the arrival of the baby, but when faced with the reality of motherhood, some found themselves unable to bond — to the child's detriment. Given that women with SSA are already prone to depression, post-adoption problems can be expected.

Same-sex relationships — whether called "marriages" or not — are less enduring than traditional marriages. Although no adoption agency can guarantee that the married couple to whom they give a child will remain together, same-sex couples are less likely to remain together and to be faithful to one another.[205]

If children adopted by married couples ask, "Why was I given up for adoption? Why didn't my mother keep me? Why didn't my father want me?" then what will the children who are given to same-sex couples ask? Won't they wonder why their mother would give them over to a permanently and purposefully motherless or fatherless family? Children adopted by husband/wife couples are told that their mother wanted to give them a better home than she

---

[204] Sandfort, 88.

[205] Timothy Dailey, "Comparing the Lifestyles of Homosexual Couples to Married Couples," April 6, 2004, http://www.frc.org.

could provide. How does adoption by a same-sex couple, which everyone admits will at the very least expose the child to societal stigma, protect a child from the stigma of being raised by a single mother? Sooner or later, the child will ask, "Why was I treated by society as a second-class baby, to be placed in a second-class situation?"

Gay activists, of course, see adoption by same-sex couples as part of an ongoing effort to drive tolerance for diversity into the public consciousness. But all the "diversity training" in the world won't prevent children raised by a same-sex couple from noticing that other children have mommies and daddies and they don't. Reading *Heather Has Two Mommies, Daddy's Roommate*, and *Gloria Goes to Gay Pride* to kindergartners is not going to convince the average child that the sex of one's parent is a matter of indifference. Children know better. And even if it were possible at some time in the future to create the perfectly non-"heterosexist" society that gay activists dream of, children placed today must live with the current reality. To ignore their best interests in order to forward the gay agenda amounts to human experimentation.

All this isn't to imply that persons with SSA who adopt don't love their children, or that their children don't love them. But precisely because there *is* love, there will also be denial: the same-sex couple won't be able to admit to themselves or to the child that the situation is less than optimal — that their decision has caused real harm. Same-sex couples won't be able to admit the possibility that they've harmed their children, and so will blame "homophobia" for the problems they face. The child won't be able to voice his dissatisfaction with his situation, and at the same time will feel guilty for not being wholly grateful. The combination of parental denial and the child's guilt will lead him to conclude that there's something wrong with his natural desire for a parent of both sexes.

Rosie O'Donnell was asked what she would do if her adopted son wanted a father. Rosie replied that he had already expressed that desire. When he was six, he had told her, "I want to have a daddy." Rosie said she had replied, "If you were to have a daddy, you wouldn't have me as a mommy, because I'm the kind of mommy who wants another mommy. This is the way mommy got born." He said, "Okay, I'll just keep you."[206]

Although Rosie undoubtedly sees this as a positive affirmation of same-sex adoption, there's another interpretation. She gave her son the message that his very natural desire for a father was a rejection of her — his mother. She forced him to choose.

• *Children adopted from another country.* Because so few children are available for adoption in the United States, many people are choosing to adopt them internationally — more than 20,000 a year. Although some countries allow an unmarried single person to adopt, most of the countries from which children are available for adoption do not countenance same-sex relationships and do not knowingly place children with same-sex couples or with persons with SSA.

For example, China, which allows approximately 7,000 children a year to be adopted in the United States, requires single parents to sign an affidavit stating they're not homosexual. This has led some same-sex couples to hide their status. According to an article in the *Boston Globe,* "gay friendly adoption agencies" have been advising same-sex couples to have one partner apply as a single parent.[207] Some countries have caught on and have begun sanctioning adoption agencies that break the rules.

[206] Rosie O'Donnell interview with Diane Sawyer on ABC *Primetime,* Thursday, March 14, 2002.

[207] Franco Ordonez, "Marriage May Hinder Gays' Foreign Adoptions," *Boston Globe,* May 8, 2004.

Adoption from foreign countries raises difficulties over and beyond those that come with domestic adoption. Children available for adoption from foreign countries are generally not newborns. They come to the United States having to learn a new language and adjust to a different culture. They might be of a different race from their parents. Children who have languished for years in orphanages and institutions often have serious psychological and physical problems. Many suffer from severe attachment disorders and require years of special care. Some of these children are prone to becoming violent, a danger to themselves and their siblings. Tragically, some never recover and end up having to be institutionalized.

Such adoptions present challenges even to stable husband/wife couples. Placing such a child with an SSA couple immediately handicaps his process of adaptation and healing, because it deprives him of a father or a mother. This might be particularly harmful for children who spent their early life in institutions where the caregivers were all women, if they continue to be deprived of a significant male influence.

Some boys from such orphanages demonstrate the classic early symptoms of Gender Identity Disorder. This is understandable, given the absence of males and the substandard conditions in many of these institutions. Placing such at-risk boys with same-sex couples only hinders their development further, sometimes severely so: we know, for example, that lesbian adoptive mothers are often unwilling to support strong masculine identification; some might be openly hostile toward it. Such placements cannot be considered to be in the child's best interests.

• *Children placed for foster care.* Children are placed in foster care because their biological parents can't care for them or have been judged unfit. Many of these children have been victims of abuse or neglect. Once in the foster-care system, they're often moved from home to home, and many suffer additional abuse, particularly sexual abuse at the hands of other children. State agencies in charge of placing children are always struggling to find suitably stable homes. Some children are never adopted or returned to their parents, remaining instead in foster care until they come of age.

What additional dangers do foster children face in homes of persons with SSA? George Rekers, professor of Neuropsychiatry and Behavioral Science at the University of South Carolina's School of Medicine, argues that children in foster care are far more vulnerable to stress than other children, need the best placement possible,[208] and therefore should not be placed with persons with SSA. In his eighty-page "Review of Research on Homosexual Parenting, Adoption, and Foster Parenting," he makes the following points (emphases in original):

I. The inherent nature and structure of households with a homosexually behaving adult uniquely endangers foster children by exposing them to harmful stresses over and above the usual stress levels in heterosexual foster homes.

II. Homosexual partner relationships are significantly and substantially less stable, and more short-lived on the average, compared to the marriage of a man and a woman, thereby inevitably contributing to a higher rate of household transitions in foster homes with a homosexually behaving adult.

III. The inherent structure of foster-parent households with one or more homosexually-behaving members deprives

---

[208] George Rekers, "Review of Research on Homosexual Parenting, Adoption, and Foster Parenting," http://www.narth.com/docs/ RationaleBasisFinal0405.pdf.

foster children of vitally needed positive contributions to child adjustment, contributions that are only present in licensed heterosexual foster homes.[209]

Children placed in foster care are often victims of sexual abuse. This, combined with attachment disorders, can lead many to experience same-sex attractions in late childhood or early adolescence, and they might act out with other children — particularly with other children in the same residence.

They might also exhibit non-gender-conforming behavior or the symptoms of GID. Gay activists typically want such children labeled as gay or "pre-gay" and placed with a person or couple with SSA:

[C]hildren who themselves are gay or lesbian . . . may benefit from being raised by a lesbian or gay parent or couple. Homosexual parents would serve as positive gay and lesbian role models.[210]

While this might sound like a neat solution to a difficult problem, labeling a child as "born gay" and placing him with a same-sex couple would only be to ignore the effects of sexual abuse or to deny him treatment for GID, or both. Such children are far more likely to be encouraged by a same-sex couple to "come out" and experiment with homosexual behavior. This, in turn, could put the child at high risk for negative outcomes, including substance abuse and exposure to HIV.[211] Conversely, placement in a home with a

[209] George Rekers, "Summary: A Rational Basis for the Arkansas Regulation," http://www.narth.com/docs/RationaleBasisFinal0405 .pdf, 2-3.

[210] G. Dorsey Green and Frederick Bozett, "Lesbian Mothers and Gay Fathers," *Homosexuality: Research Implication for Public Policy* (Newbury Park, New York: Sage, 1991), 211.

[211] Mary Jane Rotheram-Borus, et al., "Sexual and Substance Use Acts of Gay and Bisexual Male Adolescents in New York

positive same-sex role model, who supports healthy identification, could have a healing effect, averting or resolving the SSA.

Finally, it's important to remember that children are in foster care because their biological parents haven't fully relinquished their parental rights, or have had those rights removed. The hope is that some kind of relationship between the biological parents and children can be maintained. But placing children with same-sex couples might well cause additional stress between biological families, the foster families, the authorities, and the children. Parents who disapprove of such placements risk being charged with "homophobia" and permanently losing their parental rights. Although gay activists see such skirmishes as inevitable — even necessary — in their fight for justice and tolerance, they're obviously not in the best interests of children, who don't deserve to be used as pawns in a political struggle.

• *Children conceived by artificial insemination.* Artificial Insemination by Donor (AID) has been used for decades by married couples when the husband is unable to produce viable sperm. In most cases, the use of a donor's sperm is kept a secret from friends, family, and from the child. But in recent years, as the first generation of children conceived by this procedure came of age and learned the truth, many of them began voicing their objections to the process. Some told how they sensed something was wrong, how they wondered why their "father" was so distant.[212]

City," *Journal of Sex Research* 31, no. 1 (1994): 27-57; Dennis Osmond, et al., "HIV Infection in Homosexual and Bisexual Men 18 to 29 Years of Age: The San Francisco Young Men's Health Study," *American Journal of Public Health* 84, no. 12 (1994), 1993-2007.

[212] "New Research Highlights Concerns Over Children Born Through Donor Insemination," September 27, 2005, http://www.surrey.ac.uk/news/releases/8-3100dono.html.

One Man, One Woman

Margaret Brown wrote a column for *Newsweek* about her experience as the product of AID. Her parents divorced when she was seven, and when she was sixteen, her mother told her that the man she thought was her biological father wasn't. She wrote:

> I don't see how anyone can consciously rob someone of something as basic and essential as heritage. Parents must realize that all the love and attention in the world can't mask that underlying, almost unconscious feeling that something is askew . . . I feel a strange little twinge of something deep inside me — like I'm borrowing someone else's family.
>
> It seems that no one thought I might want to know the other half of my genetic makeup. But children are not commodities or possessions. They are people with an equal stake in the process.[213]

In response to this common experience, adults who discovered they were conceived by AID, longing to know who their biological fathers are, have organized a group called Donors' Offspring, Inc., which attempts to link donors and their children.

♿

Today AID has become the method of choice for lesbian couples who want children. Some women choose male friends as donors, some the brother of their partner; but many choose anonymous sperm donors. And although gay activists are now lobbying to have birth certificates list the biological mother and her partner as "Parent A" and "Parent B," there's no avoiding the reality that *somewhere* there's a biological father whom the child has a right to know.

[213] Margaret Brown, "Whose Eyes Are These, Whose Nose?" *Newsweek*, March 7, 1994.

These days, the first generation of "gaybies" conceived through AID is coming of age; now that they're able to speak for themselves, we're learning how same-sex parenting amplifies the problems and challenges that come with artificial insemination. Bronagh Cassidy (not her real name), now twenty-seven and a mother of two, was conceived via AID from the sperm of one of two gay male friends of her "mothers" (their sperm was mixed so that no one would know who the father was). Cassidy's mother and her partner, Pat, remained together until Pat's death. Three years thereafter, Cassidy's mother married a man. Cassidy says:

> When growing up, I always had the feeling of being something unnatural. I came out of an unnatural relationship; it was something like I shouldn't be there. On a daily basis, it was something I was conflicted with. I used to wish Pat wasn't there.[214]

Given her history, it is not surprising that Cassidy opposes adoption by same-sex couples:

> We shouldn't say it is a great and wonderful thing and then you have all these kids who later in life will turn around and realize they've been cheated. The adults choose to have that lifestyle and then have a kid. They are fulfilling their emotional needs — they want to have a child — and they are not taking into account how that's going to feel to the child.

In spite of everything, Cassidy remains very protective of her mother. But she questions the research that purports to find that children with parents with SSA have no extra problems, because,

---

[214] Maggie Gallagher, "Adult Children Speak Out About Same-Sex Parenting," July 6, 2004, http://www.uexpress.com/maggie gallagher/?uc_full_date=20040706.

she says, such children seldom reveal their true feelings: "They aren't going to say they are suffering because they don't want to make their parents feel bad."

Complaints from now-grown children conceived by artificial insemination have not gone completely unheeded. The British government, for instance, recently eliminated the practice of anonymous donation, giving children of AID the right to know the identity of their biological fathers (and dramatically reducing the number of men volunteering to be sperm donors).

*

Artificial insemination, like adoption, carries with it risks and difficulties even for stable married couples, particularly when it involves anonymous sperm donation. For same-sex couples, with their inherently less-stable relationships and with the stigma and confusion that children will have to endure, the risks are greater still.

For female same-sex couples, there's often an additional problem: only one woman can be the biological mother. Only one gets to bond with the baby through pregnancy, childbirth, and nursing. Roles become confused; jealousy and bitterness can set in. In a relationship that strives for perfect "equality," this stands out as an enormous and irreconcilable point of inequality.

• *Children conceived for male couples by surrogate mothers.* If a man with SSA wants to raise a child who is biologically his own, he can pay a surrogate mother to conceive via AID and bear the baby. This option, too, is fraught with risks for the child.

An article by Barbara Eisold, "Recreating Mother," gives us insight into the problems created by surrogate mothering for men in same-sex relationships.[215] "Nick" was conceived for a male couple,

[215] Barbara Eisold, "Recreating Mother: The Consolidation of 'Heterosexual' Gender Identification in the Young Son of

"Daddy" and "Don," using a surrogate mother who was paid for her services. Daddy, who was twenty years older than Don, was present at the birth, and then brought Nick home and hired a nanny to care for the boy. When Nick was two, the couple felt that the nanny had become too emotionally involved with the family, and she was fired. They hired another nanny, who was replaced six months later by a third. Nick's life was further complicated by the arrival of an adopted baby brother. He was then sent to nursery school.

By the time Nick was four, he was suffering from profound psychological problems, and Eisold was hired to treat him. According to Eisold:

> Nick was often beside himself with anxiety. He wanted desperately to be liked by the other children and by [his teacher]. He had trouble waiting and was not certain what would make him likeable.

One of his problems was that he wanted to "buy" a mother. Eisold asks:

> How do we explain why this child, the son of a male couple, seemed to need to construct a woman — "Mother" — with whom he could play the role of loving boy/man? How did such an idea enter his mind? What inspired his intensity on the subject?[216]

The answer is tragically obvious. Little boys need mothers. Nick had become attached to the nanny and was devastated when she was fired. His father had already bought a surrogate's services,

---

Homosexual Men," *American Journal of Orthopsychiatry* 68, no. 3 (July 1998): 433-442.

[216] Ibid., 436.

employed the services of three nannies, sent the boy to daycare, where female workers were paid to watch him, and then hired a female therapist; it was therefore logical for Nick to conclude that if he collected enough money, he could buy himself a mother too.

This case provides more evidence that children aren't able to adapt to "family diversity" as easily as gay activists claim. Activists can change the laws, they can modify public opinion over time, but they can't redesign the hearts of children or restructure their fundamental needs.

Surrogacy Creates Family Chaos

In another case of surrogacy gone wrong, in 2000, a New York court awarded custody of a boy to a male couple over the protests of the birth mother, Courtney St. Clements, who claimed that she was not a surrogate. According to St. Clements, who was in her late forties when the child was born, the plan had been for the three of them to raise the child as a parental trio. But the male couple, Gerald Casale and Ernest Londa, claimed that they had made a deal with St. Clement for her to carry Casale's child and then surrender custody. When the boy was six months old, the male couple prevented her from seeing the boy and she sued for custody. The case marked the first time that a New York court awarded custody of a child to a gay couple over the mother. At the age of six, the boy began to demonstrate serious behavioral problems: punching and kicking his teachers, hitting and biting himself, and threatening to commit suicide.[217]

The imprecision of surrogate motherhood combined with the instability of male same-sex relationships can create some truly awful circumstances. Michael Meehan and Thomas Dysarz employed a

[217] Brad Hamilton, "War Over Boy Raised by Gays," *New York Post*, May 30, 2004.

surrogate, who conceived quadruplets — Meehan's biological children.[218] A year and half later, the men employed the same surrogate mother to conceive and bear Dysarz's biological child. She agreed, because she wanted the children to be biological siblings.[219] The men have since separated, Meehan charging Dysarz with domestic violence. Each has custody of his own biological children, and the surrogate mother has petitioned the court to terminate her relationship with all of them.

How strange that the surrogate mother should recognize the importance of the blood relationship between siblings, yet fail to see the dangers of the surrogate arrangement itself. None of the adults in this case put the best interests of the children first.

Comparing the Risks

Some activists will argue that same-sex parenting is no more risky for children than the traditional two-parent family. "After all," they say, "married couples sometimes break up, or relate dysfunctionally, or fail to provide good models of manhood and womanhood to their children."

It's true that human beings can be weak, selfish, and sinful, and not every married couple will be good parents. But a male/female married couple nonetheless has built into it all the things children need for healthy child development: a mother and a father to fulfill parenting roles and to model gender identity, a vowed bond of permanent commitment between two persons with sexual complementarity, and freedom from the stigmas and distractions that accompany "experimental" family forms.

[218] "Gay Dads Keeping Busy with Quadruplets," http://abcnews .go.com/GMA/story?id=125775&page=1.

[219] Valarie Honeycutt Spears, "Gay Parents of Quads Have Separated," *Lexington Herald-Leader*, June 20, 2004.

Same-sex parenting, in contrast, has intrinsic flaws and deficits that amplify the risks intrinsic to adoption, artificial insemination, surrogate parenting, and foster care. To place a child into the legal care of a same-sex couple, or for such a couple to acquire a child via technology or surrogacy, unnecessarily endangers that child's health and happiness by forcing him to grow up in what is unarguably a suboptimal environment. All the "tolerance of diversity" in the world can't change the facts on the ground.

To summarize, same-sex parenting is intrinsically riskier for children because:

• Each of these situations is either fatherless or motherless. Children flourish when they can identify with a parent of their own sex and feel loved and accepted by a person of the other sex.

• These children are fatherless or motherless because of adult decisions — often based on a need to feel validated or "complete" — not unavoidable circumstances. Either by adopting them or conceiving them artificially, their caregivers deliberately choose to deprive their children of a mother or a father.

• In every same-sex household, one or both parents have no biological relationship to the child. Often compounding the situation are complicated and often contentious legal and emotional relationships with sperm donors, surrogate mothers, former spouses, and ex-partners.

• Persons with SSA have a psychological disorder rooted in childhood trauma, which can negatively affect their relationships, their attitudes toward the other sex, and their attitudes toward parenting. They are also more likely to have psychological disorders and therefore are more prone to engage in behaviors that might negatively impact their children.[220]

• Adults with SSA are part of a community that views itself as oppressed and in conflict with the greater society. This at-war-with-the-world stance places a burden on the children.

• Homosexual behavior is considered sinful by many religions, and same-sex parenting is otherwise stigmatized to some degree in mainstream society. The majority of people in most communities believe marriage should be between one man and one woman. Right or wrong, this can't help but isolate the children raised by same-sex couples, creating feelings of differentness and inferiority.

• The community of adults with SSA tends to have attitudes toward sexuality that encourage sexual experimentation and don't adequately protect minor children from exposure to sexually explicit materials and sexual exploitation.

Failure of the Adoption System

Some might assume that in the case of adoption or foster care, the social-service system would weed out those applicants who have serious problems. But this doesn't appear to be the case. We would expect that given the special circumstances and the known risk factors, adoption agencies and social workers in jurisdictions where persons with SSA are allowed to adopt would carefully screen applicants for problems. However, there's evidence that many

---

[220] It's certainly possible that one or even both members of a same-sex couple will exhibit none of these problems. But the cumulative and combined risks for a same-sex couple choosing to parent are, by objectively measurable criteria, higher, and these risks are compounded by the intrinsic difficulties associated with parenting a non-biological child.

agencies and social workers are so committed to promoting same-sex relationships as equal to marriages that they actually *lower* their standards for same-sex couples.

The National Association of Social Workers (NASW), for example, actively supports the gay agenda. Its "Official Statement Concerning Homosexuality" reads in part (emphasis added):

> Social workers are guided by the NASW Code of Ethics, which bans discrimination on the basis of sexual orientation . . . NASW believes that non-judgmental attitudes toward sexual orientation allow social workers to offer optimal support and services to lesbian and gay people. *NASW affirms its commitment to work toward full social and legal acceptance of lesbian and gay people.* The profession must also act to eliminate and prevent discriminatory statutes, policies, and actions that diminish the quality of life for lesbian and gay people and that force many to live their lives in the closet.[221]

A 1996 study by Sarah Holbrook,[222] published in a journal for social workers, examined the attitudes of more than three hundred social workers and found that, as a group, they strongly supported "the rights of single people, gay men and lesbians, and older women past menopause to have families." Social workers were most likely to reject "the traditional approach to families where couples are favored over single people" and "where the ideal for a child is always a two-parent home."

---

[221] National Association of Social Workers: Lesbian and Gay Issues (Washington: NASW Delegate Assembly, 1993).

[222] Sarah Holbrook, "Social Workers' Attitudes Toward Participants' Rights in Adoption and New Reproductive Technologies," *Health and Social Work* 21, no. 4 (November 1996): 257 ff.

This support for the gay agenda affects their decision-making process. There's substantial anecdotal evidence of discrimination by colleagues and professors against social workers, and those studying for the field, who don't accept the entire gay agenda. Several ex-social workers shared with me how they left the field in exasperation because they saw that same-sex couples were favored over husband/wife couples and could do nothing about it.

A woman named Susan Esbenshade experienced this first-hand. She and her husband

> had adopted one child by a troubled unwed mother. When her child's birth mother again became pregnant, Esbenshade and her husband wanted to adopt that child, too (twins, as it turned out). The birth mother requested this placement. But the Esbenshades say they were (falsely) told by social workers in Mecklenburg County (North Carolina) that the twins could not be placed in a home outside the county. In a letter to Mecklenburg County Commissioner Bill James, Susan said she was "shocked" to later discover "that DSS would place the twins in a home with two men rather than placing them in a home with a mother and father and a biological sibling."[223]

Social workers in such cases might claim that they have a duty to overcome societal prejudices and bigotry, and to use affirmative action to promote diversity in family style. But such high-minded aspirations ignore the reality that children have only one chance at childhood, and their best interests shouldn't be sacrificed, no matter how noble you think your cause.

[223] Maggie Gallagher, "Marriage and Adoption Law," January 14, 2005, posted on Family Institute of Connecticut website: http://www.ctfamily.org/editorial45.html.

These social workers might also argue that their actions are supported by scientific studies showing that same-sex parenting does not harm children. A large number of such studies do exist, but as we will see in the next chapter, what they prove is a different matter.

Chapter 12

＞

Dangerous Lies:
The Politicization of Research

*What do studies really say about the
impact of same-sex parenting on children?*

*How are activists misusing these studies
to make them support their agenda?*

What rights do children have in the family?

What is best for the children? The legal battles over marriage frequently revolve around this very question. Gay activists argue that many same-sex couples already have children, and these children need the protections afforded by legal recognition of their relationship. To support this line of argument, they present the courts with numerous studies claiming to prove that children raised by persons with SSA are just as happy, healthy, and academically successful as children raised by their married biological parents.

But just as the "ten percent" myth and the "born that way" myth have been debunked as unsupported by science, so too has the "just like other children" myth failed to pass careful examination. Or put less charitably: it's a lie, and a dangerous one.

They're Really Not Like Other Children

In her book *Children as Trophies?*, European sociologist Patricia Morgan reviews 144 published studies on same-sex parenting and concludes that it fosters homosexual behavior, confused gender roles, and increased likelihood of serious psychological problems later in life. The French report on the rights of children observed, "The lack of objectivity in this area is blatant." in much of the pro-gay research in this area, and concluded with the warning that "we do not yet know all the effects on the formation of the adopted child's psychological identity. As long as doubt persists, however slight, is it not in the child's best interests to apply the precaution-ary principle to adoption, as to other areas?"[224]

Even a recent meta-analysis by two gay activists failed to sup-port the "just like other children" myth. In 2004, Judith Stacey and Timothy J. Biblarz,[225] both supporters of gay parenting, pub-lished a study entitled "(How) Does the Sexual Orientation of Parents Matter?", which re-examined twenty studies of same-sex parenting that had supposedly shown no difference, and charged their authors with ignoring the differences they had indeed found. There *were* differences: children raised by parents with SSA showed empathy for "social diversity," were less confined by gender stereo-types, more likely to have confusion about gender identity, more likely to engage in sexual experimentation and promiscuity, and more likely to explore homosexual behavior. Stacey and Biblarz characterized these as positive differences, suggesting that same-sex parenting might in fact be superior.

Conservative columnist Mona Charen commented on the Stacey/Biblarz article:

Biblarz and Stacey deserve credit for their honesty. But their breezy embrace of gay parenting is highly reminiscent of the cheerful accounts offered in the 1970s for divorce and single parent households. In those days, we were told that whatever made for a happier parent also made for a happier child. We are sadder and wiser now. The children are much sadder.[226]

---

[224] Parliamentary Report on the Family and the Rights of Children.

[225] Judith Stacey and Timothy J. Biblarz, "(How) Does the Sex-ual Orientation of Parents Matter," *American Sociological Re-view* (April 2004).

[226] Mona Charen, "Are Children of Gay Parents Worse Off?" http://www.townhall.com/columists, May 21, 2004.

Paula Ettelbrick of the National Gay and Lesbian Task Force admitted that Stacey and Biblarz had "burst the bubble of one of the best-kept secrets" of the gay community — namely, that the studies it had been using didn't actually support the claims it was making. Not all gay activists saw this as a problem. Kate Kendall, head of the San Francisco–based National Center for Lesbian Rights, who raises two children with her partner, took the Stacey/Biblarz article as good news:

> There's only one response to a study that children raised by lesbian and gay parents may be somewhat more likely to reject notions of rigid sexual orientation — that response has to be elation.[227]

Gay activists have tried to put the best spin possible on the study, but they also know there are political consequences to admitting that there are real differences. Comments such as Kendall's, although meant to be supportive, throw into relief the ongoing dissonance between the public face of gay-rights activism, which pleads for acceptance into the "heteronormative" world, and the majority of its committed ideologues, who want to unmake it.

Boys in Woman Space

Any same-sex parenting scenario will be "different" from ordinary families, with consequent effects on children, but as evidence suggests, none more so than two women raising boys.

As we have noted, many women with SSA have extremely negative attitudes toward men. Some are still very angry with their fathers, and that antagonism carries over to males in general.

---

[227] David Crary, "Professors Take Issue with Gay Parenting Research" and "Report: Kids of Gays More Empathetic" AP, *Los Angeles Times*, April 27, 2001.

Some women with SSA extend their hostility to masculinity it-self, and frown on traditional boyish pursuits. It's common for par-ents with SSA to discourage play with gender-typing toys and games, but women seem to do it more thoroughly than men.[228] Some women with SSA go so far as to advocate "lesbian separat-ism," which Ruthann Robson defines as

> an ethical forward/moral/political/social/theoretical lifestyle in which lesbians devote their considerable energies, inso-far as it is possible, exclusively to other lesbians or, in some cases, exclusively to other women.[229]

Needless to say, a fatherless boy living among women who are deeply hostile toward masculinity itself will find it difficult to de-velop a healthy masculine identity.[230] The book *Lesbians Raising Sons* — a collection of essays by lesbian mothers of boys — reveals numerous cases of boys who, by their mother's admission, exhibit symptoms of Gender Identity Disorder. One mother defends her adopted son's cross-gender behavior and castigates society for not accommodating him. She herself is pleased with it:

> He has watched the college girls who student-teach, the video mermaids, the female heroines of the silver screen.

---

[228] Pauline Turner, "Parenting in Gay and Lesbian Families," *Journal of Gay and Lesbian Psychotherapy* 1, no. 3: 55-66.

[229] Albert Mohler, Jr., "Lesbians Raising Sons; Got a Problem with That?" *Baptist Press*, December 30, 2004, http://www.sbcbaptistpress.org/bpnews.asp?ID=19814.

[230] Since relatively few male couples have raised girls from birth without a female caregiver, the effects of such arrangements on a girl's development have not been fully studied. Although girls raised by male couples still don't have a female model, men with SSA aren't generally as openly hostile toward femi-ninity as women with SSA are toward masculinity.

He knows how to toss his head just so, to tuck a lock behind his ear, to suck on a strand that reaches the mouth.[231]

When the son is asked whether he's a girl or a boy, the mother encourages him to say, "Well, it doesn't matter to me what you think . . . whatever you decide."[232] The school also accommodates his problem. The kindergarten class was asked to line up for races, boys on one side and girls on the other.

> My son stood in the middle, a little dumbfounded that such a request was being made, then slid himself to the girls' side. Afterwards a confused Mr. M. went to the teachers for clarification. They recommended he no longer divide the children by gender and that was that.[233]

A sad scene like that is made possible not just by lesbian hostility toward men, but also by the Constructionist ideology, which denies that there are essential differences between the sexes. No matter how strong the evidence for such differences, radical feminists will not relinquish their vision of a world where we can choose our gender. Every little victory ("and that was that") for their side shows once again how the rest of society can't avoid being caught up in the battle.

Lesbians raising boys think they can fully compensate for the absence of a father — that fatherlessness isn't a problem unless an oppressive society makes it one. But the children don't see it that way:

> Parents reported a number of instances where children age four and older would ask about their father. Children would ask someone to be their daddy, ask where their father was,

---

[231] Sara Asch, "On the Way to the Water," *Lesbians Raising Sons*, 4.

[232] Ibid., 6.

[233] Ibid., 4.

or express the wish to have a father. They would make up their own answers, such as their father was dead, or someone was in fact their father.[234]

Can the "second mommy" compensate for the absence of a father? There's substantial evidence that children benefit from having a second sex represented in the home — not just a second person. Developmental psychologist Norma Radin and her colleagues studied the relationship between grandparents and grandchildren born to adolescent unwed mothers living with their parents. The young children who had positively involved grandfathers displayed more competence than those with an absent or uninvolved grandfather. The presence of the grandmother, on the other hand, did not have a clear-cut impact, suggesting a redundancy between the two forms of maternal influence.[235] Children, especially boys with involved grandfathers, showed less fear, anger, and distress.[236]

Even gay-affirming therapists are noting the problem. In spite of the pretense that two "mothers" are the same as a mother and father, in an article entitled, "A Boy and Two Mothers," Toni Heineman recognizes how a boy with two mothers must cope with the reality of an absent father.[237]

---

[234] Barbara McCandlish, "Against All Odds: Lesbian Mother Family Dynamics," in Fredrick Bozett, Gay and Lesbian Parents, 30.

[235] N. Radin, D. Oyserman, and R. Benn, "Grandfathers, Teen Mothers, and Children Under Two," in P. K. Smith, ed., The Psychology of Grandparenthood: An International Perspective (London: Routledge, 1991), 85-89.

[236] Comments on Radin, in H. Biller, Fathers and Families: Paternal Factors in Child Development (Westport, Connecticut: Auburn House, 1993), 17.

[237] Toni Heineman, "A Boy and Two Mothers: New Variations on an Old Theme or a New Story of Triangulation? Beginning

☞

Having two adults of the same sex in the home is objectively different from having a parent of both sexes, a point that's central to the entire "gay rights" debate. As conservative social commentator Michael Medved explains:

> The real issue behind the gay marriage dispute isn't the validity of homosexual attraction, it's the importance of gender differences . . . If men and women remain irreducibly different, it's dishonest to suggest that marrying a man is the precise equivalent of marrying a woman.[238]

Men and women grow up with certain natural expectations about what it means to be a man or a woman. Although activists might claim that these feelings are mere social constructions that they can overcome, in practice nature will always have its way.

Parenting Strains Same-Sex Relationships

Apart from the additional risks and stresses borne by a child raised by same-sex parents, having a baby can strain and even destroy a same-sex relationship. Sometimes the strain begins even before the baby is conceived: in some cases, both women want to bear a child, and they have to "negotiate" who gets to go first. In cases where a female couple is deeply enmeshed, the child can threaten to drive a wedge between them. If one or both of the women entered the relationship hoping to have her deep need for mothering met, a baby can destabilize it.

Thoughts on the Psychosexual Development of Children in Nontraditional Families," *Psychoanalytic Psychology* 21, no. 1 (2004): 99-115.

[238] Michael Medved, "Gender Difference, Not Gay Marriage, at Center of Family Fight," August 2, 2006, http://www.town hall.com.

In some instances, the woman's needs are so completely met by the baby that she no longer is interested in meeting her partner's needs. One woman explained:

> What can I say? I loved our baby and didn't know how to love two people at the same time. I fell in love with the baby and my lover felt neglected, rejected, and understandably totally abandoned.[239]

Often compounding the stresses is the fact that most persons with SSA come from dysfunctional families. The addition of a child often serves to resurrect old traumas:

> My parents fought all the time when we were growing up. I didn't have any idea that would happen to us. But it did. We were totally unprepared for the way being parents brought up all those old issues from the past.[240]

Of course, having a baby can cause problems for a husband/wife couple also, particularly if either spouse came to the marriage with deep, unresolved problems. The difference is that solving those problems will strengthen their relationship, with the child's presence deepening the bond between them. When spouses "fall in love" with their children, it doesn't diminish their love for the other spouse, but enriches it. Same-sex couples might seek children, hoping they will provide this same effect, but will more often find them an obstacle to and a competitor for affection. And when persons with SSA do succeed in solving their deep problems and meeting their unmet needs, it tends to diminish the attractions

---

[239] Cheri Pies, "Lesbians and the Choice to Parent," *Homosexuality and Family Relations* (New York: Harrington Park Press, 1990), 150.

[240] Ibid.

that form the very basis of their relationship, and it likewise undoes it.

Doesn't Everyone Have a Right to Children?

Persons with SSA are human beings. It's natural for them to want to experience the joy of having children: to love, to nurture, to leave a legacy. There's nothing wrong with a woman wanting to become pregnant and bear a child, or a man wanting to experience the joy of seeing his son grow into manhood or his daughter develop into a beautiful woman.

But children are not trophies, or a way to meet one's personal needs, or props to help forward an ideology. People aren't a means to an end; they're meant to be loved for their own sake. Therefore, no one has a "right" to a child. It's *children* who have the rights. When circumstances separate a child from one or both biological parents, adults should try to create a situation for him that is as normal as possible. No matter how honorable the intention, no one has the right to compound the tragedy of separation from biological parents by subjecting a child to another suboptimal situation.

Activists might claim that couples with SSA are "rescuing" children by adopting them out of poverty or other hard circumstances. Although laudable, this intent doesn't negate the real problems caused by same-sex parenting — problems deeper and longer-lasting than material deprivation. This argument also loses force when you consider the many roadblocks to adoption faced by stable, well-to-do married couples. Same-sex adoption doesn't provide more homes for needy children; it just keeps those children away from married couples who would otherwise adopt them.

Of course, when AID and surrogacy are used to create babies for same-sex couples, these children aren't being "rescued" from anything. Instead, they're being intentionally conceived to be placed in suboptimal situations. This is child abuse.

As more persons with SSA acquire children, society will increasingly be pressured to ignore the problems caused by same-sex parenting — just as it ignores the problems caused by divorce — and join in the pretense that having two mommies is just the same as having a mommy and a daddy. But no matter how many people praise "family diversity," children being raised by parents with SSA will always know that it's not the same, and someday they will resent how their needs have been sacrificed for the sake of a social experiment. In a sad irony, the more that cultural elites insist that there's nothing wrong with their situation, the more these children will feel guilty about resenting it, and this guilt will lead them to conclude that there must be something wrong with *them*.

The push to redefine marriage is only one aspect of the Sexual Left's assault on marriage and the family. Infidelity, premarital promiscuity, selfishness, and easy divorce have all helped to destabilize marriage and, in so doing, endanger children. Gay activists point to these problems and argue that same-sex relationships are no worse than bad marriages. William Eskridge and Darren Spedale, for example, public advocates for the redefinition of marriage, argue that same-sex marriage will have no extra negative effects on marriage or children, because traditional marriage is already self-destructing.[241] In its place they recommend that society normalize a menu of family options, so that people can choose what suits them.

In other words, because society no longer ostracizes male/female couples who neglect their responsibilities, conceive children outside of marriage, or divorce to pursue self-centered desires, there's

[241] Kurtz, "Zombie Killers."

nothing wrong with encouraging same-sex couples to likewise ignore the needs of children in favor of their own desires.

Stanley Kurtz points out the dangers of such menu schemes:

> Shifting to a broad "menu of experimental family forms"
> may feel liberating to some, but it is really a recipe for thin-
> ning out society's commitment to children. Each unconven-
> tional experiment reinforces the others, ultimately yielding
> a significantly less stable family regime. Which is to say, gay
> marriage undermines marriage. Or, as we say in some pre-
> cincts, the "queering of the social" calls into question the
> normativity and naturalness of heterorelationality.[242]

What the menu scheme does *not* allow is for children to choose
the family that best suits their needs. Children must instead rely
on society to protect their interests. Thus, the battle to preserve
marriage as the union between a man and a woman is ultimately a
battle for the rights of children.

Children's rights is probably the most important area in which
larger society is threatened by efforts to redefine marriage. But
there are others. As we shall see, marriage law, and the sexual
ethic that both informs and is informed by it, do not exist in a
vacuum.

[242] Ibid.

Part V

❧

Beyond Same-Sex Marriage

*"The common good requires that laws recognize,
promote, and protect marriage as the basis of the
family, the primary unit of society. Legal recognition of
homosexual unions or placing them on the same level
as marriage would mean not only the approval of deviant
behavior, with the consequence of making it a model in
present-day society, but would also obscure basic values
which belong to the common inheritance of humanity."*

Joseph Cardinal Ratzinger
Now Pope Benedict XVI

❧

*"In the past, predictions of catastrophe following
the integration of openly gay people into
mainstream social institutions have been
consistently wrong. The sky never falls."*

Jonathan Rauch
*Gay Marriage: Why It's Good for Gays
Good for Straights, and Good for America*

Chapter 13

Same-Sex Marriage and the Slippery Slope

*How would same-sex marriage pave the way for
further changes that would threaten families and society?*

*How are persons of conscience already being
punished for rejecting the ideology of the Sexual Left?*

Gay activists frequently challenge the defenders of traditional marriage by asking how same-sex marriage could possibly affect anyone but the couple involved. As columnist Steve Blow put it in the *Dallas Morning News*, "How does anyone's pledge of love and commitment turn into a fatal blow to families?"[243]

It's in some ways a disingenuous question, because no one suggests that the existing marriages of couples who have pledged themselves to be faithful until death would suddenly fall apart. *But everything around them would change.*

More Changes to Come

If marriage is redefined to include same-sex couples, the Sexual Left will score a major victory and be in a position to claim more. Sexual Leftists will demand — and indeed, in some places, already are demanding — that children be protected from other discriminatory ideas such as chastity, fidelity, purity, and the importance of the biological relationship between parent and child. Marriage will be further dissociated from procreation. Parenthood will be primarily "affective" rather than biological — based on the way

[243] Steve Blow, quoted by Dr. James Dobson, "Gay Marriage: Why Would It Affect Me? Eleven Arguments Against Same-Sex Marriage," *The Dallas Morning News*, March 14, 2004.

adults feel, rather than on natural ties of blood. Children who want fathers will be told that their desires are selfish, a rejection of their mothers' love.

Furthermore, the redefinition of marriage to include same-sex couples will pave the way for other legal changes. Activist justices will be emboldened. Having thrown out one precedent, there will be no reason to respect another. Gay activists and their allies in the media ridicule this "slippery slope" argument, but evidence for it can already be seen in the growing polyamory movement. After all, if same-sex couples have rights, why not those whose preferred family form involves three or more partners?[244]

Because sexual license can never fulfill the deepest longings of the human heart, no concession, however sweeping, will ever be enough. When government-imposed tolerance fails to solve their problems, gay activists will look to blame some other source of "oppression." Those who oppose them will be labeled — indeed, already are being labeled — as prejudiced, intolerant bigots, guilty of "hate." In our society, persons so labeled are second-class citizens who lose their right to participate as equals in the life of their communities.

In Canada, we can see this very phenomenon unfolding before our eyes. In 2004, the Canadian parliament passed a bill effectively making it a hate crime to speak or write against homosexuality. As James Dobson observed after one of his *Focus on the Family* radio programs was judged by the Canadian Radio and Television Commission to be "homophobic":

> In order to get a perspective on where the homosexual activist movement is taking us, one can simply look at our

---

[244] See, for example, Elizabeth Emens's case for polyamory in the *New York University Review of Law and Social Change* (2004): "Monogamy's Law: Compulsory Monogamy and Polyamorous Existence."

neighbors to the north. Canada is leading the way on this revolutionary path . . .

Pastors and priests in Canada are wondering if they can preach from Leviticus or Romans 1 or other passages from the writings of the apostle Paul. Will a new Bible be mandated that is bereft of "hate speech"? A man who owned a printing press in Canada was fined $3,400 for refusing to print stationery for a homosexual activist organization . . .

Is that kind of censorship coming to the United States? I believe that it is. Once homosexual marriage is legalized, if indeed that is where we are headed, laws based on what will be considered "equality" will bring many changes in the law. Furthermore, it is likely that non-profit organizations that refuse to hire homosexuals on religious grounds will lose their tax exemptions. Some Christian colleges and universities are already worrying about that possibility.[245]

Gay activists will say they're simply fighting for their right for "acceptance," but as conservative commentator Thomas Sowell has pointed out, there is no such right:

The issue is not individual rights. What the activists are seeking is social approval of their lifestyle. But this is the antithesis of equal rights. If you have a right to someone else's approval, then they do not have a right to their own opinions and values. You cannot say that what "consenting adults" do in private is nobody else's business and then turn around and say that others are bound to put their seal of approval on it.[246]

---

[245] Dobson, "Eleven Arguments Against Same-Sex Marriage."

[246] Thomas Sowell, "Gay Marriage 'Rights,'" http://www.town hall.com/columnists, December 31, 2004.

Is the Sky Really Falling?

Despite such warning signs, gay activists insist that the defenders of family are running around like Chicken Littles, exaggerating the dangers of redefinition of marriage, foolishly warning everyone that the sky is falling.

Are we? History suggests that it's more likely that activists are simply — or willfully — blind to the real effects their policies have caused. The Sexual Left has for decades warred against our culture's sensible restrictions on sexual activity outside marriage. They decried marriage laws designed to protect women and children as "patriarchal oppression." They mocked as "puritans" those who sought to protect the innocence of children, and they betrayed their hostility to religion by castigating them as religious extremists who wanted to impose sectarian dogma on a secular society.

Pleasure is seductive, restraint difficult. The post-war era saw a loosening of traditional morals that culminated in the sexual revolution of the 1960s, leaving for subsequent generations a legacy of abortion, disease, broken families, and personal misery. The sky has fallen on us before.

Members of the Sexual Left have never taken responsibility for the suffering their ideology caused; instead, they have sought scapegoats. They blamed teenage pregnancy on residual modesty. If girls weren't afraid to be openly sexual, they would all keep condoms in their pocketbooks. They blamed the pandemic of sexually transmitted diseases on the government, claiming that not enough money had been appropriated for the development of vaccines and effective therapies. When public health officials suggested the commonsense approach of chastity before marriage and monogamy after, the Sexual Left lashed out at them and demanded that prevention strategies must accommodate unlimited sexual activity with multiple partners and extreme practices. When no-fault divorce failed to eliminate suffering in unhappy marriages, they blamed it on outmoded and unrealistic concepts of marital duty.

The sky has fallen on Massachusetts. In the 1960s and '70s, opponents of the Equal Rights Amendment argued that it could open the door to same-sex marriage. ERA supporters insisted that the suggestion was ridiculous. In October of 1976, just before the vote on the Massachusetts state ERA, a government commission issued a report that explicitly denied that an ERA would impact future decisions on gay marriage. The report cited court decisions in Washington state and Colorado that had so held. Editorials in the *Boston Globe* and the *Boston Herald* ridiculed claims that a state ERA would affect marriage law, calling them "exaggerated" and "unfounded."[247]

Yet in spite of the clear record on the intent of the Massachusetts ERA, Justice John M. Greany cited that amendment in support of his concurring opinion in the *Goodridge* case.

The sky has fallen on the Boy Scouts. In various jurisdictions, gay activists have worked to add "sexual orientation" to the list of categories in which discrimination is legally prohibited. When opponents of this change argued this would lead to attacks on institutions such as the Boy Scouts and churches, they were shouted down; yet when James Dale was dismissed as a troop leader because he came out publicly as gay, he sued, charging discrimination, and won in the state court. Fortunately the U.S. Supreme Court supported the Boy Scouts of America's (BSA) right to exclude openly homosexual men from leadership — for now. They were not out of the woods, however. The BSA's refusal to capitulate to the demands of the gay activists has cost them funding from United Way campaigns and led to ongoing efforts to deny them resources and use of public facilities.

[247] Cordy dissent in *Goodridge*.

One Man, One Woman

The sky has fallen on the Episcopal Church. The Sexual Left has infiltrated Christian denominations, demanding that Christian doctrine make room for "tolerance" and "inclusion." This meant blessing same-sex relationships with ceremonies that were indistinguishable from weddings and ordaining homosexually active priests and ministers. When the American Episcopal Church decided to ordain an openly gay man as a bishop, Anglican churches in Africa refused to recognize the ordination, opening a fissure in the international Anglican Communion that continues to widen.

The sky has fallen on persons of conscience. Until May of 2004, Linda Gray Kelley was a justice of the peace in Massachusetts. When the Massachusetts Supreme Judicial Court ordered that same-sex couples be issued marriage licenses, Kelley assumed that she and other justices of the peace would be able to refuse, on the basis of conscience, to "marry" same-sex couples. The president of the Massachusetts Justices of the Peace Association assured her and other like-minded members that they needn't worry. Then, on April 26, 2004, a government official came to speak to the association. He told them that if any justice of the peace, for any reason, refused to marry a same-sex couple, that person would be sued for $1 million and found guilty of discrimination. He told them that if such a situation occurred, "Don't come to us for help. We are always on the side of the victim." Shortly thereafter, Kelley resigned.[248]

All this will be nothing in comparison with the effects of a judicial ruling forcing the redefinition of marriage on the entire country. If marriage is redefined, the sky will fall on every person and institution that refuses to surrender to the gay agenda.

[248] Joseph D'Agostino, "She Resigned in Protest Over Massachusetts Marriages," *National Catholic Register*, September 12-18, 2004.

Farther Down the Slope

Defenders of traditional marriage do indeed see society perched on a slippery slope, and fear that redefining marriage will push it over the edge. Once that happens, there might be nothing to break its fall. For example, if same-sex couples are granted marriage licenses, on what grounds can society justify its legal discrimination against polyamorists? The case for polygamy is in some ways stronger than the case for same-sex marriage. In contrast to same-sex marriage, there is historical and cultural precedent for it. Unlike same-sex marriage, polygamy provides a father and mother (and then some) for children. There are people in this country who have already petitioned the courts for recognition of their polygamous relationships, and there are people in jail for practicing polygamy. Hollywood has begun churning out polygamy-themed entertainment.[249]

Although patriarchal families with one man ruling over a harem of wives and a host of children might not have much appeal to the Sexual Left, polyamory understood as a group of men and women engaging in various combinations of sexual intimacy and reproduction does have its supporters in the Sexual Left. At the National Gay and Lesbian Task Force conference in November of 2004, there was a workshop promoting that very concept. (There was also a "genderqueer" caucus, promotion of cross-dressing, hormone treatment and surgery for those who want to pretend to be the other sex, and promotion of a recent innovation, so-called sex-change operations for adolescents.[250]) Gay activists deny any link between opening marriage to same-sex couples and encouraging multiple-partner marriage, but given the

---

[249] For example, the HBO series *Big Love*.

[250] Linda Harvey, "How Shall 'Gay' Activists Now Live?" *World Net Daily*, November 15, 2004.

track record of judicial activism, polyamorists will undoubtedly see legalized same-sex marriage as a logical and legal precedent for multiple-partner marriage.

Indeed, if marriage comes to be defined as whatever the participants want it to be, regardless of tradition, popular opinion, or the effects on children or society, the current restriction on number of spouses can be viewed only as another unjust societal prejudice against diversity in family forms.

*

But polygamy can't be considered the bottom of the slope. Courts could find ways to strike down laws protecting children under the guise of protecting "the right to privacy." They could lower or abolish the age of consent for sexual activity; eliminate restrictions on pornography, including child pornography; make illegal any regulation, practice, or official language that differentiates in any way between the sexes; legalize all forms of prostitution; demand the right for transsexuals, transgenders, and other "sexual minorities" to dress or act any way they want in public or in the workplace; even force the public to pay for sex-change surgery. Sound far-fetched? Each of these demands has already found advocates and is already being pushed in courts here and abroad. Each already has a constituency claiming rights, advocates who know how to work the system, and wealthy supporters. And as we slide down the slope, we can only expect the list to be expanded.

To some, there might be no apparent connection between changing the definition of marriage on the one hand and legalizing child pornography or lowering the age of consent on the other, but that doesn't mean that an activist court couldn't find one. We have only to look at the history of court-mandated social change. In the 1960s, the Executive Director of the Planned Parenthood League of Connecticut challenged a state law that restricted a couple's ability to be counseled on the use of contraceptives. In 1965, the Supreme Court ruled in *Griswold v. Connecticut* that:

> Though the Constitution does not explicitly protect a general right to privacy, the various guarantees within the Bill of Rights create penumbras, or zones, that establish a right to privacy. Together, the First, Third, Fourth, and Ninth Amendments create a new constitutional right, the right to privacy in marital relations. The Connecticut statute conflicts with the exercise of this right and is therefore null and void.

Just eight years later, in *Roe v. Wade*, the Supreme Court appealed to the "right to privacy" discovered in *Griswold* to invalidate every state law that restricted abortion. The effect of *Roe* and subsequent decisions based on *Roe* was to grant a virtually unrestricted right to abortion for the entire nine months of pregnancy. In 1992, in *Planned Parenthood v. Casey*, the Supreme Court completed the ideological journey from inventing a "right to privacy" to concluding that "the heart of liberty is the right to define one's own concept of existence, of meaning, of the universe, and of the mystery of life." And in 2003, in *Lawrence and Garner v. Texas*, the Supreme Court ruled that laws making certain sexual acts illegal violated the "due process clause" of the Constitution.

The justices in the *Goodridge* case, which changed the definition of marriage in Massachusetts, referred to these decisions, plus the state ERA, to throw out settled law, tradition, and legislative intent. They usurped the power of the legislators, ignored the will of the popular majority, and invented a new right. Other judges who believe in "changing paradigms" could well decide to extend to children this unlimited right to privacy. Already we have a ruling in Washington State that parents don't have a right to eavesdrop on children's phone conversations because children on the phone have an expectation of privacy.[251] This was particularly troubling, since the case involved a parent overhearing evidence of a crime and behavior that clearly put a minor child at risk.

Based on the evidence of the last forty years, there is every reason to expect that a judicial ruling mandating the redefinition of marriage will become a precedent for additional and more radical changes. The slippery slope is real. The Sexual Left is counting on it. Those who honestly think we are hysterical Chicken Littles simply haven't been paying attention.

[251] Bill O'Reilly, *Culture Warrior* (New York: Broadway Books, 2006), 121-124.

Chapter 14

The Threat to Religious Freedom

*Why do gay activists identify conservative
religion as their number-one enemy?*

*How could our free exercise of religion
be threatened by the gay agenda?*

*What is the attitude that most people
of faith take toward those with SSA?*

The redefinition of marriage would ultimately affect the entire culture, but in two areas, the negative impact would be especially immediate and severe: religious freedom and public education. Let's look first at religion.

"Toxic" Religion?

Religious freedom has already begun to run afoul of the global gay-rights movement. In July of 2004, Ake Green, pastor of a Swedish Pentecostal Church, was sentenced to one month in prison for "hate speech against homosexuals," for giving a sermon in which he quoted Bible passages condemning homosexual behavior. According to the prosecutor, citing the Bible on homosexuality amounted to "hate speech." Green was later acquitted on appeal, causing prosecutors to re-appeal to Sweden's highest court. There the acquittal was upheld, but Green had to promise never to preach on the topic again.[252]

Rowan Williams, the Archbishop of Canterbury, was forced to protest the decision of some colleges and universities to refuse to recognize Christian associations because these groups took a stand against homosexual behavior. Those institutions characterized the traditional position of religious groups as equivalent to

---

[252] http://www.akegreen.org.

Holocaust-denial or racial bigotry, and therefore without a place on campus.[253] In Great Britain, laws prohibiting discrimination on the grounds of sexual orientation don't exempt educational institutions run by religious groups. Those supporting these regulations argue that people may believe whatever they want — as long as they don't act on it:

> In our view, the Regulations prohibiting sexual orientation discrimination should clearly apply to the curriculum, so that homosexual pupils are not subjected to teaching as part of the religious education or other curriculum, that their sexual orientation is sinful or morally wrong. Applying the Regulations to the curriculum would not prevent pupils from being taught as part of their religious education the fact that certain religions view homosexuality as sinful. In our view there is an important difference between this factual information being imparted in a descriptive way as part of a wide-ranging syllabus about different religions, and a curriculum which teaches a particular religion's doctrinal beliefs as if they were objectively true.[254]

They defended their restriction on religious education by claiming that sexual orientation is an inherent characteristic comparable to race and sex — a myth without scientific support. They further fail to note the distinction between homosexual orientation (that is, same-sex attraction) and homosexual acts. The Catholic Church

---

[253] Archbishop Rowan Williams, "It Is Not a Crime To Hold Traditional Values," *The Times Higher Education Supplement,* December 10, 2006, http://www.thes.co.uk/search/story.aspx ?story_id=2034475.

[254] House of Lords and Commons, Joint Committee on Human Rights, Sixth Report Session of 2006-2007, "Legislative Scrutiny: Sexual Orientation Regulations," par. 67.

does not, as a point of fact, teach that SSA in itself is sinful (since a temptation is not sin), but only that homosexual acts — along with other unnatural sexual acts, and all sexual acts outside marriage — are contrary to God's law. Catholics hold that this moral teaching is objectively true. Forcing teachers and priests to hide this truth from students is a clear abridgement of freedom of religion.

These examples demonstrate how the strategy that gay activists devised in the 1980s is bearing fruit. By constantly equating opposition to their agenda with "discrimination," "bigotry," and "hate," by labeling opponents as oppressors, gay activists have succeeded in forcing ordinary people of faith to defend their right simply to participate as equals in society.

Gay activists recognize that the major opposition to their agenda comes from religious people. Thus, they know that if they're going to win, they'll have to undermine the influence of traditional religion in society.

In 2005, an article entitled "Purging Toxic Religion in Canada: Gay Marriage Exposes Faith-Based Bigotry" began appearing on the websites of gay activists. The article attacked the Catholic bishop of Calgary, Fred Henry, for his forceful public statement against the redefining of marriage, and branded Catholicism generally as a "toxic" religion that promotes prejudice and hate. In a clumsy pun, it declared that "Rome is where the hate is," and confidently forecast further successes for the gay agenda and the eventual demise of Catholicism and other traditional faiths:

[W]e predict that gay marriage will indeed result in the growth of acceptance of homosexuality now underway, as Henry fears. But marriage equality will also contribute to the abandonment of toxic religions, liberating society from the prejudice and hatred that has polluted culture for too long, thanks in part to Fred Henry and his kind.[255]

If one accepts the claim that religion is the cause of hate, the next logical step is to call for the repression of religion. This option was actually suggested by gay pop music icon Elton John:

I think religion has always tried to turn hatred towards gay people. Religion promotes hatred and spite against gays. But there are so many Christian people I know who are gay and love their religion . . . From my point of view I would ban religion completely, even though there are some wonderful things about it. I love the idea of the teachings of Jesus Christ and the beautiful stories about it, which I loved in Sunday school and I collected all the little stickers and put them in my book. But the reality is that organized religion doesn't seem to work. It turns people into hateful lemmings and it's not really compassionate.[256]

Gay activists understand that their vision of our culture's future is incompatible with the traditional religious message that homosexual behavior is contrary to God's law. In op-eds and in front of cameras, gay activists might insist that persons who hold to ancient and unchangeable faiths have nothing to fear from same-sex marriage, yet anyone who doesn't capitulate to their demands is a bigot and a hate-monger. Are we really supposed to believe they'll let us keep our bigoted, hateful ideas in peace? We

[255] Kevin Bourassa and Joe Varnell, "Purging Toxic Religion in Canada: Gay Marriage Exposes Faith-Based Bigotry," January 18, 2005, www.samesexmarriage.ca/equality/toxic180105.htm.

[256] John-Henry Westen, "Elton John: Religion Causes Hatred of Gays"; "I Would Ban Religion Completely," quoting from an interview by Jake Shears, published in *The Observer Music Monthly*, November 12, 2006.

already hear a growing chorus of voices from the Sexual Left insisting that traditional religions, and in particular the Catholic Church, change their teachings to conform to their ideology of "tolerance."

Of course, in a country (unlike Sweden or England) that has historically valued both freedom of speech and freedom of religion, it won't be easy to deny pastors the right to quote Scripture or penalize people of faith for speaking out against the gay agenda. For gay activists, the solution is hate-crimes legislation. If "hate" is a crime, then "hate speech" is a crime, and from there, it's only a short step to declaring that anything that makes a person with SSA feel "hated" is a crime. That would have to include mentioning what Scripture says about homosexual behavior, because teaching that homosexual behavior is wrong creates a climate of "hate" against people with SSA, and is therefore the cause of all violence against them.

As "proof," the gay activists hold up the awful torture and death of Matthew Shepard in 1998. There's no evidence that his killers — meth addicts looking for money to buy drugs — were particularly bigoted against persons with SSA, still less that they had been influenced in any way by religious education, or sermons against homosexuality, or by reading the Bible. But this hasn't stopped Shepard's story from being cited far and wide as the logical terminus of Christian "homophobia."[257]

It's true that there's a tiny number of high-profile anti-gay crusaders who call themselves "Christian" and yet use ugly and abusive language toward persons with SSA. They're an exception. The great majority of people of faith condemn violence against

---

[257] "New Details Emerge in Matthew Shepard Murder," November 26, 2004, http://abcnews.go.com/2020/story?id=277685&page=1.

people with SSA. Neither is there any evidence that perpetrators of anti-gay "hate crimes" have been influenced by religious teaching against homosexual behavior. Indeed, if they looked at that teaching, they'd find that it's not about hatred but *love*. Love demands that we seek what's best for all God's children. And what's best for every person is to come to the knowledge of God and of the truth in all its fullness: the truth that can set them free to be the healthy, fully human persons God made them to be. To truly love persons with SSA, we must want their highest good, which is freedom proper to the sons and daughters of God.

Judge Not . . . Unless You're Judging Christians

Gay activists accuse Christians of failing to follow Christ's admonition to "judge not, lest ye be judged." Doesn't this, they say, prohibit Christians from "judging" persons with SSA by telling them their sexual tastes are disordered, or by forbidding them to marry each other?

Clearly Scripture does warn against judging others. But confusion comes from a false understanding of what constitutes "judging." To judge, in this context, means to hear the evidence, render the verdict, pass the sentence, and see that it is enforced. In this sense, God is the sole judge; none of us can judge the heart and eternal destiny of any person. Today, the Sexual Left has confused this sense of judging with a more limited sense: that is, simply having a set of moral principles and applying them in order to make judgments about what is right and what is wrong.

To say that homosexual acts are always wrong isn't to judge the personal culpability of any individual. Neither is it to belittle the real needs and sufferings of people with SSA. In fact, a correct understanding of the origins of SSA and of the serious problems caused by the gay lifestyle ought to move us to greater compassion for them.

It's not surprising that those who engage in sexual sin should feel judged. Although they deny having any doubts about their situation, gay activists have consciences, and at some level, they must sense the truth about their behavior. Words spoken against that behavior, no matter how lovingly they are spoken, bring that feeling of judgment. The truth shines a light on their lies. We should not, therefore, be surprised when they lash out at us. Their pain is real. They think that silencing us will eliminate the prick of their own consciences. It won't.

Ironically — although no one should be surprised by this inconsistency — members of the Sexual Left don't apply their "judge not" standard to themselves. In fact, they're constantly judging not only the actions and convictions, but the motives, and indeed the very hearts and souls, of their opponents. To them, traditional Christians and other defenders of marriage are never simply wrong; they're oppressive, sanctimonious, intolerant, and always, of course, "hate-filled."

The Gay Agenda's Christian Cronies

In the realm of religion, gay activists aren't all on the outside looking in. Many have established themselves in places of influence within religious organizations and have won support from fellow travelers who do not themselves experience SSA, but reject other aspects of Christian sexual morality. In support of the gay agenda, some of these appeal to the supposed "Christian spirit of inclusion," or tolerance.

For example, on December 19, 2003, two dozen Catholic priests from Chicago, while claiming to respect "the teaching authority of the Church," issued an open letter accusing the Church hierarchy of assaulting and violating "our gay and lesbian brothers and sisters" by using "violent," "abusive," and "mean-spirited language." They called upon the Catholic Church to be inclusive and embracing.[258] They don't explain precisely how a church dedicated to calling people to repentance can embrace and include what it considers sinful and self-destructive behavior.

Many of those who want the Church to be "inclusive" have accepted the myth that some people are "born gay" to justify changing the unchanging and unchangeable teaching. They argue that since God made some people "gay," how could God condemn them for being what He made them to be? At the same time, these "includers" reject Scripture as divinely revealed truth, as well as the moral teaching authority of the Church in general.

It's true that Jesus issued an invitation to all men and women to share in loving communion with him. He didn't shun even the worst sinner. However, Jesus also called his followers to obedience. He told the woman caught in adultery to go and "sin no more." He warned that evildoers would be cast out of God's presence. The kind of "inclusion" he preached is not the same thing as unconditional toleration of sin.

Christianity calls every person to repentance. This necessarily requires mentioning the things we have to repent of. Homosexual acts are only one kind of sexual sin, and sexual sins are only one kind of sin. However, to tell Christians they can't mention specific sexual sins is to tell them that they can't preach the full gospel. Calling people out of sin into freedom isn't rejection. Not to point out specific sins would be the worst form of discrimination.

Religions Offer Healing and Hope

We must never underestimate the power of Christ's undiluted message, and the reality of true conversion. Charlene Cothran,

---

[258] "An Open Letter to the Hierarchy of the Roman Catholic Church Regarding the Pastoral Care of Gay and Lesbian Persons," *National Catholic Reporter Online*, January 5, 2006.

publisher of *Venus* magazine, a periodical dedicated to African-American gays and lesbians, shocked her readers by announcing that she had given God her heart, and that henceforth:

> The new mission of *Venus* magazine is to encourage, educate, and assist those who desire to leave a life of homosexuality. Our ultimate mission is to win souls for Christ, and to do so by showing love to all God's people. We believe that homosexuality is outside of the will of God. We know that many new and longtime *Venus* readers have been instilled with a belief system that is in line with this teaching but are still living "in the life." Many desire change and wonder if they can be accepted into the family of God "just as they are." The answer is YES![259]

Christianity doesn't reject persons with SSA — it offers them *hope*. Although for some, just saying yes to God works miracles, for others, the yes must be followed by a long road of healing. In the last thirty years, many Christian denominations (and groups from other religions as well) have recognized that such people also benefit from specialized help: religious ministries to help them carry their burden and eventually to find freedom from it. This movement can be compared to the treatment of alcoholics. Simple conversion worked for some, but most alcoholics needed something more. Alcoholics Anonymous provided that something, with its twelve-step program and regular meetings. In the same way, persons with SSA can receive specialized counseling and support to help them develop their true personhood.

Evangelical Christians have been the most active in this area. For example, under the umbrella organization Exodus International, many ministries have sprung up around the world, based on

---

[259] Charlene Cothran, *Venus Magazine* website.

the belief that faith in Jesus can be combined with practical professional support to help people come out of homosexuality. Homosexuals Anonymous is a Christian ministry that uses a modified twelve-step method to help men and women find freedom from SSA. Father John Harvey's group Courage ministers to Catholics with SSA who want to live chastely and faithfully. A recently formed organization called JONAH helps Jewish men and women with SSA who desire to live according to the Torah. Evergreen ministers to Mormons; there's also a group for Muslims. The ongoing work and success of some ministries has helped create a growing ex-gay movement, whose mounting testimonies provide more evidence of the effectiveness of ministry and therapy for persons with SSA.

Some of these ministries focus on helping men and women develop their heterosexual potential with the hope that they'll eventually be able to consider marriage, but the primary focus for most of them is freedom from sexual acting-out and the healing of childhood wounds. Many of those who have been in the gay life for a number of years are content to live chastely and don't see marriage as their ultimate goal.

True Inclusion vs. False Compassion

No person struggling with SSA ought to feel excluded from the love of God or from his faith community. No matter how many times they fail, such persons can be welcomed back. The problem is with those who want to continue acting out their SSA and, moreover, who demand to be affirmed in that choice by their religion. In this case, they're in the same position as anyone who wants God's laws to change to accommodate his behavior; they'll feel excluded and guilty.

There *is* unjust prejudice here, but it isn't from Christians; rather, it's from those who believe that persons with SSA can't control their sexual impulses. They're prejudging persons with SSA as different from the rest of humanity; inferior; incapable of change or chastity. This is a far crueler form of discrimination. Although they think they're being kind, their pity leads them to treat persons with SSA as second-class human beings whose handicap needs to be accommodated rather than challenged.

On the other hand, those who really care about persons with SSA believe in their masculine and feminine potential, and recognize that every person has free will, and can choose to seek help and find real change. They know that persons with SSA can respond to God's grace, and count on his mercy.

Chapter 15

The Threat to Public Schools

How are gay activists working to
spread their ideas in the public schools?

How are educational
organizations helping them to do this?

Why are their programs especially
dangerous for children at risk for SSA?

Apart from overcoming religious opposition, the Sexual Left knows that the key to ultimate victory for its agenda lies in winning over the younger generation. This is why gay activists have made "tolerance education" in public schools a central part of their strategy.

The larger movement for ever-more-explicit sex education in public schools has been underway for decades, but it was at their 1993 march on Washington, DC, that gay activists unveiled their demand for gay-friendly curricula to be incorporated at "all levels of education" — federal, state and local, grades K-12.[260] Toward this end, they had been working for over a generation to solidify their influence within the educational establishment, enlisting the support of the National Education Association (NEA), the American Federation of Teachers, the American Association of School Administrators, and the National Association of School Psychologists. With these influential soapboxes under the control of gay activists and their allies, they were ready to make a more overt push into America's schools.

"One in Ten," Repeat After Me

One of the initial strategies, called "Project 10," sought to spread Kinsey's false claim that ten percent of the population is

[260] http://www.afa.net/homosexual_agenda/ha1993.htm.

homosexual (the figure is closer to two percent).[261] In sex-education classes supposedly geared toward helping students avoid pregnancy and STDs, teachers would assert the "one in ten" figure as established fact. This would cause the students to look around and try to guess which of their friends were gay — or wonder if they were among the ten percent. A number of school-based programs, in fact, were given the very name "One in Ten."[262] Widespread acceptance of the ten-percent figure has been, of course, an important element in the long-term plans of gay activists. And to judge by the frequency with which we still hear or read this long-discredited claim, they seem to have succeeded.

"There Is No Other Side"

According to its own literature, the NEA supports the aims of the gay agenda, and it has encouraged many initiatives designed to assist it: advocating the recognition of sexual orientation as a protected "civil right" for both students and staff, developing sex-education classes to include information on the "diversity of sexual orientations," and teaming with gay-rights groups to promote gay-oriented programs and educational products.[263]

One such product in which the NEA had a hand was the 1997 pro-gay video *It's Elementary.* Simply put, its aim was to teach schoolchildren that homosexuality was normal, and that to think otherwise was wrong. As then-president of the NEA Bob Chase explained that this was not about tolerance but acceptance.[264]

---

[261] Fergusson et al., "Is Sexual Orientation Related to Mental Health Problems?": Sandfort et al., "Same-Sex Sexual Behavior."

[262] http://www.oneinten.org; http://www.1n10.org.

[263] Executive Summary of the Report of the NEA Task Force on Sexual Orientation, January 2002, www.vtnea.org/taskforce.htm.

[264] Malcolm A. Kline, "The NEA vs. Teachers," www.academia .org/news/nea_teachers.php; "NEA Pres. Bob Chase's Historic

One portion of the video showcased a sixteen-year-old boy named Noe Gutierrez, who talked about his experience as a gay teenager. Now twenty-four, Gutierrez says he is no longer "gay"[265] — but that didn't stop educators from the Montgomery County, Maryland, school district from using the video as a resource. When Gutierrez wrote a letter to the school committee asking that students watching the video be informed he was no longer "gay," he was rebuffed.

The story is a familiar one. Activists of the Sexual Left claim that introducing the gay agenda into schools is the only way to promote tolerance of "diversity," yet when ex-gays like Noe Gutierrez ask — in the name of diversity — to present their point of view, the activists change their tune. As Kevin Jennings, cofounder and executive director of the Gay, Lesbian, and Straight Education Network (GLSEN), put it:

> [E]x-gay messages have no place in our nation's public schools. A line has been drawn. There is no "other side" when you're talking about lesbian, gay, and bisexual students.[266]

Seeking Converts in the Classroom?

Gay activists publicly insist that SSA is something people are born with and the sooner they recognize it, "come out," and are accepted as unchangeably gay or lesbian, the easier their lives will be. This Essentialist line is used to justify pro-gay education in

Speech from 2000 GLSEN Conference," October 7, 2000, www.glsen.org/cgi-bin/iowa/all/news/record/143.html.

[265] Warren Throckmorton, "Hiding Truth from School Kids: It's Elementary Revisited," June 16, 2004, http://www.drthrock morton.com/article.asp?id=78.

[266] "First-of-Its-Kind Publication Urges Educators to Support Gay Students, Reject 'Ex-Gay' Messages," November 23, 1999, http://www.glsen.org/cgi-in/iowa/all/news/record/279.html.

schools, where pro-gay educators insist they're not "recruiting," but merely facilitating the inevitable.

The problem with this is twofold. First, not every child who has a same-sex attraction eventually becomes identified as a "gay" or "lesbian" adult. Studies suggest that while same-sex inclination might be common in adolescence, by their mid-twenties the vast majority of those who had such feelings or who experimented with homosexual behavior consider themselves firmly heterosexual.[267] Encouraging sexual experimentation among adolescents with even faint same-sex temptations is thus more about steering them toward SSA rather than easing their journey toward a preordained destination.

Second, although pro-gay educators insist that all they're doing is protecting adolescents who are naturally gay, a review of the programs themselves reveals that they have the much broader aim and effect of promoting casual attitudes toward sexual activity among students across the presumptive spectrum of orientations. For the gay agenda to succeed, the next generation of "straights" must be sexually liberated, too.

According to GLSEN, "coming out" is a normal and positive experience, and children with SSA should be encouraged by teachers and parents to publicly announce and explore their sexuality. But GLSEN's interest goes beyond encouraging adolescents with strong SSA to "come out"; they also target "questioning" teens and those whose sexuality is "fluid."

A manual published by GLSEN entitled *Tackling Gay Issues in School: A Resource Module* contains the following statement: "Each of us should have the freedom to explore our sexual orientation and find our own unique expression of lesbian, bisexual, gay,

[267] Dr. Jeffrey Satinover, "M.D. Testifies in Mass. in Defense of the Family," April 29, 2004, www.satinover.com.

straight, or any combination of these."[268] *Explore* in this context means to engage in promiscuous sex. In schools where this environment prevails, troubled students might decide to act out sexually, or claim to be gay or lesbian, as a way of rebelling against their parents. In such cases, teachers with SSA, having not resolved their own conflicts with parents, might identify strongly with the student and even come to see themselves as the student's true parents.[269]

Apart from leading vulnerable adolescents into homosexual experimentation, the gay movement also seeks to use schools to indoctrinate students into its political agenda. In classrooms and peer groups, opposing viewpoints are categorized as merely "religious" and therefore out of bounds. Objections are ridiculed as narrow-mindedness or bigotry. In the movie *It's Elementary*, a teacher voices concern about children whose parents held religious beliefs that were contrary to the gay movement's goals. Another teacher made it clear that such opinions were not allowed in the classroom.

If marriage is redefined to include same-sex couples, we can expect increased pressure to promote the gay agenda even more thoroughly in public schools. It's already happening in Massachusetts. According to a report on National Public Radio, Deb Allen, who teaches eighth-grade sex education in Brookline, has been pushing a gay-friendly curriculum for ten years. But the recent debate and legal decisions involving gay marriage have further encouraged her. Now, in her classroom, she draws a chart illustrating sexual activities such as kissing, hugging, and different kinds of intercourse, and then asks her students:

[268] Leif Mitchell, *Tackling Gay Issues in School: A Resource Module* (Watertown, Connecticut: GLSEN, 1999), 78.

[269] Gilbert Herdt and Andrew Boxer, *Children of Horizons* (Boston: Beacon Press, 1993), 250.

So can a woman and woman kiss and hug? Yes. Can a woman and a woman have vaginal intercourse? And they will all say no. And I'll say, "Hold it. Of course they can. They can use a sex toy. They could use . . ." and we talk, and we discuss that. So the answer there is yes.[270]

Activists Appeal to Parents' Fears

When parents and family groups complain about the promotion of the gay agenda in schools, activists and their fellows in the education industry respond that it's in the best interests of the students. First, they say, identifying GLBT students early will help to provide them with support and "safe sex" education, and thereby avoid negative outcomes — particularly teen suicide and STDs. Second, they argue that gay-positive education will prevent teasing and bullying of such children by other students. Without gay education, they say, such children might commit suicide.

It's true that teenagers who self-identify as gay or lesbian are at high risk for a number of negative outcomes, including suicide. Homosexual behavior is a high-risk activity, particularly for teenage boys. Why do schools encourage this behavior? In every other parallel case of high-risk activities, government *restricts* the rights of children and adolescents, in order to protect them. Laws governing driving, drinking, smoking, and sexual activity include arbitrary age limits, which involve weighing the risks against liberty rights. Likewise, when it comes to most risky behaviors — drugs and drinking, for example — school education takes an "abstinence" line. Why, then, in this one instance, do government-run schools try to affirm and promote the risky behavior? Schools do

---

[270] Deb Allen, "Debate in Massachusetts Over How to Address the Issue of Discussing Gay Relationships and Sex in Public School Classrooms," National Public Radio, September 13, 2004.

not encourage "safe smoking" or "safe drunk driving," yet so-called "safe sex" carries a higher risk than either. Why do they think that with regard to sex and sex alone, the way to protect teens from risky behavior is to encourage them to engage in it?

Apart from the broad category of physical and emotional woes associated with teen sexual promiscuity in general, research shows that adolescents who self-identify as GLB are at an even higher risk than their classmates. In a 1992 study of 4,159 ninth- to twelfth-grade students in Massachusetts, just over a hundred (or 2.5 percent) of them self-identified as gay, lesbian, or bisexual.[271] These GLB students were found to be more likely than non-GLB students to have engaged in thirty different high-health-risk behaviors, including the following:

	GLB	non-GLB
Alcohol use (<age 13)	59.1%	30.4%
Cocaine use (<age 13)	17.3%	1.2%
Inhalant use (life)	47.6%	18.5%
Ever had sexual intercourse	81.7%	44.1%
Three or more sexual partners (life)	55.4%	19.2%
Alcohol or drug use at last sexual episode	34.7%	13.3%
Sexual contact against will	32.5%	9.1%

According to the study, "students with six or more sexual partners in their life" were nearly eight times more likely to have been classified as gay, lesbian, or bisexual than students who had never had intercourse. It also found, unsurprisingly, that the greater

[271] R. Garofalo, R. Wolf, S. Kessel, J. Palfrey, and R. DuRant, "The Association Between Health Risk Behaviors and Sexual Orientation Among a School-Based Sample of Adolescents" (Youth Risk Behavior Survey), *Pediatrics* 101, no. 5 (1998): 895-903.

the number of sexual partners, the greater the risk of contracting an STD.

The study's authors are not social conservatives; in fact, following the usual line of gay activists, they blame those excess problems on "stigmatization." Nonetheless, they were forced to conclude that:

> GLB youth who self-identify during high school report disproportionate risk for a variety of health risk and problem behaviors, including suicide, victimization, sexual risk behaviors, and multiple substance use. In addition, these youth are more likely to report engaging in multiple risk behaviors and initiating risk behaviors at an earlier age than their peers.[272]

Those who encourage boys to self-identify at an early age nonetheless argue that "coming out" raises boys' self-esteem, making them more receptive to "safe sex" (condom) education, thereby protecting them from HIV infection. But statistics collected by the Centers for Disease Control show that, in spite of all the condom education and support for "coming out," an unacceptably high percentage of young men who have sex with men (MSM) are infected with HIV.[273] Studies confirm what common sense tells us: when an adolescent boy begins to have sex with men, he's *more*

---

[272] Garofalo et al., "The Association Between Health Risk Behaviors and Sexual Orientation."

[273] *"HIV Incidence Among Young Men Who Have Sex With Men — Seven U.S. Cities, 1994-2000,"* MMWR 5, no. 21 (June 1, 2001): 440-444. CDC analyzed data from the Young Men's Survey (YMS), a study that found a high prevalence of HIV and associated risks among MSM aged 15 to 22 years sampled in seven U.S. cities. This report confirms high HIV incidence among these young men. The average was 7.2% and increased with age.

likely to take risks and become infected with HIV than a man who begins homosexual behavior later in life.[274]

When confronted with the evidence that their "education" does not protect adolescents from SSA-related risks — and in some cases, might increase the risks — gay activists have only one answer: more gay-affirming education is needed.

A Higher Risk of Suicide

When it comes to SSA and teen suicide, the numbers tell a similar story. Gay activists have played on the fear of teen suicide to insist that vulnerable teens need gay-friendly schools and teachers to help them "come out" and overcome self-hatred. But a study by Gary Remafedi, who has published many articles on the subject, revealed that suicide attempts by teenagers with SSA were not lessened or averted by early "coming out." Neither were they appreciably increased by peer influences. On the contrary, Remafedi found that the five factors connected to suicide attempts among young MSM were:

1. *The age at which the teenager self-labeled. The later an adolescent self-labeled as "gay" or bisexual, the lower the odds of a suicide attempt.*

2. *Gender non-conformance. The more feminine a boy was, the higher the likelihood of suicide attempt.*

3. *Involvement with drugs and alcohol.*

---

[274] George Lemp et al., "Seroprevalence of HIV and Risk Behaviors Among Young Homosexual and Bisexual Men," JAMA 272, no. 6 (August 10, 1994): 451 (15.2% of the 79 young men in the study who began anal sex with men were found HIV positive, versus 3.8% of the 53 men who began the practice age 20 to 22).

4. Criminal apprehension.

5. Previous childhood sexual abuse.[275]

The last three items on Remafedi's list are common factors in many teen suicide attempts, not just for teens with SSA. But adolescents with SSA are more likely to have been sexually abused, more likely to have problematic home lives, and more likely to use drugs. The link between gender non-conformance in adolescence and suicide attempts is one more reason for identifying and treating Gender Identity Disorder. But gay activists want such treatment banned and want children with this problem to be labeled as "born gay." For some, this course of action will prove deadly.

Gay activists encourage "safe sex" without considering the real risks. Many suicide attempts by teenagers with SSA come after the breakup of an intense emotional and sexual relationship. For a boy with SSA, the first intense relationship feels like the solution to all his longing, so when the relationship falls apart, as almost all teenage sexual relationships do, the teen with SSA feels the loss even more deeply, because he already has psychological deficits and is frequently alienated from his parents. Discouraging teens with SSA from becoming sexually involved would protect them from intense emotions they can't handle and help lower the suicide risk.

There's no question: students with SSA need help. But there's every reason to believe that encouraging them to "come out" early will only make their problems worse. Instead, educators should focus on identification, diagnosis, and treatment of young boys with GID. While there's no guarantee that treatment of GID will

---

[275] Gary Remafedi, James Farrow, and Robert Deisher, "Risk Factors for Attempted Suicide in Gay and Bisexual Youth," *Pediatrics* 87 (1991): 869-875.

prevent same-sex attraction in adolescence, treatment can allevi-
ate the problems associated with GID in childhood. Teachers
should also be sensitive to the symptoms of sexual abuse, particularly in boys. Given that some forty percent of persons with SSA
have a history of child sexual abuse, school counselors should consider the possibility that a teenager with SSA is an abuse victim
who needs counseling, not condoms.

Many of the boys who are encouraged to come out early might,
like Noe Gutierrez, discover later that they are not "gay." Using fig-
ures from the National Health and Social Life Survey (NHSLS)
study of sexuality, researcher Jeffrey Satinover explains:

> Roughly ten out of every hundred men have had sex with
> another man at some time — the origin of the ten percent
> gay myth. Most of these will have identified themselves as
> gay before turning eighteen and will have acted on it. But
> by age eighteen, a full half of them no longer identify them-
> selves as gay and will never again have a male sexual part-
> ner. And this is not a population of people selected because
> they went into therapy; it's just the general population.
> Furthermore, by age twenty-five, the percentage of gay-
> identified men drops to 2.8%. This means that without any
> intervention whatsoever, three out of four boys who think
> they're gay at age sixteen aren't by twenty-five.[276]

There is no evidence that a pro-gay school environment protects students with SSA from the risks inherent in homosexual
behavior. There's a real possibility, however, that the boys who
discover they aren't gay at twenty-five might also discover they
are HIV-positive.

---

[276] Dr. Jeffrey Satinover, "M.D. Testifies in Mass. in Defense of
the Family," April 29, 2004, www.satinover.com.

One Man, One Woman

A Battle for the Minds and Souls of the Next Generation

Gay activists want to use issues of real concern in schools — teen health, suicide, bullying, and harassment — to introduce programs that promote the gay agenda, starting as early as kindergarten. They want children taught all the gay myths and never exposed to any other point of view. By positioning gay indoctrination as diversity education, gay activists have been able to force children with strong religious convictions to participate in what are essentially brainwashing sessions.

At Arcata High School in Arcata, California, during a sex-education lesson led by a representative of Planned Parenthood, students were asked if they believed homosexuality was a sin. Those who said yes had to remain alone in the center of the room. The goal of the exercise was to make religious children identify with gay students by making them experience alienation and humiliation.[277]

In Boyd County, Kentucky, the ACLU sued the school board over the right of a Gay-Straight Alliance student group to meet on campus. The school board settled the lawsuit by agreeing that all students, staff, and teachers would be required to receive "tolerance training," including "mandatory anti-harassment workshops" and an hour-long "training" video on sexual orientation and gender identity issues for middle- and high-school students.[278] Ten months after the settlement, a third of the students had failed to see the film. On the day the training was scheduled, 324 students

[277] Peter LaBarbera, "When Silence Would Have Been Golden," www.cwa.org, April 10, 2002.

[278] "The Law of the Land," *WorldNetDaily.com*, November 28, 2004, http://www.worldnetdaily.com/news/article.asp?ARTICLE_ID=41667; Susan Brinkman, "Gay History Month in City Schools Part of Larger Trend," *Catholic Standard and Times*, November 2, 2006.

didn't show up for school. So the ACLU went back to court to demand that the students be forced to undergo gay indoctrination against their parents' wishes. In a comment that illustrates with stunning clarity the sense of entitlement gay activists have when pushing their agenda in public schools, James Esseks, litigation director for the ACLU's Lesbian and Gay Rights Project, remarked:

> [T]he training is now part of the school curriculum . . . Parents don't get to say, "I don't want you to teach evolution" or this, that, or whatever else. If parents don't like it, they can homeschool, they can go to a private school, they can go to a religious school.[279]

The Sexual Left is only too happy to see traditional Christians and other objectors taking their kids out of public schools, effectively yielding the battlefield to them and their agenda. There will be a time in the future to put pressure on religious schools, too. In the meantime, divide and conquer.

Anthony Romero of the ACLU insists that those who oppose the redefinition of marriage are "on the wrong side of history." According to Jason West, the mayor of New Paltz, New York, who gained his fifteen minutes of fame when he performed rogue same-sex weddings in 2004, "It's inevitable that we'll have same-sex marriage in this country, because it's a generational question . . . Give it ten or twenty years when we're holding state legislatures and Congress. It will just be a non-issue."[280] Gay activists are confident that as young voters, who have been subjected to intensive

---

[279] "View Homosexual Film, or School Faces Lawsuit," http://www.worldnetdaily.com/news/article.asp?ARTICLE_ID=41667.

[280] Quoted by Joshua K. Baker and Maggie Gallagher, "Not Inevitable: On the Future of Gay Marriage, the Future Is Not Yet Determined," *National Review Online*, December 1, 2004.

in-school indoctrination, replace the older generation, the percentage favoring the redefinition of marriage will shift.

Their optimism might be misplaced. According to Maggie Gallagher and Joshua Baker:

> After the Massachusetts Supreme Court ruling in *Goodridge*, opposition to gay marriage among adults skyrocketed. In June 2003, according to Gallup, young adults favored gay marriage 61 to 36 percent. By December 2003, opposition among young adults had jumped 17 percentage points (more than twice the 8 percentage-point shift among all adults), resulting in 53 to 44 percent *opposition* to gay marriage.[281]

This trend continues. According to a Gallup poll in 2004, sixty-three percent of teenagers disapprove of marriages between homosexuals.[282]

History shows that trends move like a pendulum; they reach a certain peak and then swing back. The excesses of the previous generation — the generation of the sexual revolution, with its divorces, abortions, and plague of sexually transmitted diseases — will generate a backlash. The only question is how far the pendulum will go before it starts to swing back. How much will have to be destroyed before people say, "No more"?

And they will say it. The increasingly radical demands of gay activists are causing a growing number of people to question uncritical "tolerance." The debate over the redefinition of marriage is leading to increased public awareness about the origins, prevention, and treatment of SSA. Eventually there will be a sexual counter-revolution.

---

[281] Baker and Gallagher, "Not Inevitable."
[282] Ibid.

G. K. Chesterton once wrote of the dangers of tearing down what appears to be a useless fence, without fully understanding why a previous generation invested the time and effort to build it. Ideologues of the Sexual Left want to tear down the fence of traditional marriage; but the more people come to realize that the fence was erected for the good of individuals and of society, by people who understood the laws of nature, the more they will rise up to halt its destruction.

Conclusion

What Must Be Done?

What can we do to preserve traditional marriage, protect children, and show real compassion to those with SSA?

After their defeat in the 2004 election cycle, realizing that they might have overreached in their demands for an immediate redefinition of marriage, gay activists acknowledged the need to modify their strategy.

John Corvino, a member of the Independent Gay Forum, suggested that instead of pushing for marriage as a right, they focus first on civil unions:

> Properly crafted civil-unions legislation could grant ALL of the legal incidents of marriage (albeit under a different name) . . . Our best strategy (in most states) for securing the tremendously important legal incidents is to fight for them under the name "civil unions." Our best strategy for securing the social endorsement (i.e., marriage under the name "marriage") is first to secure the legal incidents. Then people will look at our civil unions, realize that they are virtually indistinguishable from marriages, start calling them marriages, and gradually forget why they objected to doing so before. That's what happened in Scandinavia, and it's happening elsewhere in Europe.[283]

[283] John Corvino, "Civil Discourse on Civil Unions," *Between the Lines,* January 19, 2005, http://www.pridesource.com/article .shtml?article=10939.

A corollary to this strategy is a push to secure economic bene-fits for partners in same-sex relationships; as more corporations grant these to their employers, the more logical it would seem to standardize those scenarios by recognizing some type of civil union or domestic partnership. These would then be unofficially solem-nized with "wedding" ceremonies, and same-sex couples would claim they were married — thus re-defining marriage informally. Not long afterward, it will seem foolish to go on prohibiting same-sex marriage by law.

And so the future fight will continue to be waged on ever-changing ground, as gay activists seek to press any advantage they can find.

It's important to recognize that marriage is not the activists' ultimate goal, but an important step toward total acceptance of homosexual behavior, and in the bigger picture, toward the tri-umph of the Sexual Left. This will require not merely passive tol-erance of homosexuality in society, or even active affirmation of it in the schools and courts, but elimination from the culture of all "heterosexism" and "heteronormative" ideas of marriage, family, and human nature. Since traditional religions hold these ideas as articles of faith, the Sexual Left's victory must include restrictions on the religious freedom of those who refuse to cooperate with the program.

The activists are skilled and smart: for every inch they're given, they will find a way to take a foot. Therefore, in formulating a strategy to defeat them, it's proper and prudent first of all to refuse any demand they make, no matter how harmless it may appear on the surface.

Then we must follow up with strong statements of the truth about SSA. We must make the public understand that the best thing we can do for persons with SSA is to offer them help to resolve the psychosexual developmental disorder responsible for their condition. If they don't want the help, so be it; that's their decision. But society doesn't then have a duty to pretend that SSA and other psychosexual problems are just normal variations in human development. And gay-rights activists don't have a right to use their positions in government, social work, and education to thwart the popular will or to put children at risk in the name of social change.

Politically, the only permanent answer is to codify human civilization's age-old preference for marriage in a form that activist courts can't touch: a federal marriage amendment.

Ten years ago, many were reluctant to take on this challenge; many couldn't imagine that there would come a time when marriage would be redefined. That attitude has allowed the gay agenda to gain ground. Some people were afraid to take part in this battle because they didn't know how to do so in a loving, compassionate way. They were afraid of being labeled "homophobic." They had friends, family members, and co-workers with SSA — people they genuinely cared about — and it seemed that to fight the gay agenda meant to fight those loved ones. And it must be admitted: some were turned off by the uncharitable words and actions of a small minority of social conservatives.

It's therefore also essential that anything we do to respond to gay activism be done in a spirit of vigilance, love, and real compassion. The threat to marriage is real. This is truly a time to speak the truth in love.

A Twelve-Point Practical Strategy

Because this is a battle for the whole culture, it must be fought on a number of fronts simultaneously. Here are twelve points outlining the major initiatives we must pursue if we are to defend marriage, protect children, ensure religious freedom, and safeguard society's foundations.

1. Expose the Frauds.

In his book *Hoodwinked*, Jack Cashill documents how the far left has consistently used false science, fraudulent reporting, and other deceptions to forward its agenda. The Sexual Left is no exception.[284] Its intellectual "hucksters" receive honors and awards from a sympathetic academe and are lionized as innovative thinkers, while those who have documented their lies are ignored or marginalized. The mainstream media have been willing accomplices to this fraud.

We must shine a spotlight on the Sexual Left's consistent pattern of deception, and the accompanying cover-up by academics, professional organizations, and mainstream media. We must never tire of pointing out the flaws, misrepresentations, and outright fabrications in the research that Sexual Leftists tout. By focusing on their lies, we can create a climate of skepticism around the Sexual Left's claims of "scientific proof" — countering its influence in popular culture, and lending courage to scientists, social researchers, journalists, and other professionals who must risk their careers to proclaim the truth. Once the public fully comprehends how gay activists play loose and fast with the facts, it will be harder for them to market their myths.

In order for this to succeed, we must be absolutely sure of our own data, carefully documenting everything we claim, and when possible, using data and material from pro-gay sources.

2. Present the Truth about SSA.

If we're to defend marriage and family, we must teach the truth about same-sex attraction. And this means educating ourselves

---

[284] Indeed, in his book, Cashill mentions three icons of the Sexual Left: Margaret Mead, Margaret Sanger, and Alfred Kinsey.

first. In the decade since I attended the UN Conference on Women in Beijing, I've seen countless instances where Christians and other defenders of marriage, due to sheer ignorance, have failed to answer challenges posed by gay activists. We've made progress, we've become more educated and more organized, but too many would-be defenders of marriage — especially those sitting next to us in the pews — still believe many of the gay activists' myths and still underestimate the stakes of the battle.

Perhaps the best way to educate people about SSA is to let them hear from men and women who have come out of homosexuality. This helps them to put a face on the problem. They'll be able to understand how these people suffered, struggled, and eventually found their way out. Their stories are beautiful and inspiring, stories of faith and love, stories that can change hearts and minds.

Several years ago, I took some friends to a Courage conference, where they had a chance to meet women who were struggling with SSA. This personal exposure changed my friends' attitudes. They became more compassionate and more committed to spreading the truth about SSA. Although my friends had never been troubled by SSA, they had struggled with abusive family situations and could identify with the Courage members' struggles.

At each step along the way, it's important that the key spokesmen be not just people who have come out of homosexuality, but mental-health professionals who have worked directly with people with SSA. If we're going to convince people that SSA is a psychological developmental disorder, we need to put forward victims and experts. Ministers, professional activists, and lawyers aren't as credible.

We can't count on the mainstream media, or even the sympathetic conservative media to do this work for us. We have to educate our own communities. Richard Cohen, an ex-gay therapist and President of Parents and Friends of Ex-Gays (PFOX) called on people of faith to commit themselves to educating others:

> Let us all make a determination . . . to stand up and share the truth about homosexuality. Let us enlighten our family, friends, neighbors, teachers, pastors, rabbis, priests, and therapists. They won't know unless we tell them that no one is born with same-sex attraction and change is possible. Share your personal stories. I know it's a risk. You risk rejection. But the greater risk is that people continue to live in ignorance and sell out this country to a false paradigm, thus imprisoning the homosexual community into a life of disease and destruction. We can make a difference. Let's make a goal to share the truth about homosexuality with one person each day, or one person per week. It's that simple. You and I can make a difference. Please do it for the sake of all those who desire freedom. They are counting on us.[285]

Ex-gay Randy Thomas of Exodus International exhorts others to overcome their fear of standing up on this issue:

> At one time, I was fearful of conflict and against speaking into venues that came in direct opposition with the gay-identified community. Each passing year brings deeper revelation that the Gay Elite — past and present leaders of some of the wealthiest organizations in the world — market a bill of goods that keeps people trapped in a perpetual "gay" victim mentality, ungrateful for the tolerance they actually experience. Silence is not an option . . . If the Gay Elite will take every opportunity to uphold their version of

[285] Richard Cohen, *You're Not Alone* newsletter, Winter 2004-2005.

faith and morality, why are we silent? The time is now. Speak out, stand up and be counted.

We can't be content until everyone has heard the good news that SSA is a preventable and treatable psychosexual developmental disorder. No matter how hot the political battle, we must remind ourselves that persons with SSA have been denied something they really needed — not marriage, but non-sexual same-sex love. They need our love and understanding. We betray them if we join the pretense that SSA isn't a disorder, or that their relationships are marriages.

3. EMPHASIZE THE DANGERS TO CHILDREN AND WOMEN.

When social change is rapid and radical, you can't accurately predict all the negative consequences that will follow. But when it comes to the potential redefinition of marriage, we can at least point out the more obvious ones. We can be fairly sure that the triumph of the gay agenda would have effects far beyond their "community." It would signal the definitive ascendancy of the Sexual Left. Chastity, purity, and faithfulness would be treated as, at best, personal preferences; at worst, obsolete and oppressive hangups. The obstacle of childhood innocence would be eliminated by early and intense indoctrination. There would be pressure to lower the age of consent and abolish laws against public sex and public nudity and pornography. And marriage between biological parents would become less common (as the current European experiment proves), meaning that more children would suffer from suboptimal family structures.

One thing that hasn't received much attention is the effect on attitudes toward women. Where gay activism prevails, true feminine virtues are denigrated. The particularly female need for a stable marriage in which a woman can become pregnant and rely on her husband to protect and provide for her and her children is already under attack. This will increase.

The gay-male community exhibits a high degree of sexism by glorifying the male weakness for sexual variety. This will influence heterosexual males — indeed, it already has — who will find themselves in a relationship-paradigm that places ever less value on fidelity and self-control. The lesbian community is also ambivalent about what it means to be a woman: a substantial portion of them seems intent on looking like and acting like men. This might lead to girls who are natural tomboys being labeled "pre-lesbian." Subsequently, girls may avoid sports and other healthy activities for fear of being thought a lesbian.

Radical feminism portrays men as violent monsters, rapists, or abusers. Yet the Sexual Left encourages behaviors that inevitably demean women, helping to further cycles of abuse and denigration as prematurely sexualized girls become abused women who are unable to make wise choices or protect their daughters. *Sexual Utilitarianism*, by definition, means using people as sexual objects, and that means treating women without due regard for their needs and feelings. It means that more women will be used for the pleasure their bodies can give, left pregnant without support, or infected with nasty diseases. It means more mothers will have to struggle alone to support their children. In their world, the very problems that radical feminism seeks to remedy only increase.

4. CONNECT THE SHOCKING TO THE DISORDER.

When dealing with gay activism, it's easy and very tempting to focus on the extreme behavior of some members of the gay community — the blasphemous obscenities that occur at gay-rights parades, the shocking propaganda handed out by gay activists, and the extreme sexual behaviors of men who have sex with men. It isn't unjust to do so: many of these shocking elements come not from the fringes but from the heart of the gay movement. And many extreme behaviors are the norm, not the exception, in parts of the gay subculture.

But highlighting this behavior might not be the prudent thing to do. There's a simple communications rule we need to remember: when you display something ugly and shocking in order to turn people against your opposition, they might associate the image with you. Thus, while such images might be red meat for the committed and might motivate them to action, they might have exactly the opposite effect on the larger group of moderates. Such presentation might cause the unsure or the uncommitted to see our side as unpleasant, offensive, or extremist.

Therefore, if we're forced to present shocking material — and sometimes this is necessary; for instance, when explicit materials are being distributed to schoolchildren — it must be done carefully and with reticence. Most important, we should always take care to point out the connection between extreme behaviors and the psychological disorders (and the childhood abuses and deficits that cause them) that are at the root of SSA.

5. COUNT THE COST.

The Sexual Left must be held accountable for the suffering its policies have caused. The world is in the midst of a deadly pandemic of sexually transmitted diseases, millions of unborn babies die every year from legal abortion, families are devastated by divorce, and children are separated from their parents. Now, Sexual Leftists don't get up in the morning and say to themselves, "Let's abort some babies," or, "Let's infect some gay men with HIV," but they do know that the effect of their ideology will be behaviors that lead to the abortion clinic or the AIDS hospice. But they're willing to sacrifice a few innocent lives in their quest for absolute sexual freedom. The Sexual Left views the rampant promiscuity, extreme sexual practices, and other shocking aspects of gay life not as aberrations to be condemned, but as a model for society in general. If a measure of misery and death must be borne by innocents in order to achieve that goal, well, no great fight is won without a cost.

When faced with this cost, those on the Sexual Left might say they just need more money (for programs) and more time (to indoctrinate the public); they promise a future utopia in which everyone is protected from sexual harms. But even they know that the "protection" they promote is at best a "risk reduction" strategy. They know that no matter how many condoms they hand out, people in the throes of illicit passion will forget to use them. They know that their condom campaign has failed among men who have sex with men — and not because these men felt compelled to obey the Pope. The experts despair as high-risk behavior increases.

We must work ceaselessly to show the world what the cost has been and who is to blame for it. The Sexual Left must be made to answer for the suffering it has caused.

6. BUILD COALITIONS.

Defenders of marriage must seek strength in numbers with all those who are sympathetic to the cause. Our most likely allies in this fight will be those who are already most committed to the battle against the Sexual Left — pro-life and pro-family activists. A further step would be to reach out to members of churches that haven't yet compromised their traditional teachings. From there we'll have a strong base for making political allies. Many leaders of black churches are particularly offended when gay activists equate racial bigotry with "homophobia," particularly since most of them strongly support the scriptural prohibitions of homosexual acts.

The foundation for such coalitions is already in place, but it's important that they be maintained and deepened. Evangelical

Christians, Catholics, Orthodox Jews, Muslims, and Mormons have, in spite of their theological differences, agreed on the importance of marriage and family and been able to define shared goals. As important as it is to work within our own religious communities, it's just as important to build bridges of common cause with others.

7. TAKE BACK EDUCATION.

Parents must firmly and resolutely resist the imposition of the gay agenda in public and private schools. They need to educate their children, organize with other parents, and pursue effective means to communicate their message to educators. Churches can help by bringing in speakers who can explain the origins of SSA, and speakers who have been converted from homosexuality, to talk to youth and young-adult groups. There are also videos and other materials that can help in this effort. All our children should be taught how to explain the truth to their classmates, and how to pray for and show compassion for at-risk friends.

Taking back the schools won't be an easy task. In some areas, parents might have no choice but to withdraw their children and set up separate schools; but even in those cases, they shouldn't withdraw from the system completely. They can support candidates for school boards who will oppose the gay agenda, preventing public money from being used to propagandize children. An organization called Mission America has developed a "Risk Audit"[286] to help parents ask the right questions and evaluate the extent of the gay activists' influence in their school.

Parents faced with a pro-gay curriculum can learn from the experience of parents in Montgomery County, Maryland. Faced with a revised sex-education program that was thinly disguised gay

[286] http://www.missionamerica.com/agenda.php?articlenum=45.

advocacy, the parents organized, sought help from nationally known experts and organizations, and took the school board to court — and won. U.S. District Court Judge Alexander Williams, Jr. ruled that "The revised curriculum presents only one view on the subject — that homosexuality is a natural and morally correct lifestyle — to the exclusion of other perspectives" and therefore violated the parents' free-speech rights.[287]

It's also important to prevent schools from taking students who are confused about their sexual identity and, without their parents' knowledge or permission, turning them over to be counseled by gay activists. One way to stop this is for parents whose children have been encouraged to "come out," or young men and women who were falsely told they were "gay" or "lesbian," to sue the schools. A few well-placed lawsuits can inhibit programs that expose students to greater risk. Another way is to work to pass state laws that prohibit this kind of interference with parental rights.

Given the stranglehold that the Sexual Left has on the higher levels of the educational establishment, the task of taking back the schools will be long and hard, but it must be attempted.

8. TAKE BACK SOCIAL AND PROFESSIONAL INSTITUTIONS.

Virtually every institution in society — churches, professional organizations, businesses, universities, political parties — is having its fundamental principles and practices challenged by gay activists. First, the gay activists organize and ask for recognition. They then begin to ask for "statements" of support. Once they gain this foothold within an institution, it's very difficult to remove them. Opponents of their agenda can fight to wrest control

[287] LifeSiteNews.com, "Maryland Judge Halts Sex-Ed Curriculum," May 6, 2005. The Throckmorton/Blakeslee critique can be found at www.drthrockmorton.com/montgomeryhealth revision2005.pdf.

back from the activists, which usually results in nasty internal battles.

Or they can leave the organization and join a competing group. We've seen this happen in mainstream Protestant denominations that have abandoned scriptural teachings for pro-gay stances; their more traditional members leave to join conservative Evangelical congregations. Mainstream pro-gay churches have seen dramatic decreases in membership in recent years, but unfortunately, those who remain are left in control of their buildings, endowments, and other resources.

When an organization has been totally co-opted by gay activists, dissenting members might have to start an entirely new one. This can occur in universities, and in professional organizations whose original mandate has been totally subverted and in which differences of opinion have become forbidden.

Surely one of the most frightening consequences of the growing power of the gay activists is the subversion of professional associations, peer-reviewed publications, and academia. A. Dean Byrd, Jeffrey Satinover, and others have documented the takeover of the American Psychological Association (APA) and other professional mental-health organizations by gay activists.

Byrd has accused the APA of committing scientific fraud by falsely representing to the public and to state and federal courts the results of scientific research on issues relating to same-sex attraction. Byrd documents how the APA has blocked research, misrepresented the research on areas related to gay activism, and penalized professionals who refused to go along with this deception.

When Robert Perloff, a former president of the APA, agreed to speak in support of "the individual's right for self-determination of sexuality" — the right of a client to seek therapy to change his sexual-attraction pattern — he received a phone call from a former

APA board of directors member warning him of their "deep concern" at his audacity and political incorrectness.[288]

The APA has released several statements supporting the gay agenda. Such statements are the product of a committee that includes gay activists such as Candace McCullough, whose partner, Sharon Duchesneau, was artificially inseminated with sperm from a deaf donor in hopes that the child would be deaf.

Satinover, a psychiatrist and lecturer on constitutional law, and author of the article "The Trojan Couch: How the Mental Health Guilds Allow Medical Diagnostics, Scientific Research and Jurisprudence to Be Subverted in Lockstep with the Political Aims of the Gay Subcomponents,"[289] analyzed APA briefs in important cases and found that the material referenced came from a small group of gay activists who falsified or misrepresented their own or other research. The judges in *Lawrence v. Texas* and *Romer v. Evans*, as well as the Vermont and Massachusetts marriage cases, relied on such briefs.

The APA bases its activism on its claimed commitment to diversity and open-mindedness, yet it's openly hostile toward those who hold conservative political and religious beliefs. Even a researcher with impeccable ideological credentials will find it difficult to pass "peer review" if the conclusions of his work challenge the gay agenda. On the other hand, patently invalid research is

---

[288] A. Dean Byrd, "Former APA President Supports NARTH's Mission Statement, Assails APA's Intolerance of Differing Views," *NARTH Bulletin* (December 2004): 1-2.

[289] Jeffrey Satinover, "The Trojan Couch: How the Mental Health Guilds Allow Medical Diagnostics, Scientific Research and Jurisprudence to be Subverted in Lockstep with the Political Aims of the Gay Subcomponents," *National Association for Research and Therapy of Homosexuality*, Conference Report, 2005.

published and referenced — if it lends weight to gay activists' claims.

The APA today continues its pattern of material misrepresentation of the research on same-sex attraction, the psychological and physical health of persons with SSA, the effects of parenting by same-sex couples, and the possibility of change. Although the evidence of misrepresentation is obvious even to those not trained in the field, the media reports its statements as "scientific fact," while those who expose the fraud are ignored. Over the long term, this corruption of science and denial of patients' right to know can only have a negative effect on the entire field, undermining respect for the mental-health profession.

In 1992, a group of concerned therapists formed the National Association for Research and Therapy of Homosexuality (NARTH) to stand up for their clients' right to choose therapy to change their sexual orientation. The Catholic Medical Association is another professional organization working to defend professional integrity and stand up against the gay myths. Focus on the Family, too, has organized doctors and other professionals in opposition to the gay agenda.

Given gay activists' takeover of professional organizations, the defenders of the truth about the human person must take a two-pronged approach: 1) build separate organization where solid research can proceed; 2) work to undermine the control of gay activists within professional organizations by alerting other members to the long-term threats that politicized research poses. We must emphasize the inappropriateness of using professional organizations to push political agendas.

9. CREATE LAWS TO PROTECT MARRIAGE.

The federal Defense of Marriage Act (DOMA) won't be enough to prevent activist courts from finding constitutional warrant for overturning state laws and state constitutional provisions protecting marriage. For this reason, we must support a federal marriage amendment. Stand firm against the politicians and op-ed writers who protest that a constitutional amendment is an "extreme" measure and an unnecessary one. Most of them know full well that nothing less will serve to prevent a nationwide redefinition of marriage by judicial imposition, but they want to appeal to the conservative spirit of many voters, a spirit that, as a matter of principle, prefers to leave the Constitution alone.

A federal marriage amendment would be wholly in keeping with the sentiments expressed in the Declaration of Independence:

> That to secure these rights, Governments are instituted among Men, deriving their just powers from the consent of the governed — That whenever any Form of Government becomes destructive of these ends, it is the Right of the People to alter or to abolish it, and to institute new Government, laying its foundation on such principles and organizing its powers in such form, as to them shall seem most likely to effect their Safety and Happiness.

When an unchecked judiciary at the federal and state levels capriciously throws out laws passed by legislatures or through referenda, and forces its own ideology on society, the people have a right and a duty to resist with any legal means they have.

10. LIVE MARRIAGE WELL.

We must defend marriage by example. That means living our marriages well. Sexual Leftists delight in pointing out how marriage has been falling apart for years. Why complain about infidelity and instability in same-sex couples, they ask, when husband/wife marriages suffer from the same problems? Of course, they don't mention the part they've played in undermining marriage. It isn't surprising that boys and girls who are encouraged to be "experi-mental" and promiscuous, who are exposed to pornography and marriage-mocking TV shows, who are taught to put pleasure above all else, grow up into men and women who have a problem remaining faithful in marriage.

The push for the redefinition of marriage has caused people of faith to look at marriage, recognize its importance, and work to strengthen it. For example, in 2006, the influential Institute for American Values issued a statement of principles, initially signed by more than a hundred scholars, therapists, policy-makers, church leaders, and marriage activists, calling for a "marriage renaissance" in the United States:

> We unite around a vision of America where more children are raised in nurturing homes by their married mother and father, and where more adults enjoy mutually fulfilling and lifelong marriages.[290]

Such efforts are beginning to bear fruit. The pendulum might already be swinging in the other direction. According to the same statement:

> Divorce rates are now modestly declining. Rates of unwed childbearing, after increasing sharply year after year for de-cades, have changed very little since 1995. Teen pregnancy rates have declined dramatically. Rates of reported marital happiness, after declining steadily from the early 1970s to the early 1990s, have stabilized. Perhaps the more encour-aging news is that, from 1995 to 2000, the proportion of Af-rican American children living in married-couple homes rose by about four percent.

[290] Institute for American Values, *Marriage and Law: A Statement of Principles*, www.americanvalues.org/ht.

A related group, Therapists in the Marriage Movement, believes that with the right kind of help, many marriages in trouble can be saved. They're convinced that, too often in the past, therapists encouraged couples to give up on their marriages, when in fact they could have been saved. While recognizing that it's important to respect clients' decision-making, they assert that a neutral or negative attitude toward marriage isn't the best approach to therapy, nor is it in the best interest of the couples or their families.

11. DEFEND OUR RIGHTS.

The Constitution and other international human-rights documents don't mention the sexual and reproductive rights claimed by the Sexual Left. They do, however, guarantee the inalienable right to freedom of religion and freedom of speech, including the right to speak prophetically and proclaim the word of God in the public square without being threatened with prosecution for "hate speech."

One of the foundation-stones of a free society is that, in order to protect our right to free speech, we must tolerate speech we find offensive. Yet, as is becoming increasingly clear to many people, passing ordinances against "hate speech" gives those with a particular political agenda a legal way to silence the opposition. The political left argues that only the oppressed have the right to speak hatefully and threaten their oppressors; the oppressors have no rights and must be prosecuted for offending the oppressed. Such attitudes are obviously incompatible with democracy.

12. PRACTICE CONSCIENTIOUS OBJECTION.

In 2003, the Catholic Church's Congregation for the Doctrine of the Faith issued a document defending marriage as "established by the creator with its own nature, essential properties and purpose.

No ideology," it said, "can erase from the human spirit the certainty that marriage exists solely between a man and a woman."[291]

The statement exhorts believers, in places where same-sex relationships have been given legal recognition, to engage in conscientious objection:

> One must refrain from any kind of formal cooperation in the enactment or application of such gravely unjust laws and, as far as possible, from material cooperation on the level of their application. In this area, everyone can exercise the right to conscientious objection.

There might come a time when conscientious objection is our only option. We need to be ready. It may mean making sacrifices, such as taking our children out of public schools, refusing to send them to certain universities, refusing to join certain organizations, leaving a particular political party, or boycotting various products. The only way for such actions to be effective is if they are massive and coordinated.

The Spiritual Battle

Although such practical steps must be taken, they are not enough. This is also a spiritual battle, and it must be fought with spiritual weapons.

• *Repentance*. If we're going to be a credible voice against gay activists, we must collectively and individually repent for past failures. This is a spiritual imperative. Our side has publicly and privately said things about persons with SSA that are uncharitable

---

[291] Joseph Cardinal Ratzinger, Congregation for the Doctrine of the Faith, "Considerations Regarding Proposals to Give Legal Recognition to Unions Between Homosexual Persons," June 3, 2003.

and un-Christian, and for this we need to demonstrate our real repentance: in both God's eyes and the public's. Our opposition knows our failures and will use them against us.

Homosexual acts are objectively sinful; religious believers cannot compromise this point. But none of us "chooses" our temptations, and people with SSA didn't choose their feelings. Most of them have no idea why this happened to them and not their brother or sister. They wanted to be like other people, but they always felt "different." It's our job to be there with information, with real help and with prayer, and too often we fail.

Forty years ago, when therapists knew how to prevent and treat same-sex attraction, few people cared. Churches certainly didn't take up the cause. We knew that our friends, family members, and coworkers were experiencing SSA. They thought they were hiding in the "closet," but their closets were made of glass. We abandoned them to their suffering. They lived through years of teasing, humiliations, lies, rejection, and shame. Of course "coming out" felt like a solution — acceptance feels better than rejection — but "coming out" really meant "giving up" hope. Why did they give up hope? *Because we never gave them solid reasons to hope.* We just added to their shame until the burden became unbearable. Most of all, we didn't pray for them as we should have.

We know that same-sex attraction is a developmental disorder, but sometimes we don't act as though we believe it. If we're going to speak of the very real problems of those in the gay community — infidelity, sexual addiction, extreme sexual behaviors, sexually transmitted diseases, substance abuse, violence — we must also speak of their origins, for these problems are but symptoms. The more wounded the child, the more that child needed early intervention, protection, and help. If the child wasn't helped, then it isn't surprising that the adult will act out. The more extreme the behavior, the more that person needs our prayers.

We must rededicate ourselves to prayer and to sharing our hope, even in the midst of the fierce political battles in which we're engaged. We must love our enemies and do good to those who persecute us. That doesn't mean giving in to their agenda, but it does require constantly praying for them.

It isn't what we oppose that shapes who we are, but what we support. It is our *hope* that compels us to refuse to call the relationship between persons of the same sex a "marriage." We're for reality, for truth, and for love. This is where we must stand.

• *Prayer.* I'm convinced that the current threat to marriage came upon us because we didn't pray for persons with SSA. Now we need to besiege heaven for help. Our right to speak, to preach, and to educate our children is at stake. If we are to prevail in the political and public relations battles that lie ahead, we need more than a coordinated political campaign; we need a concerted prayer campaign. Without God's help, we can't succeed.

A man who had been involved in a same-sex relationship for over twenty years was sitting at the hospital bedside of his dying partner. Both had been Catholic but had left the Faith. The dying man began to pray the *Memorare*, which he had learned as a child. But he could only remember half of it. On the way home, his partner thought, "My friend is dying, and he's Catholic. He needs to see a priest." He found a priest and brought him to his friend, who passed away not long after. Since then, the man has lived a pious life — and it all began with half a *Memorare*.

As spiritual patrons for this campaign, the Maccabees are a logical choice. The story of their battle for religious freedom has many similarities to our current struggle. In 175 BC, Antiochus Epiphanes ascended to the throne of the Seleucid Empire, which ruled the land of Israel. Antiochus was enamored of all things Greek. He believed that all the local religions, with their gods and goddesses, were really forms of the Greek religion. At first, Antiochus merely encouraged Greek practices, but soon he demanded that all his subjects conform to Greek ways. He desecrated the holy Temple in Jerusalem. He mandated religious uniformity in his kingdom. The Greeks considered circumcision a barbaric practice (Greek males participated in athletics in the nude and went to public baths where it would be evident whether or not a man had been circumcised), and Antiochus ordered it to be banned. Babies who had been circumcised were brutally executed along with their mothers. Likewise, Jews who refused to eat pork were executed.

These might seem like small things, but faithful Jews understood that they were not small things, not mere tokens of tolerance for modern ways, but a denial of their covenant with God. No story is more moving than that of the mother and her seven sons who, under the tyranny of Antiochus, accepted torture and death rather than deny God's law.

Mattathias and his sons finally rose up against this tyranny, gathered a small army, and waged war against Antiochus and his mighty empire. The sons of Mattathias took the name *Maccabees*, from the Hebrew word for *hammer*. In spite of the odds, the Maccabees succeeded and re-conquered Jerusalem. The feast of Hanukkah celebrates the rededication of the Temple after its defilement by the forces of Antiochus.

We must stand like the Maccabees as a light against the darkness of the Culture of Death, and be ready to re-consecrate the holy but defiled institution of marriage.

• *Love and forgiveness.* This is, of course, the hardest. To love our enemies, to do good to those who persecute us, to forgive everyone who has injured us; not just to mouth the words, but really love, really forgive — this is no easy task, but it's necessary. We will be judged by a higher standard.

Real love means wanting what is best for another person, and what is best for persons with SSA is that they find the love they need, the freedom they've been denied. As long as we keep that in mind, we won't be swayed when they claim that if we *really* loved them, we would give in to their demands. It's precisely because we really love them that we won't.

Perfect love drives out all fear. Many people are afraid to speak out on this issue. Some say it's because they love persons with SSA too much, but it might be that they don't love them enough. If we really loved these neighbors as we love ourselves, we would be eager to share the truth that could set them free.

I have many dear friends with SSA who have come out of the life. Most say they came out because someone loved them: someone witnessed to them about the love of God. They didn't get their lives in order first; they were *loved* first, then they said yes to God. Slowly they found their way home.

One friend had been brought up Catholic, but left the Church when she "discovered" her attraction to women. She spent twenty years in a same-sex relationship. Then she and her partner went to a prayer service where the minister invited the congregation to accept Jesus — it didn't matter, he said, that the women were involved in a lesbian relationship.

But as soon as my friend had opened her heart to Jesus, she knew it *did* matter. She left her partner, but didn't know what to do next. For two years, she spent an hour a day in a small adoration chapel before the Blessed Sacrament, asking God to help her. She received the grace to be free.

When I first met her, she looked like a pudgy boy — masculine haircut, clothing, and mannerisms, but a year later, I didn't recognize her. The prayer had transformed her. It wasn't just her more feminine clothing; there was a joy in her face that hadn't been there before.

Some people are afraid that befriending persons with SSA will be seen as an endorsement of their sexual or parenting choices; yet Jesus ate with tax collectors and sinners, and by that means, brought them to conversion. If we really believe that what each person needs is conversion, we must find ways to be instrumental in that process. Men and women who have experienced inadequate fathering almost always have warped images of God's love. They need real examples of love in order for that image to change. We need to be images of God's fatherly, merciful, and just love.

No matter how difficult the battle for marriage, we must never let bitterness take root in our hearts, even if it means making continual acts of forgiveness. Only then we can fulfill in our time what as the prophet Isaiah foretold long ago:

> Your ancient ruins shall be rebuilt, you shall raise up the foundations of many generations, and you shall be called the repairer of the breach, the restorer of the paths of rest.[292]

---

[292] Isa. 58:12.

⮽

Dale O'Leary

Dale O'Leary is a freelance writer and lecturer. As a reporter for several Catholic magazines and newspapers, she covered the pro-life movement, Operation Rescue, and the United Nation's conferences in Cairo, Beijing, and New York. Her book *The Gender Agenda: Redefining Equality* has been published in Italian, and other translations are in the works. For a number of years, she wrote a column that appeared in the religion section of *The Providence Journal*. She has lectured across the United States and in Italy, Ireland, Austria, Hungry, Switzerland, El Salvador, Mexico, and the Philippines. Her articles have appeared in *Catholic World Report*, the *NARTH Bulletin*, and *L'Osservatore Romano*. She has also made frequent appearances on television and radio.

In preparation for this book, she spent ten years researching same-sex attraction and interviewing therapists and persons who have come out of homosexuality.

Sophia Institute Press®

Sophia Institute® is a nonprofit institution that seeks to restore man's knowledge of eternal truth, including man's knowledge of his own nature, his relation to other persons, and his relation to God. Sophia Institute Press® serves this end in numerous ways: it publishes translations of foreign works to make them accessible for the first time to English-speaking readers; it brings out-of-print books back into print; and it publishes important new books that fulfill the ideals of Sophia Institute. These books afford readers a rich source of the enduring wisdom of mankind.

Sophia Institute Press® makes these high-quality books available to the general public by using advanced technology and by soliciting donations to subsidize its general publishing costs. Your generosity can help Sophia Institute Press® to provide the public with editions of works containing the enduring wisdom of the ages. Please send your tax-deductible contribution to the address below. We welcome your questions, comments, and suggestions.

For your free catalog, call:
Toll-free: 1-800-888-9344

Sophia Institute Press®
Box 5284, Manchester, NH 03108
www.sophiainstitute.com

Sophia Institute® is a tax-exempt institution as defined by the Internal Revenue Code, Section 501(c)(3). Tax I.D. 22-2548708.